THE SILENT GOD AND THE SILENCED

THE SILENT GOD AND THE SILENCED

Mysticism and Contemplation amid Suffering

MIN-AH CHO

GEORGETOWN UNIVERSITY PRESS / WASHINGTON, DC

© 2025 Min-Ah Cho. All rights reserved. No part of this book may be reproduced or utilized in any form or by any means, electronic or mechanical, including photocopying and recording, or by any information storage and retrieval system, without permission in writing from the publisher.

The publisher is not responsible for third-party websites or their content. URL links were active at time of publication.

Library of Congress Cataloging-in-Publication Data

Names: Cho, Min-Ah, author.
Title: The silent god and the silenced: mysticism and contemplation amid suffering / Min-Ah Cho.
Description: Washington, DC: Georgetown University Press, [2025] | Includes bibliographical references and index.
Identifiers: LCCN 2024020682 (print) | LCCN 2024020683 (ebook) | ISBN 9781647124915 (hardcover) | ISBN 9781647124922 (paperback) | ISBN 9781647124939 (ebook)
Subjects: LCSH: Silence—Religious aspects—Christianity. | Suffering—Religious aspects—Christianity. | Spiritual life—Christianity. | Mysticism—Christianity.
Classification: LCC BV5068.S55 C48 2025 (print) | LCC BV5068.S55 (ebook) | DDC 248.4/7—dc23/eng/20241011

LC record available at https://lccn.loc.gov/2024020682
LC ebook record available at https://lccn.loc.gov/2024020683

26 25   9 8 7 6 5 4 3 2   First printing

Cover design by Nathan Putens
Cover image by Ja Woonyung, *A map of fear*, drawing, graphite on paper, 2019
Interior design by Westchester Publishing Services

To my mother and father

CONTENTS

Preface ix

Acknowledgments xvii

1 Encountering Silence: Silence in Everyday Life and in Christian Spiritual Traditions 1

2 To Dwell and to Flow Out with Love: Silence in Scripture, Liturgy, and Christian Mystical Traditions 35

3 The Silence of Jesus's Empty Tomb: Listening to Silent Cries amid Suffering 69

4 The Silent Women and the Empty Tomb: Listening to Unheard Stories 101

5 The Silent Joy of the Empty Tomb: Attention to the Void 137

Epilogue: The Concentric Circle of Listening and Paying Attention to Silence 171

Bibliography 177

Index 197

About the Author 203

PREFACE

Be still and know that I am God!
—Psalm 46:10 (NRSV)

This book emerged as a tangible idea during the years of the COVID-19 pandemic, though it had long been burgeoning in my mind. As the world desperately struggled to survive through the unprecedented event, the various ideologies and trusted values of individual freedom, conquest, success, and prosperity, which had sustained the world for centuries, were put into question and torn apart, making disturbing and harrowing clamors. In the time we needed to grieve for the losses of millions of lives, inflammatory words ran through social media—Twitter, Facebook, Instagram, TikTok, and many others—agitating, obscuring, and manipulating our minds. Speech and images proliferated electronically at a rapid and overwhelming pace. We spoke too much, too fast, too easily, and too divisively. Language was caught in clichés of false convictions, lubricating anxiety, misunderstandings, and hatred. Language lost its creative force and pulse of imagination. Words were too small, too shallow, and too flimsy to describe the calamity and the pain that the pandemic and subsequent events caused. Weakened language became a senseless slogan, an irrelevant trademark, a shout from the back, whether one hears it or not. I mourned over the infertility of language.

As a lover of language, it was sad and painful for me to accept this reality. Nevertheless, I pressed on and endeavored to uncover meaning amid the confusion and commotion. Amid the swirling trap of chaos and noise, I was drawn into the presence of something absent. It was not new, of course, but existed before language and has always been around. With or without being noticed, it had been deep underneath every word, even the words not yet born, bearing meaning that language alone could not fully convey. The absence that has a stronger presence than anything in the midst of grief and destruction was *silence*.

There has been an excessive interest in silence as a spiritual pursuit of our time. When discussed and practiced, silence is often understood as a space free from conflict and suffering. Such perception of silence dilutes the power of silence I encountered during the pandemic—the silence in many cities across the world, where people were all gone, and only refrigerated trucks lined up, carrying hundreds of corpses. The silence of the most defenseless members of society, who sat on the deserted streets of those cities after losing everything in the global tragedy, even though they had nothing more to lose. The silence of sons and daughters whose last encounter with their dying parents was from the other side of a window. The silence that swallowed the final words of George Floyd, who lost his breath under the knee of White police officer Derek Chauvin, and yet turned into the cries of millions of people on streets demanding racial justice.

Yet there was also another face of silence. The silence we witnessed after all the sounds of street noises, traffic, and night life ceased was "both uncanny and profound," but it made us actually *listen* to rarefied sounds and the moans of vulnerable creatures in nature, some of which may have existed before the pandemic but had been unheard due to louder ones.[1] Silence also attuned us to what we had lost in public life—a much-needed period of solitude during our daily routines and activities. There was also the silence I shared with my fellow Asian and Asian American feminist theologians and ministers, who gathered online to mourn and remember the victims of the Atlanta shooting in March 2021. We were all speechless, just feeling each other's presence. The first sound that broke the long silence was not a word but a song, "Arirang," that one of us started with her shaking voice.[2] As such, silence bore our suffering intimately and carried different meanings and compound emotions that I could not name. Silence wandered here and there like a ghost, sometimes as gloomy as the underworld; its aroma was death and ominous uncertainty. Yet silence also provided immeasurable support, revealed a glimpse of hope, and robustly united people.

Witnessing such powerful existences of silence that provided depth and breadth beyond words, I pondered over the silence of God. I am a Catholic Christian and have engaged with many faith communities across different cultures. As in many theistic traditions, there is a question always raised among people of Christian faith in hard times: Why is God silent? While this question echoes the cries of all the biblical figures who were in desperate need of God's response, the grandiose silence and the vast emptiness I witnessed during the pandemic invited me to meditate particularly on the silence of God in the empty tomb of Jesus, where his disciples were left alone after the Incarnate Word of God was gone. Just like the disciples, I wanted to envision a sense of hope for life that must go on amid fear, confusion, and uncertainty. This compelled me to look at the question about the silence of God differently from before.

If God speaks in silence, or more precisely, if silence is God's language, how can we listen to God and communicate with God in and through silence? What does the silent God listen to and want us to listen to in times of suffering? How can we cultivate the ability to embrace a moment of silence, as the disciples lingered by Jesus's empty tomb, without immediately resorting to the triumphalist rhetoric of the Resurrection that overlooks the suffering we endure in our daily lives? What would be a mode of theology, whose task is *theo-logia* (θεο-λογία)—reasoning and explaining about God—to engage with the silence of God and the God of silence in the midst of suffering? These questions eventually led me to examine my manner of speaking, writing, and doing theology.

I know that to write about silence is oxymoronic because whatever is uttered about silence is not silence anymore. To write about the silence of God, furthermore, would be futile at best and impossible in general because no language can adequately capture both silence and God. It is a project destined to fail if not turn out to be erroneous. Readers of my book may wonder why a book on silence has so many words. Perhaps simple silence is the best medium by which to meditate on both silence and God. While I appreciate the value of numerous spiritual writings on silence that invite us to the simplicity of silence, this book explores silence not only from the perspective of spiritual traditions but also through the lens of everyday life, especially within the context of suffering. Silence in a world filled with violence is a complex and multifaceted phenomenon that requires careful attention and examination. Therefore, though I resist conceptualizing silence or the God of silence, I dare to explore ways to engage with and reflect on silence as a source for our compassionate attendance to the suffering of humans and the biosphere and the silent God who is present with them.

Meanwhile, my fellow feminist, liberation, and decolonial and postcolonial theologians may raise concerns about presenting silence as a constructive means of addressing the reality of suffering, given that silence has often been used as a tool to perpetuate injustice against vulnerable members of society. Although I am fully aware of the risk of discussing the spirituality of silence in connection with the suffering of disenfranchised members of society, I took up this project neither as an escape from the responsibility of the theologian to address the pains of those who are silenced nor as a way to spiritualize their suffering. Rather, I write about silence to renew my use of language and confront the bigotry and hatred that permeate public discourse so that I can speak more authentically and more earnestly. I intend to witness the multifaceted manifestations of silence by listening to those who are silenced as well as those who want to remain silent for various reasons, and search for the spiritual and theological implications of their silence. I believe that when we open our ears to both the ineffableness of suffering and the ineffability of God, we can facilitate silence to help us connect to the deepest needs and desires of ourselves, of others, and of the divine—even as we are surrounded by the networks of raucous, boisterous, and noisy power.

Thus, my book will argue that theology in our time must take silence more seriously and the task of listening more strenuously for the furtherance of genuine accountability. I vouch that theology is not only a matter of speaking about or to God but a matter of listening and attending to God, who reveals the divine self through silence. Theology must be able to hold us and discipline us to stay with the silence that cradles the silent cries of Creation and "the sound of sheer silence" of God (1 Kings 19:12).[3] Theology ought to muster the courage not only to speak but also to unspeak to renew its language, just as the emptiness of tomb proceeded the Resurrection of Jesus. If we want to be directed toward the divine revealed among the realities of suffering, it is available for us through our exercise of unsaying and attentive listening.

Before delving into the discussion, let me offer a brief overview of this book. The book intertwines two distinct yet interconnected threads. The first thread, comprised of chapters 1 and 2, establishes a connection between the silence of everyday life and Christian spiritual traditions, laying the foundation for my study of silence. Through my research on the experiences of silence among disenfranchised individuals in both society and Christianity, I identified a gap in methodology, metaphors, and theological vocabulary to describe the theological and spiritual aspects of silence in relation to the intersections of cultural difference, gender, race, and class. To address this gap, I drew upon the Christian mystical and contemplative traditions to construct a theoretical framework that describes silence in a way that addresses both the political and spiritual needs of vulnerable individuals. As theologian Andrew Prevot astutely observes, "Christian mystical theology learns from past contemplatives who experienced intimacy with the unknown God of incarnate love. But to be all that it promises to be, it must not only look to the past. It must also search hidden places in this troubled word for new forms of the grace of divine union."[4] I find myself in full agreement with this view. In the tapestry of life, Christian mysticism and contemplation stretch far beyond the confines of mere individual quests, esoteric knowledge, or elitist pursuits for inner tranquility. The lives of numerous mystics, both past and contemporary, bear witness to this, revealing how their profound spiritual encounters were woven through the fabric of their everyday joys and sufferings. I believe that these profound experiences resonate meaningfully with the lives of those navigating the complexities of their quotidian existence, especially in these times of tumultuous change and widespread yearning for renewal. The first two chapters of my book thus aim to make the spiritual tradition of silence accessible to people in their everyday lives, grounded in the ineffable mystery of the divine.

Expanding on the discussion of mystical and contemplative silence provided in chapters 1 and 2, the second thread weaves through chapters 3, 4, and 5 by exploring mystical and contemplative silence in various contexts of contemporary suffering. This thread runs parallel to the different manifestations of silence in the Gospel narratives of Jesus's empty tomb. The empty tomb represents the place where Christians encounter the most solemn and obscure silence, where all speech about God "lies dead in the grave with the Son of God."[5] The silence of the Incarnate Word in the tomb, nonetheless, is turned into a space for the Resurrection. I hear the silence of Jesus's empty tomb echoing the silence of the vulnerable and the subjugated in our contemporary reality of suffering, those who often fail to find expression and instead choose silence for various reasons amid atrocity. Each of the three chapters offers a different angle to approach the manifestation of silence in the empty tomb—the silence of Jesus's dead body, the silence of the women disciples upon finding the empty tomb, and the mysterious silence that kept the disciples not only in fear but in ecstatic joy.

Chapter 1 establishes the theoretical foundation for the subsequent chapters of the book by examining how silence intersects with social, political, and religious contexts. Drawing on my own experiences encountering silence in different cultural contexts, I suggest that silence in ordinary life is a site of struggle, observation, and creative engagement where diverse forms of expression converge. I propose a new metaphor for a holistic understanding of silence, which will serve as a guiding principle for the following chapters. By contesting the binary between speech and silence, meaningful discussions on the spirituality of silence become possible. Then, I redefine key concepts and terminology of Christian spirituality useful for studying silence and reference notable scholarly investigations into the topic to demonstrate the interdisciplinary nature of the book. I conclude this chapter by defining mystical and contemplative silence, which will be the focus of my discussion throughout the book. By offering a refreshed understanding of silence and its connection to Christian spirituality, the first chapter aims to provide a framework for exploring the intersection of silence and suffering in contemporary contexts.

Chapter 2 delves deeper into the exploration of mystical and contemplative silence, examining its expression in biblical and Christian liturgical contexts, as well as in mystical literature. Specifically, I focus on two Christian mystics, Evagrius Ponticus (AD 345–399) and Hadewijch of Antwerp (thirteenth century), who offer profound insights into the understanding of silence in the face of exterior and interior suffering. By drawing upon their teachings, I highlight the characteristics of mystical and contemplative silence, which facilitate a deeper understanding of silence in both the context of suffering and the Christian spiritual tradition. Rather than compartmentalizing spiritual experience from the mundane, I emphasize the interrelated but distinct aspects of mysticism and contemplation. By taking this approach, the renewing facet of the mysticism of silence enhances our awareness of the reality of suffering while also grounding and aligning our daily existence with the contemplative tradition of the ineffable mystery of God. I argue that while contemplative silence represents the perfection and goal of prayer, mystical silence is a path and progress. Both dimensions of silence guide us toward communion with others and with the divine while also compelling us to resist the violent disruption of human constructions.

Chapter 3 examines the transformative potential of mystical and contemplative silence in the aftermath of violence, drawing upon the emptiness of Jesus's tomb as a metaphor for the harrowing trauma left by suffering. Challenging the rhetoric of triumphalist theology, this chapter highlights the role of silence in recognizing and embracing the pains and sorrows of our reality. The chapter employs the heartbreaking tragedy of the 2014 South Korean ferry disaster that claimed 304 lives, predominantly high school students on a field trip, to exemplify the critical role that mystical and contemplative silence can play in political activism by creating a space for remembrance, active listening, and healing. Through the practice of unsaying and bearing witness to the tragedy of life, mystical and contemplative silence can encourage us to continue on a path of hope, connect with others who share our grief, and remain open to the transcendent.

In chapter 4, I explore my experience as an Asian woman, navigating the roles of educator and writer within a US academic environment while also actively participating in interactions with racial minority communities. Through drawing parallels between the silence of women disciples at Jesus's empty tomb and the experiences of Black and Asian American women, I reveal the subversive use of silence to challenge and survive in a society that marginalizes women in vulnerable situations. Although coercive and complicit silences contribute to their discrimination by depriving them of their language, silence also offers multifaceted mystical and contemplative opportunities. I examine various modes of silence that manifest in the experiences of women of color, such as "loud" silence, melancholic silence, and defiant silence, emphasizing how silence creates space for shared struggle and resistance. By prioritizing the practice of listening, I propose a way to move forward with this mystical and contemplative opportunity of silence. The artwork of Theresa Hak Kyung Cha (1951–1982), a Korean American poet and artist, serves as an inspirational source for envisioning a "concentric circle" of listening together while acknowledging the uniqueness of each other's pain.

In chapter 5, I probe into whether silence amid suffering can bring joy in a world plagued by violence, hatred, bigotry, and killing. I revisit the story of the women disciples' silence in Jesus's empty tomb and explore the paradoxical nature of their silence, born out of "terror and amazement." I interpret their experience as an ecstatic jouissance that transformed their perspective from the mundane to the divine order brought about by Jesus's Resurrection. From there, I turn my attention to two women writers, Simone Weil (1909–1943) and Arundhati Roy (1961–present), whose works reveal the diverse dimensions of silence in the realities of suffering. By drawing parallels between the women disciples' ecstatic encounter in the empty tomb and the two writers' insights—Weil's concept of void and Roy's depiction of the graveyard, I underscore the transformative potential of silent attention amid the void of suffering reality. Such attention can turn the pains and sorrows of reality into joy and freedom, paving the way for communion with God and others. This final chapter concludes by suggesting that attention is a practice of mystical and contemplative silence that opens a venue for listening to the silent God, who emptied the divine self into silence to be present with the silenced.

NOTES

1. de la Barre and Momchedjikova, "Introduction," 2.
2. Christine Yi Suh, "Arirang," sung at a Pacific Asian North American Asian Women in Theology meeting, March 21, 2021.
3. Unless otherwise indicated, all biblical references in this book are from the New Revised Standard Version (NRSV).
4. Prevot, *Mysticism of Ordinary Life*, 1.
5. McLauchlan, *Saturday's Silence*, 1.

ACKNOWLEDGMENTS

Writing has always been a refuge for me. Writing this book, in particular, became a cherished sanctuary that sustained me, kept me alert, comforted me, and inspired me during the time I was bidding farewell to what might have been the most beautiful and painful period of my life. Completing this book felt as if I was finally ready to step into a new chapter and embrace new joys and friendships. I am deeply grateful to all those who have influenced, accompanied, molded, challenged, remembered, and patiently followed my journey, even if I cannot name them all here.

I extend my deepest gratitude to my teachers Mark D. Jordan, Wendy Farley, and Don E. Saliers, who listened to and nurtured my writing voice, which I once doubted. Their guidance has shaped me not only as an academic but also as a writer. I am also deeply thankful for the late Rev. Suk-mo Ahn, whose encouragement propelled me forward. I miss him dearly.

My Georgetown University colleagues encouraged me to write and publish. I am grateful to them, particularly to Ariel Glucklich and Mark Bosco, SJ, for the resources and opportunities they offered me. I also want to thank the two reviewers whose words of encouragement provided assurance during the manuscript stage. I appreciate my editor at Georgetown University Press, Al Bertrand, for believing in the potential of this book. I also thank Carol Sargent for her inspiration and practical wisdom and Kaeley McEvoy, Caitlin Parsons, and Billie Smith-Haffener for their careful manuscript reading and helpful suggestions.

My heartfelt thanks go to my sisters in Pacific, Asian, and North American Asian Women in Theology and Ministry, especially Nami Kim, Jin Young Choi, and Boyung Lee, for their caring support, which was always accompanied by gentle humor and shared life experiences. I deeply value Jinho Kim for his unwavering support and friendship, and I am profoundly grateful to

Ja Woonyung for her beautiful artwork that graces the front cover of this book. My friend of prayer, Kyeongil Jung, deserves gratitude for his dedication to the vulnerable. I'm thankful to my colleagues at the Woori Theology Institute for their resilience and hard work.

The sisters of the Religious of the Sacred Heart, particularly Mary Frohlich, Mary E. McGann, and Mary Pat White, have been steadfast friends, and I am so grateful for their presence in my life. The companionship and support of Jung Eun Sophia Park, SNJM, are deeply appreciated. I also cherish my enduring friendship with Liz Sully, OP, and the numerous handwritten letters she has sent me.

To my dear friends Yunkyoung, Katie Junghee, OhSung, Miyeong, Meg, and Koonyong, I owe each of you a great deal. I'm also grateful to my friends in the DMV area, Echo, H.K., Kate Youngjoo, Heejun, Ryan, Tony, Myung Ji, Joan, and Keiji.

When it comes to expressing my gratitude to my family, I am at a loss for words. To my beloved parents, Hyeon Jea Cho and Wonsook Oh, my brother, Hyung Rai, sister-in-law, Jin Ran, and nephews, Hyun Seok and Hyun Jun, your profound love and trust in me have brought me this far, and I will continue forward because of it. There are no words to express my love for you except silence.

1

ENCOUNTERING SILENCE

Silence in Everyday Life and in Christian Spiritual Traditions

> As the prestige of language falls, that of silence rises.
> —Susan Sontag, "The Aesthetics of Silence"

> God works in silence, and God is silence.
> —Thomas Merton, *The Waters of Silence*

Silence is not simply the absence of sound or speech. There cannot exist a space that is entirely devoid of sound in the realm of living beings. There cannot be an expression that is completely devoid of meaning in human communication. Rather, silence is a particular type of presence that becomes apparent when other forms of sound and speech are negated. Silence exists both before sound or word arrives and after they have departed. Its unique nature lies in the fact that it is vastly open to embracing meanings conveyed through sound and speech, yet it cannot be defined by them. The mode of existence of silence emulates that of God, as expressed and experienced in the *via negativa*. It is no wonder that many mystics, in both the past and present, have referred to silence as the language of God.

Silence's undefinable nature makes it the most suitable means of expression available for the experiences that surpass human language and reason. Thus, it is the medium through which human beings can express the ineffable mystery of God, and at the same time, it is the medium to which humans can resort when they are stripped of everything in times of extreme suffering. Silence contains the experiences of both the ineffable divine and the ineffable suffering of humanity. Then, one may ask: In times of inexplicable suffering, how can we listen to the silent God while also engaging with the silence of our own and others' suffering?

My book aims to navigate the ineffable aspects of both God and human suffering and to illustrate the role of silence in making the ineffability of human suffering heard, seen, and enfolded within and through the ineffable mystery of God. However, in order to situate silence in the theological discussion of the silent God and suffering, I need to undertake many tasks along the way. These include examining the various ideological constructions about silence and the diverse cultural contexts that interpret and misinterpret both the silence of God and the silence of vulnerable individuals, and analyzing the social and political circumstances that manipulate both.

Silence becomes a highly complex matter when it pertains to a culturally bound human experience. The meaning of silence is often interpreted based on one's personal experiences and expectations, regardless of the intentions of the person who is silent. My own complicated relationship with silence substantiates that silence carries different meanings depending on one's culture. As a bilingual writer, educator, and researcher, I have lived between two tongues: Korean and English. A seamless connection between the two languages is impossible and undesirable, yet slippage between them taught me that human communication inherently includes the unsaid and unaddressed. I often experience a failure to convey the meaning of my silence when navigating across the two languages and diverse cultures. Silence is viewed as virtuous in some settings within my native culture. However, in Western intellectual and democratic culture, it is more commonly associated with passivity, lack of agency, and complicity. In both cultures, nonetheless, marginalized individuals may find that silence is used both as a means of oppression and as a symptom of it. At the intersection of race, gender, and class, they are often denied the opportunity to speak out and are left silent. While coercive silence must be contested and broken, my bilingual sensitivity made me more interested in the unaccountable omission and unspeakable juncture within and outside the speech and silence binary and enabled me to observe the impact of silence and both positive and negative aspects of it. Silence is an important element in everyday communication, political struggles, and spiritual practice. Drawing from my personal experience, I believe that challenging the binary opposition between silence and speech is crucial for meaningful conversation about silence.

The speech and silence binary pervades the everyday experience of marginalized groups and individuals, and it also leaves a mark on the Christian practice of silence. The dominant culture that is uncomfortable with silence is equally uncomfortable with the silence of God, namely, the unfathomable nature of the divine. Despite the rich sources of spiritual traditions that have venerated silence, the binary holds great weight on the words used to preach the word of God and express one's experience of God. Consequently, it implements the idea either that silence is uncomfortable, dull, lifeless, and suspicious, or that it must be set apart from lived experience and remain pure in order to be spiritual. The lacuna within this tendency is that silence is not an authentic or available spiritual experience for Christians. The silence of God simply means God's nonresponse. Thus, the diverse aspects of silence that people experience and adapt for communication in their daily life are lost in the context of spiritual practice and access to the divine. The privilege given to speech impedes a nuanced understanding of silence that accounts for cultural differences and power imbalance and also keeps Christians from having a holistic spiritual experience through silence.

My experiences and observations of silence at the crossroad of the mundane and the religious motivated me to discern and discuss the ways of engaging the silence of God in theological inquiry and to explore the implication of silence in the diverse context of human suffering beyond the binary between silence and speech. The spiritual traditions, particularly the Christian mystical and contemplative traditions that I am most familiar with, offer ample resources to discern the role of silence in both spheres. While I found the tradition helpful, delving into the silence of God in contexts of political and social oppression requires a culturally sensitive approach that accounts for the experiences and perspectives of those who have been silenced. The aim of chapter 1 is to suggest methodologies, vocabulary, and metaphors to translate and make the traditions of mysticism and contemplation more accessible for engaging the silence of human suffering. In what follows, I lay out the rudimentary ideas and approaches that serve as the foundation for the rest of the book.

I commence this chapter by elucidating my personal encounters with silence across different cultures and contexts, ranging from the mundane to the spiritual. Drawing on a diverse range of studies and perspectives, I aim to move beyond the limiting binary of speech and silence and explore the complex nature of silence and its relevance to those who are silenced in society. Next, I explore ways to facilitate meaningful discussions on silence by introducing a new metaphor for silence to further explore silence in the sphere of everyday life. This investigation highlights the need to develop a theoretical framework to study silence and to define the notions of mystical and contemplative silences that guide the discussion of this book.

AN OBSERVATION ON SILENCE IN EVERYDAY LIFE

I was raised in Korea, where traditional culture affords greater significance to silence than mere absence of speech. Silence, conceived as "reticence," is often respected, honored, and perceived to be more valuable than speech. Silence naturally flows into everyday social interaction and, furthermore, is expected on many occasions because it reflects the virtues of modesty, humility, and consideration of others in communication. Silence can manifest one's strength in "not possessing words"; it can imply one's wisdom in "not needing words."[1] Silence also expresses sensibility to the presence of others. Remaining quiet in conversation allows participants to think deeply before speaking and to avoid the possibility of embarrassing themselves and others.[2] Along with silence, body language—the use of hands, gesture, posture, facial expressions, or eye contact—is also considered as an integral part of human communication. The unarticulated does not simply remain the background of the articulated in communication. Sometimes, it is taken even more seriously than the articulated, requiring the participant's attention and ability to read and respond to it.

The virtuous silence, of course, is not free from power. Even in Korean culture, the expectation of silence weighs much more heavily upon women and the marginalized than men and the privileged. Growing up in a heteropatriarchal culture, women and marginalized individuals in Korea develop silence as an alternative means for communication, similar to the experiences of those who are subjugated across diverse cultures.[3] Silence can be an instrument to express disagreement, defiance, self-protection, and resistance when one is deprived of authority to speak and is overpowered by lies, hate speech, and ignorance. Silence can also occur when one is overwhelmed by emotions such as shock, fear, guilt, shame, and sorrow. In vulnerable situations, individuals often communicate their anguish and distress through silence, not only because they cannot perform effective discursive action but also because silence keeps them from lying or pretending. A refusal to speak in such cases can be understood as a coping mechanism and instrument to attest truth.[4]

However, in social interactions in the East Coast culture of the United States, especially in the academy and political discourse, silence generally implies an inability to speak, the absence of opinions, an expression of compliance, and a state of depoliticization. Periods of silence are avoided among people engaged in conversation because they are considered awkward.

Speech is normally placed in the foreground, and silence remains in the background, requiring no attention. The perception of silence on the US East Coast often baffles me because it conflicts with the implication of silence I adopted from Korean culture. As I live in the United States, my silence often sends a message quite different from what I intend as it converges with both the cultural difference and the general expectations of my gender, ethnicity, culture, and language. My gendered and racialized location serves to affirm my silence as a stereotypical manner of a docile, passive, or even "spiritual" Asian woman, and thus I often feel the urge to speak up, even when I neither want to speak nor think that verbal communication is the best way to respond to the moment.

The Western intellectual tradition as such has deemed silence to be subordinate to speech. Franco-American philosopher and literary critic George Steiner writes in *Language and Silence*: "Possessed of speech, possessed by it, the word having chosen the grossness and infirmity of man's condition for its own compelling life, the human person has broken free from the great silence of matter."[5] Speech is viewed as the characteristic of human beings that distinguishes them from the rest of the creatures, and it has played a pivotal role in the development of culture. In this framing, silence does not have substance; it is only defined by speech. So silence is the absence of voice, lack of meaning, and a void.

In the same vein, the liberal democratic culture, especially after World War II, has advocated testimony as a vehicle of truth and silence as the sign of timidity or concealment of truth. In discourses on human rights and justice, the subject who breaks silence, finds their own voice, and testifies vocally is at the center of seeking justice. Largely focusing on empowering voiceless individuals, the project of human rights strives to activate their agency in order to speak out and resist forced silence. Speech is automatically associated with emancipatory projects revealing systemic violence experienced by women, the subaltern, gender minorities, the economically disadvantaged, and numerous other marginalized groups. As feminist philosopher Martina Ferrari indicates, the assumptions operative in feminist theorizing about liberation are, first, coming to voice one's experience of oppression as an empowering practice to break silence that relegates its victims and, second, acknowledging silence as "a punishment equal to molestation."[6] In the speech-centered tradition, such political thought generates a set of dichotomies such as "speech versus silence, memory versus forgetting, resistance versus complicity, or power versus powerlessness."[7] Consequently, silence is equated with submissiveness, passivity, timidity, deception, and oppression across academic discipline, progressive activism, and daily life.[8]

However, in the past few decades, and particularly with the onset of the COVID-19 pandemic, the world has observed the unreliability and deceptiveness of words, and Western societies have been hit the hardest by this phenomenon. The growth of social media is not the root cause, but it allowed untruths and dangerous half-truths to permeate communication effortlessly. As the social psychologist Jonathan Haidt comments, popular social media platforms are designed to bring out "our most moralistic and least reflective selves" by encouraging us to lash out and accelerating anger that harms self and others.[9] We learned that speech can rarely be an effective instrument to confront such frivolity because an exuberance of words does not necessarily lead to a better understanding but generates another facetious reaction. What we need is an invitation to slow things down, cool passions, and listen to each other.

Although it is becoming more momentous, disquiet over the capacity of language is an age-old concern for all who are sensitive to language. Paul Celan, the Jewish Romanian poet who survived the Holocaust but lost his parents to the Nazis, was perhaps one of the writers who experienced the ambivalence of language to the extreme despite his genius to penetrate to its core. Born in Romania in 1920, Celan spoke German, Yiddish, Romanian, and many other languages fluently. Throughout his life he wrote poetry in German, his mother tongue and also the language of his parents' murderers. His poems disclose his struggle with the obscurity of language, particularly the demand to speak truth. While he held out hope that language was the "one thing [that] remained reachable, close and secure amid all losses," he avowed the limitation of language, lamenting that "language had to go through its own lack of answers, through terrifying silence, through the thousand darknesses of murderous speech."[10] He knew that toxic and superficial language conceals truth and leads one into mayhem. Celan wrote poems that express personal and historical tragedies in a succinct, restrained, and almost ascetic manner, yet his later poems demonstrate a strong tendency toward silence. The poet's poignant sensibility to language kept him longing for silence beyond words—"something that listens, not without fear," rather than being inflamed to the readers' distraction.[11] In a world where language has been devasted by pains and wounds, Celan perhaps knew that silence would open our ears to listen. He believed that silence would remember a cruel history and resist violence even more resiliently than language. In the end, however, he drowned himself in the Seine at the age of fifty. Celan's poetry is a reminder of the predicament of language—how it could portray the world painfully legible and intimate and at the same time drive us into a hazy disorientation.

Even within the Western intellectual tradition, there have been avid attempts to challenge the speech-centeredness and the binary between speech and silence. In the philosophical realm, many thinkers, including but not limited to Nietzsche, Heidegger, Picard, Wittgenstein, Foucault, Dauenhauer, and Derrida, have valued silence or critiqued speech-centered logocentrism.[12] Jacques Derrida, in particular, offered extensive discussions over the subject, revealing the incompatible possibilities for the reader and listener to settle on any unified and permanent meanings of words. Feminist and postcolonial writers have extended the discussion, highlighting the dilemma of language especially concerning those who live outside the system of language constructed by the dominant.[13] Feminist writers such as Hélène Cixous, Julia Kristeva, and Luce Irigaray have vigorously challenged the phallic-centered nature of the existing language, arguing that women's experiences cannot be described through language formed and sustained by patriarchy.[14] Gayatri Spivak, Trinh T. Minh-ha, and many other postcolonial theorists and writers have also challenged the language of the Western intellectual and indicated that the subaltern can only speak and be represented through the language of the dominant and thus are perpetually misunderstood, manipulated, and silenced by it.[15] The shared concerns of these writers offer insights into my discussion in the following section, where I examine the role and meaning of silence in relation to the complex power relations that interfere with one's desire to speak and unspeak.

SILENCE IN THE EXPERIENCE OF THE VULNERABLE POPULATION

Addressing silence in conjunction with suffering entails a different set of questions, looking into the intersections of gender, race, class, culture, and religion. The individuals and groups in vulnerable situations are often silenced and unheard rather than choosing silence for themselves. As Tillie Olsen writes in her influential book *Silences*, "unnatural silences" may result from social contexts that numb, muffle, distract, impede, and steal one's ability and opportunity to speak.[16]

In particular, silence is *gendered*. Assertiveness and confidence are discouraged in women during the process of socialization because these qualities are considered to be unfeminine.[17] Saint Paul's admonition in the first century remains in force in the twenty-first century: "Women should be silent in the churches. For they are not permitted to speak but should be subordinate, as the law also says" (1 Corinthians 14:34). Now LGBTQIA+ individuals are pressured to stay silent because they will face discrimination, stigma, and violence if they speak about who they are. On February 17, 2022, a Florida legislative committee advanced a bill, the so-called Don't Say Gay bill, that would restrict discussions of sexual orientation and gender identity in schools.

Silence is also *racialized*. The histories of racism in the United States and elsewhere have tied the bodies and tongues of persons of color. This silencing effect extends to people of color serving in the legislative, executive, and judicial branches of government when they address systemic discrimination. Their voices are muffled, subjected to censorship, banned, or erased. Even within the realm of social media, often associated with unrestricted freedom of expression, silencing occurs when people of color speak openly about racism and White supremacy.[18] In reaction to such attempts at silencing, the idea of expressiveness is elevated as the core of Black resistance. Yet, Kevin E. Quashie, in *The Sovereignty of Quiet: Beyond Resistance in Black Culture*, points out the constraints of associating public Blackness solely with expressiveness and instead explores a "theory of Black quiet," highlighting its role as a balance between political expression and introspection.[19]

Silence is *classed* as well. Poverty keeps individuals from accessing the abilities and means to communicate their needs, ideas, and interests. The silencing of the impoverished often stems from societal contempt or aversion, rooted in stereotypes, biases, and the misconception that poverty results from personal failure rather than systemic factors. This social stigma linked to poverty can deter individuals from impoverished backgrounds from expressing themselves, as they may anticipate criticism and doubt that their perspectives will be respected. Poverty blocks or limits their rights to fully participate in society due to lack of education, health care, and channels to speak. Vulnerable groups and individuals are left unheard, if not overtly silenced. The experience of being unheard is a "much more subtle and insidious form of exclusion."[20] Intricate challenges hinder people living in poverty from being heard, acknowledged, and included, even when they make an effort to express their viewpoints.

Religious settings are not exceptional. Silence is *segregated*. As a former member of the Society of the Sacred Heart of Jesus, a women's order in the Roman Catholic tradition committed to both contemplation and action, I have cultivated a deep-seated desire and practice of engaging in contemplative prayer—the attentive listening to the divine in silence. This commitment endures even after my departure from the community. However, as I looked for and joined faith and non-faith communities whose practices centralize silence, I felt often despondent to find that the participants in those meetings are predominantly White, intellectual, and middle class. Although contemplative silence is not foreign to people of color, the practice of silence in their communities is either detached from their experiences or unrecognized.

Among Asian Christians, for example, while it is true that the practices of religions such as Hinduism, Buddhism, and Confucianism "place great stress on silence, contemplation, detachment, and non-violence," whether silence is reflected in their liturgy and prayer remains a question.[21] Contemplative prayer is not as favored by the majority of Asian Christians as is culturally assumed. Many Asian and Asian American Catholic parishes I have attended replace silent prayer with "saying aloud" the prayers of the Hail Mary, Our Father, and the Glorias. Many Protestant communities prioritize vocal prayer over silent prayer and consider praying out loud as a "spirit-filled" prayer, an authentic expression of devotion to God and a proof of strong faith. While vocal prayer has its strength, it can also distract one from meditating on the mystery that opens in silence. Another misconception about silent prayer is a perceived division between silent prayer and activism, wherein silence is deemed "spiritual stuff" apart from political activism and an excuse to remain aloof from the needs of fellow human and nonhuman beings. The false dichotomy between contemplation and action misleads Christians who are striving for an engaged life to believe that contemplation would result simply in a fixation with our own comfort and selfish need, whereas the Christian tradition, especially mystics, considered the pursuit of silence before God as a pursuit of being fully present for the needs of others and Creation.

Meanwhile, for Black Christians, despite their vibrant traditions of contemplation, certain forms of contemplative silence are invalidated or minimized due to the speech-centered norm that only values legible speech. In her book *Joy Unspeakable: Contemplative Practices of the Black Church*, Barbara A. Holmes offers a thoughtful examination of contemplative traditions in Black Protestantism, pointing out that there is an accepted view that contemplative practices remain "a subliminal and unexamined aspect of the religious life of Black Christians."[22] The African diasporic community has a rich and diverse tradition of contemplation, and Holmes's book expands the spiritual and theological foundation of contemplation, drawing inspiration from West African cosmologies and religious practices, the experience of African enslaved people, the liturgy of the Black church, and African American social activism.[23] However, despite such a rich legacy, there exists a tendency to undermine the creativity and heterogeneity that have marked the African contemplative traditions, as if contemplation must be protected from syncretism. Holmes describes it as "the remnants of the malignant forms of Christianity offered by slaveholders."[24] This tendency to invalidate or minimize certain forms of contemplative silence among Black Christians may be attributed in part to the negative connotation silence has acquired. This negative connotation is likely the result of the church's complicit and forced silence during the colonial era regarding the genocide of Aboriginal and Indigenous peoples, as well as the issue of clerical sex abuse in present times. It is important to note, however, that this tendency is not rooted in the types of silence that are practiced by the mystics of Christian spiritual traditions. For these mystics, silence is a tool for profound, rigorous, and even painful self-reflection.

This complicated landscape of silence suggests that in order to have a meaningful discussion on silence in both everyday life and spiritual traditions, we must on the one hand examine the forms of silence attached to the negative frameworks of gender, race, class, and colonialism, and on the other hand challenge the current tendency of Christian practice of silent prayer detached from the experiences of the suffering world. Such careful approaches will pave ways to recognize the mystical aspect of silence in everyday life and reclaim contemplative silence by and for the Christian communities at the margin of society and the church.

Above all, however, I must distinguish the spirituality of silence from coercive silence, though I elaborate the differences between the two further in the following chapters. Whether in the shape of historical or political invisibility, cultural custom, or self-censorship, silence can be a symptom of oppression and a submission to structural violence. These forms of coercive silence include silence forced upon marginalized groups and individuals, silence of the privileged that neglects the suffering of others, complicit silence that protects the self while putting others in danger, or evasive silence that seeks remote peace and avoids reality. In the context of power asymmetries, silence is often abusive, manipulative, and even violent. It hinders marginalized groups and individuals from speaking up for themselves and casts shadows in their spiritual practice as well. These forms of silence must be confronted and broken, and the effort of activists, scholars, and ministers who encourage the voiceless to speak should not be undermined. The slogan that came along with the Black Lives Matter movement was "White Silence Is Violence." The #MeToo movement broke centuries of silence that had kept women and the vulnerable in the quiet shadow of sexual assault and harassment. Asian Americans must break the complicit silence that has perpetuated the myth of the model minority and aggravated discrimination and hate crimes against their own people. As Audre Lorde famously phrased, "Your silence will not protect you."[25]

I join and support efforts to break coercive silence, yet I also believe that silence in the context of power imbalance and suffering needs to be examined carefully. The dichotomy between silence and speech can disguise the complex power dynamics of communication and can also invalidate the effectiveness of silence as a tool for resistance, authentic self-expression, and spiritual practice. The binary does not allow for the illustration of the multifaceted nature of silence, in which we can observe struggles and creative engagement, convergence of diverse forms of expression, and multiple (un)speaking subjects, including the divine, finding their presence without words. In order to engage with this multifaceted nature of silence, we need a refreshed understanding and a new metaphor for silence.

SILENCE AS SPACE IN THE SPIRITUALITY OF EVERYDAY LIFE

The role of silence in human experience has been considered in diverse fields, including philosophy, literature, politics, communication studies, anthropology, and critical pedagogy. By exploring silence as a pertinent element of communication and cognitive activity, these studies address silence as an antidote to a reactive, volatile, and opinion-slinging culture, as a remedy to the violent and turbulent rhetoric of the dominant narrative, or as a means through which one genuinely listens to their own being-in-the world and to others.[26] Although many of these studies recognize the spiritual dimension of silence that transcends the rational and the comprehensible, there is a lack of focus on explicating the theological significance of this spiritual experience of silence. This gap in knowledge is what caught my attention. To address this, it is necessary to challenge the binary of speech and silence and develop a novel metaphor that can broaden our understanding of silence.

In his book *Enfolding Silence: The Transformation of Japanese American Religion and Art under Oppression*, Brett J. Esaki suggests a theory of silence that moves beyond the binary of sound and silence and recognizes multidimensional silences. Drawing on his study of Japanese American silence as manifested in the history of oppression and various artistic practices, he argues that the sacredness of such nonbinary silence lies in its ability to be "set apart" from the mundane. According to Esaki, this sacred silence can serve spiritual purposes such as healing, gaining wisdom, and finding the strength to resist and endure.[27]

I resonate with Esaki's discussion on the distinctive functions of nonbinary silence, and I expand on his proposal with the aim of understanding how silence operates within the lived realities of individuals who are often excluded or disregarded by mainstream society. As Esaki observes, when silence is understood as the absence of or opposition to sound or speech, it is framed only into the type of epistemic and normative premises at work, and thus we fail to address the multifaceted aspects of silence as a phenomenon and felt experience. Furthermore, the dichotomous understanding of sound/speech and silence hinders us from becoming aware of the vulnerable existence whose medium of expression is silence and from listening to "the sound of sheer silence" of God (1 Kings 19:11–13).

US journalist George Prochnik shares this concern in his book *In Pursuit of Silence*. Prochnik writes his reflections from his travel across various places seeking an answer to the questions, Why has contemporary society become so loud, and what we have lost as we have allowed no room for silence to be part of our daily life? On his trips to a Trappist monastery, a Quaker meeting, a library, a park, and a Zen retreat, Prochnik "hears" silence. He experiences silence not as the absolute lack of sound but as "the particular equilibrium of sound and quiet that catalyzes our powers of perception."[28] In areas free of high-decibel music and machinery, his sense was awakened and attuned to the whispering sounds of tiny little things making their presence audible and visible—a bird chirp, a spring raindrop, autumn leaves falling, and a page turning in an old book.

German Swiss theologian Max Picard, too, rejects the perception of silence as the absence of sound and pursues further theological reflection. Picard pondered deeply upon silence as a phenomenon when he wrote his book *The World of Silence* in the midst of the rapidly changing society of postwar Europe. Lamenting the machinery of growing mass communication in urban areas in the 1960s and 1970s that diminished contact with silence, he suggests that silence is a phenomenon in itself that gives us time and space to come into a deepened relationship with ourselves, with others, with nature, and eventually with God. For him, silence is not something lacking but something that surpasses the dichotomy between things and no-things. Silence precedes and embraces all beings we find in the world and ultimately prepares us for union with the divine. Picard recognizes the spiritual aspect of silence to transform human beings and connect us to the sacred. He knew that the transformation of heart—the conversion experience—takes place in silence. He says, "The silent substance is also the place where a [hu]man is re-created. It is true that the spirit is the cause of the re-creation, but the re-creation cannot be realized without the silence, for [a human] is unable wholly to free [themselves] from all that is past unless [they] can place the silence between the past and the new."[29] Silence moves, shapes, and changes the human heart.

Echoing Picard's insights, French philosopher and poet Jean-Louis Chrétien beautifully captures the profound impact of silence, describing it as "the site of a deeper transformation than all those that I would have been able to bring about myself." His statement encapsulates the significant shift that silence can induce, far surpassing self-driven changes. Chrétien delves deeper, characterizing this transformative experience as "mystic silence, in which this passivity higher than any activity corresponds to the moment when God himself acts directly within us and on us."[30] Chrétien's reflection subtly underscores the depth of this transformation, transcending human effort, and illuminates the intricate work of the divine within our hearts. In his reading of the fourteenth-century German mystic Johannes Tauler's sermons, Chrétien further endorses the mystical aspect of silence: "Silence and exodus, an exodus outside oneself, here go together. It is not a matter of the cult of inwardness complacently turning in on itself. My silence tears me away from myself and leads me to renounce myself so that within me the Other may come into being and be given birth." This mystical silence leads to transformative epiphanies, transcending mere asceticism or inner discipline.[31] The silence in which we willingly immerse ourselves for transformation is distinct from the silence defined as a depravity of sound. This chosen silence allows us to engage with its constancy, expanding our inner space both far and wide.

Esaki's, Prochnik's, Picard's, and Chrétien's writings reveal that silence is not simply devoid of sound or speech. Nor is it an experience merely of ears but of the body, mind, and heart. In silence, all our sensory organs become attuned with the whole away from external and internal noise. In silence, we experience profound relationality that connects us to our surroundings and the core of ourselves. Considering the rich, dynamic, and relational nature of silence, I am compelled to propose a new metaphor for silence that goes beyond the traditional binary of sound/speech and silence. I suggest *space* as a metaphor for understanding the distinct characteristic of the relational dimension of silence.

Space, by definition, is "a continuous area or expanse which is free, available, or unoccupied." While space denotes an empty expanse free from things and is "available to be used," it could also include a temporal sense, meaning "an interval of time." It can also have an experiential dimension, "the freedom and scope to live, think, and develop in a way that suits one."[32] When it comes to discussing human interactions within it, space is understood as a social construct, rather than an externally given entity. In other words, space recognizes the roles that people play in creating it and the interaction of human actions within it.[33]

Taking space as a metaphor for the spirituality of silence, I emphasize its unlimited capacity to encompass human experiences while preserving its undefinable and ungraspable nature. By intentionally relinquishing external and internal noises, one experiences silence as a temporal and spatial space that envelops them, offering a break from the power of speech and sounds. Silence is "the space of conjunction," as Esaki illustrates, bringing together aural, spatial, and temporal dimensions that create a space between sounds, cutting the flow of sound while also defining it.[34] This understanding of silence allows us to view it as an open area within the spheres of everyday life, separate from the realms of sound and speech yet preserving both alterity and connectivity in its relation to them.

The spatial metaphor for silence is not new. A sense of spatiality is already attached to the usage of the word. We "enter" into silence as if it is an architecture we can abide. We "rest" in silence as if it is a refuge from the verbosity of the world and the deceptiveness of the word. The exterior silence invites us to go into the interior space of ourselves, where we often hear even louder noise than we do on the exterior. However, by making room for silence exterior and interior, we become ready to discover and contact senses, feelings, thoughts, and values that we often forget, ignore, or suppress. In silence, we are embraced by something spacious that awakens the underneath of our consciousness, which has been eager to be spaced from the whirlpool of the mind. Then silence becomes "a space to breathe, freeing us from the reactionary mode to what is said."[35] The resonance of the external and internal silence creates a shelter, as theologian Martin Laird says, "a space to move into and out of, a space to be in the midst of however life happens to be at any given moment."[36] In other words, when silence is made available to us, once external and then internal, it leads us into a spacious presence of mystery beyond the dichotomy between sound and silence.

Some of the examples of our experience of silence in arts evince the spatiality of silence. Writer Morgan Meyer, who has been tracing the possibility of materializing silence in many artworks, notifies the spatiality of silence in their observation of artist Marianne Heske's *The Silent Room* of the Norwegian pavilion at the universal exhibition Expo 2000 in Hannover. Recalling the experience of sitting down on the floor in a gigantic but empty room, Meyer says that silence is not "spaceless nothingness" but is "textured" and "contained." Silence produces "*in space* and *as space.*"³⁷ Yet the writer and priest Colin Heber-Percy cautions against an ontological understanding of silence, saying, "a truly spiritual architecture would not be evocative but a-vocative. . . . A 'death' space that does not speak, but listens," and thus advocating for an apophatic turn in artistic representation of silence.³⁸

A musical sense of silence also rectifies the spatiality of silence. Silence in music is not a mere non-action but a mindful pursuit that goes against the course of action in order to pause and create space within the flow to breathe, recollect, and flow again. Music is "the art of negotiating these malleable spaces of silence."³⁹ American composer John Cage's three-movement composition 4′33″ radicalizes such silence in music. First performed by the pianist David Tudor on August 29, 1952, in Woodstock, New York, 4′33″ was composed for any instrument, and yet the score instructs performers to refrain from playing during the entire duration of the piece. While the piece is (un)performed, the listeners hear silence, or more precisely, the unnoticed sounds of the environment. Cage is a lifelong follower of Zen Buddhism, and his experiment was an outcome of his struggles to write a piece that would change our perception of sound.⁴⁰ Cage's 4′33″ presents to us the intense moment of encountering the unexpected when simply being present in the space named silence.

However, silent space is not given effortlessly. In order to become space itself, silence must be "made real" and be "recognized, understood and appreciated" by our attention.⁴¹ The English term "silence" came from the Latin *dēsinere*, meaning "stop, cease, or abandon," which adds a sense of intentional engagement with a break, a rest, a withdrawal, and an attention. Silence requires one's initiative to withdraw from skirmishes within and outside our mind. The Chinese word for silence, 沈默, is a combination of two verbs. The second character, 默, alone means "to be still and keep quiet," and yet it has another verb, 沈, meaning "to sink, fall, submerge, and subside." The Chinese word captures a gentle force drawing one into stillness that is expansive and boundless like the ocean. We do not clearly hear underwater because a sound generated underwater stays underwater. It is not because there is no sound in water but because the way our ears have evolved to hear sound in the air is not as useful in water. As soon as we sink into water, our usual sense is not much help. We are surrounded and embraced by water that entirely rearranges our mode of existence. Just like being underwater, we must train ourselves to see, perceive, and feel the presence of ourselves and others in silence. In other words, silence demands attention and discipline. We need to let go of our ordinary perception and alter all our sensory faculties in order to simply be present in silence. To be present in silence is to become part of it, a "fertile unknown," a space external and internal in which we see and feel everything resonating as our discriminating intellect stops operating.[42]

Just like space, silence is not neutral or value-free. French philosopher and sociologist Henri Lefebvre illustrates space as a social product that serves as an instrument of thought and action. According to Lefebvre, space does not simply assist the production of thought and actions, but it is a tool for creating a complex web of relations. Various traits of social relationships project and inscribe themselves into a space. In this sense, space is neither a "thing" of itself nor a repository for something but a "set of relations and forms" lived and experienced within the physical and mental realm.[43] So is silence. Like space, silence in the ordinary experience is inevitably bound to power relations, though it is not solely defined by them. Silence does not simply function in the background of social relations but it binds and unbinds relations. Even as a part of spiritual experiences, silence never remains inert and inept, free from the actors and players who take part in it. With respect to its temporal and spatial quality, intentionality, and susceptibility to the players within, I expect that the spatial metaphor for silence may highlight the experiential, relational, and participatory nature of silence in human experience.

First, the spatial metaphor for silence allows us to describe silence as an experience that we attain by relinquishing our own sound, language, or movement. When we remove the dualistic frame between silence and sound, we can focus more on the experiential dynamic within silence in which the unsaid and unseen of ours and others reveal their presences without being trapped by a discursive frame. Then, all the paralinguistic elements of communication—nonverbal and non-sound expressions such as body language, eye contact, murmurs, moans, and groans—can be part of our experience of silence. Silence as a space allows us to recognize all the beings who reveal their presence in invisible and inaudible forms and be influenced by them.

Second, the spatial sense of silence helps us recognize the relationality of silence. Silence as space, as mentioned, is affected by social relationships among the participants.[44] Such relationships include not only ones formed by interactions among humans but also those formed by nonhuman beings. In particular, the spatial sense of silence accentuates the interdependency of human beings with others and with their surroundings. Solitary engagement with silence is rarely possible in this noise-filled world. The spiritual dimension of silence, in particular, is not a phenomenon that automatically happens when sound and speech are removed, but a concerted outcome that necessitates both one's efforts and support from others. As philosopher Bernard P. Dauenhauer writes, silence reveals itself as a "yielding," which suspends and binds in a new way. "Deep silence," according to Dauenhauer, makes people realize that they have "a responsibility for letting the other appear." Thus, silence "includes and is fostered based on this relational quality," a fundamental dependency of one to other beings as well as the vulnerability of their own that is cared for and sustained by others.[45]

Third, the spatial metaphor presents silence as a workable space performed by participants, particularly decentering the authority of speech and words that determines and confines human and nonhuman relationship.[46] Unlike speech, silence includes everyone in the same space, offering everyone a chance to join. By closing an uttered word and allowing a "new stream yet-to-be-expressed" to take space, silence invites all participants to what is uncertain and indeterminate.[47] Here I draw an insight from the French historian and philosopher Michel de Certeau's concepts of space and place. In *Practices of Everyday Life*, de Certeau examines the practices of resistance made into the operations of individuals who create fluid, spontaneous, and indeterminate *space* within *place*, which is more stable, static, and ideologically informed by power. De Certeau's description of the relation between *place* and *space* can parallel with the relation between speech and silence. Silence of the marginalized creates space within the place-dominated speech and word. And it can tactically intervene, which de Certeau describes as "poaching," in the speech and word arranged and organized by the dominant. By mobilizing the unsaid and unspeakable, the spatial metaphor for silence challenges the dictating power of words and allows the (un)voice of the other to be heard.[48]

My choice of a spatial metaphor for silence aims to describe the multifaceted nature of silence in everyday experience while recognizing the diverse nonverbal expressions of groups and individuals who live outside speech-centered norms as a valuable source for investigating the spirituality of silence. Using a spatial metaphor, we can expand our cultural, political, and theological imagination of silence and shift away from the habit of privileging speech. With this spatial understanding of silence in mind, I will now turn to discuss silence in Christian spiritual traditions.

TERMINOLOGIES AND METHODOLOGIES FOR DESCRIBING SILENCE IN CHRISTIAN SPIRITUAL TRADITIONS

Religious and spiritual traditions across cultures have venerated silence as a form of prayer par excellence. The Yogic tradition cherishes *mauna* (मौनम्),

a Sanskrit word for silence, which allows the practitioner to promote mindfulness and spiritual growth and then reach a state of self-awareness and union with the higher Self. The late Buddhist monk Thich Nhat Hanh said, "Silence is essential. We need silence just as much as we need air, just as much as plants need light. If our minds are crowded with words and thoughts, there is no space for us."[49] In the Christian spiritual and mystical tradition, the practice of silence, namely contemplation, is to be taken primarily in the literal sense. Silence is considered a means to access the divine, to develop self-knowledge, and to live a more holistic life. God manifests the divine self in silence, as the Psalmist sings: "Be still and know that I am God" (Psalm 46:10). The monastic traditions of the Christian East and West developed the spirituality of silence through practice and theology.[50] "If there is no silence beyond and within the many words of doctrine, there is no religion, only a religious ideology. For religion goes beyond words and actions, and attains to the ultimate Truth only in silence and Love," says the late Trappist monk Thomas Merton.[51] The Quaker tradition epitomizes the significance of silence in liturgy and community gatherings. For Quakers silence itself is the essence of the experience, and thus music, ministers, readings, and formal prayers are considered obstacles.[52] Contemplative silence in these traditions does not remain a solitary experience but becomes a shared common journey that opens one to recognize their deepest emotions and innermost thought in relation to God. Merton wrote, "God works in silence, and God is silence."[53] For many authors and practitioners from the tradition, to dwell in silence both exteriorly and interiorly is to live within intense attention to the wholeness beyond the fragmented and multifarious perceptions of reality.

While there is a notable resonance between silence as a spiritual experience and silence as a phenomenon of everyday life, the lack of the articulation of that resonance begs questions that I take up from my theological perspective. What is spiritual about silence in Christian traditions, and how do we experience it? How can one claim the spirituality of silence in daily experiences of silence attached to forms of suffering and oppression? As someone who reveres the silence of spiritual traditions but also participates in the challenges of reality, I feel the necessity of making the spiritual tradition of silence available for its practice in our everyday life, grounded in the inexhaustible mystery of the divine silence. With a deeper theological understanding of contemplation that surpasses the rational, I believe that silence in everyday life can be altered into a spiritual practice that forms a relation of listener to listener, silent lover to silent lover, which will eventually lead to the divine at our deepest core. By contextualizing the spiritual language of silence in the contemplative tradition, yet minimizing its risk to betray silence, we can face the reality of suffering.

Albeit not termed religious or spiritual, the use of silence in the context of suffering and particular acts of resistance already indicates certain spiritual aspects that can be explored and investigated. For example, silence used in the political struggles of marginalized groups and individuals expresses multifaceted meanings at the intersection of power and agency, while disclosing a spiritual and transcendental dimension that cannot be reduced into a mere political scheme.[54] To name a few recent cases, Day of Silence became a tradition in 1995 to spread awareness about the effects of bullying and harassment of LGBTQIA+ individuals.[55] X González, a survivor of the mass shooting at Marjory Stoneman Douglas High School in Parkland, Florida, solemnly paused for four minutes and twenty-six seconds of silence during their address at the March for Our Lives 2018, denouncing gun violence. During the 2020 Black Lives Matter movement protests, protesters across the world lay on streets in silence for eight minutes and forty-seven seconds to commemorate George Floyd's last breath before his death. In winter 2022 protesters in major cities in China held up blank sheets of paper in silent protest to express their anger over COVID-19 restrictions. Blank paper was a statement about the silencing of dissent as well as a tactic to evade censorship or arrest.[56]

The sacredness of silence is evident in these political struggles, as it sets participants apart from the prevailing culture of aggression. It inspires people by forming a bond between strangers, inviting self-reflection, and inspiring refreshing insights. This spiritual potential of silence creates a "fluid, non-linear, internal, and sacred" space and provides a refuge for the vulnerable. However, the sacredness manifested here is not isolated from the urgent and profound needs of people but opens us toward the transcendental amid suffering. This silence allows us to go within before we speak or act and prepares us to shape a ground that "connects the spiritual with the political."[57]

This constructive potential of silence has garnered significant attention from scholars in the fields of feminist, postcolonial, and critical race studies as well. These scholars have analyzed the paradoxical nature of silence, particularly in its implications for women and subjugated individuals. Through their works, they have offered critical insights into the ways silence can be both empowering and oppressive. The objective of this book is to further develop the existing traditions and literature by establishing a more explicit link between the silence experienced in the face of suffering and the spiritual and theological traditions that intersect with it. Specifically, I aim to anchor the sacredness of silence in the experience of suffering in Christian spiritual traditions while also exploring the nuances and complexities that arise when considering the diverse experiences and perspectives of silence across cultures. I suggest that silence in the experience of suffering can offer an opportunity to claim and reclaim Christian mystical and contemplative traditions for marginalized Christian communities, and that it can be a support for the vulnerable in the struggle to find meaning in their suffering. In silence lies the depth and breadth of emotion that words cannot express, of the understanding that words cannot explicate, and of the strength and healing that words cannot bear. The mystics of Christian traditions, through their experience of exterior and interior suffering, may help us discern the sacred and transcendental in the silence of the marginalized and subjugated. In what follows, let me illustrate what I mean by spirituality, mysticism, and contemplation in conjunction with silence and how I approach these subjects in this discussion.

The Spirituality of Silence

The contemporary term "spirituality" encompasses a wide range of subjects and disciplines. It could mean the journey of self-transcendence with or without the higher being; the depth and breadth of human existence; the quest for ultimate values and meaning; the "process of conscious integration and transformation of one's life"; "the lived aspect of one's faith commitment in terms of values and behaviors"; and "a dialectic that moves from the inauthentic to the authentic and from the individual to the communal."[58] Furthermore, spirituality involves "what we do with the fire inside us" and "how we channel our eros," a process necessitating disciplines and habits that culminate in either "a greater integration or disintegration in the way we are related to God, others, and the cosmic world."[59] While each definition is valid in its own context and practice, this book cautions against the tendency to separate spirituality from the history, tradition, and context of a certain faith community, particularly in the case of Christianity. One's spirituality is hardly independent from the belief system and tradition that shapes and influences their imagination, language, and practice. Even though I do not privilege the language and practices shaped by organized religions, recognizing the organic connection between individual believers and organized religions provides grounds for taking individual spiritual experiences as a subject of academic discipline despite their subjective and personal nature.[60]

I am thus convinced of the approaches suggested by scholars of Christian spirituality, including Sandra M. Schneiders, Bernard McGinn, and Philip Sheldrake, whose works explore spirituality within a specific religious tradition—Christianity, in their case. I find helpful Schneiders's broader description for spirituality as "the experience of conscious involvement in the project of life integration through self-transcendence toward the ultimate value one perceives." Additionally, her definition specifically for Christian spirituality, "the life of faith, hope, and love within the community of the Church through which we put on the mind of Christ by participating sacramentally and existentially in his paschal mystery," is appropriate for my own research on silence.[61]

To be clear, I aim to explore the spiritual aspect of silence in daily life, which has the potential to open individuals to transcendence, and if the individual is Christian, their experience can be connected to participation in the paschal mystery of Christ and interpreted by the spiritual and theological language of Christianity. The reason I refer mainly to Christianity is because I have engaged with people of faith whose spiritual practices center around Christianity, so I feel more confident in naming both highlights and challenges of Christian practices of silence.

With that said, I want to underline that speaking about one's spirituality in the context of Christian belief and tradition must procced with careful consideration and nuance. Primarily, despite the value that the continuity of belief and tradition may hold, I am cautious about using them as a universal standard to assess the authenticity of one's spirituality. The symbols and languages of the Christian spiritual tradition have been constructed largely based on European Christian experiences and thus do not fully reflect the richness of Christian experiences in the non-European cultures that date back to early Christianity. As Andrew Prevot argues in his critique of the dichotomous aesthetics of the light and darkness metaphors pervading the Christian imagination, we must be aware that the symbols and languages of the European tradition inform our conscious and subconscious perception and judgment, which in turn affect cultural, political, and religious institutions and perpetuate practices of sexism, racism, and colonialism.[62] As a Catholic Christian myself, I must admit Christianity's complicity in culturally supporting violence, as well as the unreliability of its language and practice as a moral resource for the vulnerable in non-European contexts. For this reason, I assert even more strongly the critical need of historical-contextual, transcultural, hermeneutical, and theological approaches to study silence as a spiritual experience both within and outside the Eurocentric Christian tradition.

The historical-contextual approach underlies my description of silence because silence as a site for struggle and observation cannot be separated from the historical and contextual landscape of one's experience. However, when describing silence, history is inherently limited as a dependable category because history does not account for the unsaid and unspeakable. What is unsaid and unspeakable can neither be constructed as a whole narrative nor excavated by scholars whose ears are trained to hear what is assumed to be objective. The study of silence, therefore, challenges the assumption of historical methodology that objective events occurred in the past and that they can be accessed and proven through proper methods. We do not discover silence through spoken and written narratives but in the gaps and cracks within those narratives, which we can see and hear only when we approach them with careful and willing attention. Those gaps and cracks draw us to the stories hidden in the underside and margins of history—the stories of victims and the historically marginalized, women, non-Europeans, Indigenous and Aboriginal peoples, and all those whose voices were deemed unimportant and uninteresting.[63] Furthermore, the gaps and cracks created by silence serve as a reminder that the available data is inherently incomplete, and therefore the authenticity of that data must always be evaluated in light of the recognition that it is impossible to fully grasp it and that one must engage with it from within its cultural context. The experience and practice of silence depends on the embodied and situated subject, as well as their concrete perspective within a particular geographical, historical, and political context.[64] If the spirituality of silence can construct any coherent meaning, it is not through objective evidence or category but through each believer making their own engagement with silence in their cultural context.[65]

To complement the historical-cultural approach, I adopt the transcultural approach as an integrative framework for addressing diversity and plurality of silence as both daily experience and spiritual experience. The transcultural approach proves useful in describing the varied ways in which silence manifests itself, shaped and inspired by a multitude of cultures and localities.[66] The formation of spirituality is a nonlinear process, and it involves constant translation, adaptation, redefinition, and appropriation. Studying the spirituality of silence, therefore, requires what Robert Orsi, a scholar of American history and Catholic studies, has called a "hermeneutics of hybridity," which values the complicated and varied cultural appropriations of religious idioms. Terms such as "tensile, hybridity, ambivalence, and irony" are placed as "the central methodological commitment."[67] By moving beyond conceptions of a singular homogeneous culture, the transcultural approach challenges a preexisting or dominant cultural condition as a normative category for the study of silence. On the one hand, it acknowledges and explores the various cultural expressions of silence, while also seeking to prevent the dominance of power, social hierarchies, and institutions from shaping cultural interactions within the study. Yet on the other hand, it accepts "the inevitability of the tension between collective and individual interests" and thus sees conflicts and negotiations as natural and productive in understanding and practicing the spirituality of silence among different faith communities, groups, and individuals.[68] The indeterminate nature of the tension can be a source for creative invention and renewal that must affect all the parties involved with the process. To claim and reclaim the spirituality of silence for the Christians at the margin, we must consider the cultures and traditions of Christianity at all levels of theology and practice, the power relations between and among faith communities, and the positionality and self-reflectivity of individual Christians. Thus, my preference of choosing the transcultural approach expresses my desire to interrogate the dominant practices and understandings of contemplation inherited from the European monastic traditions, to welcome the instabilities of the practices and understandings of contemplation at the margins of Christianity, and to be inspired by the spiritual potential of silence experienced and practiced outside the institutional boundary.

Silence as a felt experience is contextual and involves power relations in cultural, political, historical, and ecclesiastical settings. Particularly, when the experience is expressed and preserved in literature, arts, and other artifacts, it demands a hermeneutical approach in order to understand the meaning and intention behind it, even when the experience remains unsaid and inarticulable. Michel Foucault's conception of apparatus (*le dispositif*) in his discourse analysis underscores the significance of silence as a nondiscursive practice and implicit knowledge for hermeneutics. Referring to the various institutional and administrative mechanisms and knowledge structures that amplify and maintain the exercise of power within the social body, Foucault said that the unsaid, just as much as the said, determines and defines the existence of the enunciative field.[69] Silence is a form of discourse, he reminds us, when speech and testimony are restricted as "acceptable practice of discretion." The silence of the linguistic minorities then discloses "the different ways of not saying such things, how those who can and those who cannot speak of them are distributed, which type of discourse is authorized, or which form of discretion is required in either case."[70] Silence in this way is a means of resistance for the linguistic others, a reactive tactic to survive in the oppressive social order governed by speech. Within this context, I push the interdisciplinary nature of hermeneutics forward, involving feminist, postcolonial, and critical race theory. For the hermeneutical process to account for power relations in (non)discursive interactions, a description of the experience and phenomenon of silence is necessary. However, the description and analysis of silence aim not to comprehend or decipher the meaning behind silence, which is impossible. Rather, it is limited in its role as a tentative appropriation for the subject eventually to be aware and transformed.[71]

If spirituality is to be taken as a subject of study, it must interact with theology, first because the "attempts to speak about our understanding of God (theology) and our efforts to live in the light of that understanding (spirituality) cannot be separated," as religious historian and theologian Philip Sheldrake writes in *Spirituality and Theology*.[72] Especially for the study of silence, a theological approach is critical because speech and writing about God cannot be addressed without recognizing the silence of God. In theological inquiry about God, speech and silence are dependent on each other and defined by the other. Just as there is no speech without silence, there is no speech about God without silence that surrounds, keeps, and even hides that speech. By orienting theology toward God who is beyond words and comprehension, silence can be a remedy for excessive speech and writing about God.

Emphasizing theological approaches to spirituality, nonetheless, could result in "the reduction of spirituality to a mere appendage of dogmatic or moral theology." The assumed hierarchy between speech and silence could also reinforce the hierarchy between theology and spirituality, which I avoid repeating in this book. Theology and spirituality are interrelated but they are also distinct. Theology studies "the objects of belief as it were in the abstract"; spirituality studies "the reactions which these objects arouse in the religious consciousness."[73] While holding the distinction between the two disciplines, I also affirm the task of theology argued by the theologians who prefer the term "constructive theology" over "systematic theology." Constructive theology engages with "the contingent, transigent, impermanent, and ultimately constructed reality of any theological speech, insisting on foregrounding the imaginatively constructive work that is truly at the heart of theology."[74] The task of theology, particularly in discussions of silence, should not be restrained to developing a coherent theory of doctrines and dogmas within the tradition because silence as an experience and phenomenon cannot be prescribed or regulated into a given discursive structure to fit in the overall system of speaking and writing about God. It must allow the unaddressed and unexpected pauses, breaks, cracks, gaps, and ruptures that silence creates within the speeches and writings about God. After all, "theology emerges from God's gracious act of mercy at our wrestling for meaning in our human condition," as theologian M. Shawn Copeland says.[75]

Besides locating the subject of silence in the study of Christian spirituality, I assert its transformative aspect that affects the life of Christians both in private and public spheres, simultaneously rejecting the traditional opposition between contemplation and action. Christian spirituality is rooted in a belief that God works in history and reaches out to human and nonhuman beings. It presumes a "sacramental view" that "we are opened to God's grace and to God's transformative Spirit *in and through* human history and *in and through* human affairs."[76] Christian spirituality must invite its believers to discern the divine and the sacred within all aspects of daily life, including social and political life, rather than offer a retreat into a "pseudo-spirituality that deals in escape, in avoidance of the reality of the other."[77] It must lend, furthermore, a similar passion to Black feminist ethicist Traci West's description of defiant spirituality: a "sustaining energy to the task of creating space for honoring community members' [and individuals'] intentional transgression" of certain norms of self-expression embedded in the church and everyday life.[78] To deconstruct the opposition between contemplation and action is also to challenge the binary between silence and speech and the negative frameworks attached to silence that hinder Christians from engaging in contemplative silence. If the contemplative practice must be combined with life in this world and responsibility to one's neighbors, its potential must also be recognized in daily experiences as a catalyst for transformative speech and action. The mystics of Christian traditions considered in this book exemplify the integration of the two spheres.

Mystical and Contemplative Silence

Mysticism generally refers to an immediate encounter with the mystery of God beyond an analytical and conceptual sense, and the word has been used interchangeably with spirituality in the past. Alister E. McGrath describes the three assumptions attached to mysticism in discussions of Christian spirituality: 1) an approach to the Christian faith that emphasizes "the relational, spiritual, or experiential aspects of the faith," in contrast to "the more cognitive or intellectual aspects"; 2) a term to denote spiritual issues, both in religious and nonreligious settings, that highlight "inner experience and correspondingly marginalizes or rejects any use of cognitive approaches to spirituality"; and 3) specific schools of Christian tradition that pursue the union with God through direct and personal experience.[79]

Although McGrath prefers to use the term "spirituality" over "mysticism" when he describes Christian experience due to the many unhelpful associations and misleading overtones connected to "mysticism," I use both terms for different purposes in this book. Whereas I use "spirituality" to refer specifically to the forms of spirituality connected to Christianity, I particularly emphasize the subversive and transgressive character of "mysticism," thus broadening the periphery of Christian experiences by inviting a consciousness of the transcendental that is available "intuitively" in addition to more rational, moralistic, normative, and dogmatic claims and that thus remains ineffable.[80] Rather than an elitist definition of "mysticism" as an esoteric, separate, and eccentric experience available to peculiar people, I am convinced of descriptions of mysticism offered by theologians like Karl Rahner and Dorothee Sölle, who see mysticism at the core of all human experience, including ordinary aspects of life. The sacred coexists with the secular without separation, and all aspects of human life are ultimately oriented toward "the eternal and silent mystery, which we call God and his secret grace," as Rahner said.[81] Mystical sensibility calls us to recognize the mystery of God found within ordinary life and urges us to engage with social, political, and ecological issues. The "democratization of mysticism," Sölle's term, offers non-authoritative and self-reflective language to describe human experience in relation to the transcendental, surpassing the division between the sacred and the secular, the religious and the nonreligious.[82] With these more extensive descriptions, I establish mysticism as a "vital category" that connects Christian spirituality and theology with creative imagination drawn not only from spiritual traditions but also from the arts, literature, and the personal and communal practice of everyday life.[83] My description of mysticism encompasses and embraces mystical experiences beyond the Christian realm, acknowledging their significance even when they are not rooted in theological or ecclesiastical frameworks. Their value is not diminished simply because they diverge from doctrinal approaches. Mysticism in this book is thus a concept broader than Christian spirituality, crisscrossing the boundary between the religious and the nonreligious, the sacred and the secular, the personal and the social, and the private and the public.

The work of Michel de Certeau, again, is particularly helpful in my attempt to view and describe silence as a mystical experience. De Certeau's work is hard to categorize or conceptualize, given that he brought an extraordinary breadth of intellectual interests and extensive interdisciplinary engagement, not to mention that he consciously made the definite categories of various disciplines ambiguous. His study of mysticism, too, resists any rigid boundary that tends to confine the term. Primarily focusing on sixteenth- and seventeenth-century Spanish and French mysticism, which was marked with excessive interest in the interior, experiential, and autobiographical, de Certeau saw mysticism as a kind of social practice that "inherently engaged with the public world," being driven toward "what is not known."[84] Investigating the embodied nature of mystical experiences in relation to the social, de Certeau argues that the mystics of early modernity created space for new ways of thinking, (un)speaking, and imagining the Christian tradition away from a body of doctrines. De Certeau considered silence an intrinsic part of mysticism. As theologian Fergus Kerr notes in his reading of de Certeau, de Certeau shifted the criteria to verify Christianity from "the level of theory to the ground of practice," in other words, "from reliance on the language alone" to "respect for the undefinable and incircumscriptible whole."[85] This shift vouched for various activities besides linguistic ones, including silence, to be taken as consideration for the study of mysticism. Within this understanding and given this experiential foundation of de Certeau's study of mysticism, I explore the mysticism of silence as a subversive space for new ways of thinking, (un)speaking, and imagining the divine as opposed to or complemented by the institutional place defined by words and speech—doctrines and dogmas. I take mysticism of silence as both an experience and a form of critique and practice that challenges and counters the culture of loquaciousness.

Contemplation these days flourishes in diverse forms of spiritual practice such as chanting, *lectio divina* (sacred reading), music, and art. Yet "contemplation" in the Catholic Christian tradition refers to one of three major expressions of the life of prayer: vocal prayer, meditation, and contemplation.[86] Vocal prayer uses descriptive and explicit words; meditation engages with imagination, emotion, and desire based on the Scripture; and contemplation emphasizes receptive, participatory, and experiential modes of awareness. Both meditation and contemplation are nonverbal forms of prayers, but they are different. The twelfth-century Scottish mystical theologian Richard of Saint Victor says that contemplation is "a free and clear vision of the mind fixed upon the manifestation of wisdom in suspended wonder," whereas meditation is "an industrious attention of the concentrated diligently upon the investigation of some object."[87] In other words, the Christian tradition has understood contemplation as a gift or grace from the divine in which one sees truth, instead of an effort to reach the truth.

Silence as a form of contemplation is often confused in practice with centering prayer. Centering prayer is a method of silent prayer developed in the 1970s by three Cistercian monks—William Meninger, Basil Pennington, and Thomas Keating—drawing from Christian spiritual sources such as the fourteenth-century spiritual classic *The Cloud of Unknowing* and Thomas Merton's insights. The three writers made a distinction between centering prayer and contemplation. Centering prayer is an intentional practice to sit in silence and open to God away from thoughts, emotions, or sensations, while contemplation is communion in the life of God beyond instructions or any intentional practice. In other words, contemplation in the Christian tradition is the pursuit of an uninterrupted relationship with the divine through the emptying of the images and concepts attached to our relationship with the world. "Contemplation" or "contemplative silence" in my book does not refer to a method or technique of prayer.

In my discussion of the spirituality of silence, I extend the classic definition of contemplation. "Contemplation" in this book means, borrowing the words of theologian Wendy Farley, "a general attitude for integrating all the aspects of one's life into a spiritual whole." It is a holistic way of seeing, desiring, waiting, and becoming in relation to the divine, which requires interior tranquility. Certainly, it is not confined to those in monastic orders or those who devote their lives to intense discipline. One engages in contemplation with practices of prayer, service, and meditation, but more importantly, contemplation is a way of living in which one is attracted, attuned, and united with the beauty of ordinary good things as well as the ultimate good, the divine, free from manufactured and falsified concepts and images. As Farley continues, a contemplative way of life is a "disposition" that provides mental patterns that make us constantly inclined toward and connected with the divine at the core of all beings.[88]

Contemplation is essentially relational. Contemplation is not simply finding a clear idea of the divine as if one could conceptualize it or understand it.[89] It is remaining in relationship with the divine and gazing into the eyes of the divine, by which we become the divine we look upon. The thirteenth-century German mystic Meister Eckhart poetically expresses the intimacy with God one cultivates in contemplation: "The eye with which I see God is the same eye with which God sees me: my eye and God's eye are one eye, one seeing, one knowing, and one love."[90] Theologian Mary Frohlich affirms this relational character of contemplation by saying that Christian contemplation is "the radiant embodied awareness of mutual indwelling with God and with God's people." The unity that one experiences in contemplation transcends the limits of reason, morality, norms, and dogma and thus remains ineffable. Hence, mysticism and contemplation are interconnected. Mysticism is a dimension of experience and contemplation a dimension of disposition, both of which inevitably surpass human language and therefore find the best expression in silence. Mysticism, characterized by its evocative nature, guides individuals toward transcending the discursive level of thought and perception. This process allows for brief yet transformative glimpses into the ecstatic experience of unity with the divine. Similarly, contemplation invites one to remain in this divine connection through practices that foster deep internal awareness and reflective attentiveness to the surrounding world. These two spiritual experiences can coexist harmoniously, each shaping and influencing the other in a mutually enriching journey.[91]

Considering these definitions of mysticism and contemplation, I describe mystical silence as an experience of silence that leads one to a transcendent experience beyond the confinement of an ordinary horizon, while contemplative silence fosters a relationship with the divine and others. Mystical and contemplative silence thus cannot be equated with coercive silence in its variations as forced, imposed, neglectful, complaint, and evasive silence. Coercive silence isolates one from relationship, while mystical and contemplative silence links us to the whole by allowing us to hear and see what remains unheard and unseen. Coercive silence takes and suppresses one's voice, but mystical and contemplative silence restores the voice by distancing it from the forceful demand of the words manufactured by the dominant. Coercive silence destroys one's self and erases one's presence, yet mystical and contemplative silence leads one to discover, examine, explore, and transform themself. Ultimately, mystical and contemplative silence orients one to the divine, who exists in loving communion, whose triune being is relationality itself.

I pay special attention to how mystical and contemplative silence is manifested, experienced, and claimed by people in the midst of suffering, drawing inspirations from Christian mystics. Christian mystics experienced excruciating pains externally, through their conflict with the social and ecclesiastical institutions that literally silenced and even killed them. Many of the mystics also suffered internally as they encountered the deepest shadow of their souls. The confusion and disorientation caused by suffering were so profound that it failed them to comprehend or rationalize it. They express it only as a metaphor, like an abyss, a dazzling darkness, or a dark night of the soul. Yet, in the midst of suffering, they were caught with a silence filled not only with fear but also with a deep yearning for God. Thus the mystics chose silence. Rather than remaining constricted in forced and imposed silence, they attuned themselves in silence, through which they listened to God, who was ineffable. They altered coercive silence into mystical and contemplative silence that freed them from the falsity of human constructions of God and other vulnerable beings. They understood that extreme suffering, whether internal or external, can only be approached through contemplation, which entails a complete reliance on and trust in God.

With the theoretical lens established in this chapter, the following chapters navigate the multilayered experience of silence, spanning diverse cultures, social and political circumstances, and disciplines, in an effort to create a space for mystical and contemplative silence. I consider questions about the role of mystical and contemplative silence in the realities of suffering as a solacing and transformative space for the defenseless. How might mystical and contemplative silence offer shelter for the marginalized and vulnerable and simultaneously motivate them not to be trapped in forced and imposed silence? How can we negotiate the need for creating silence for our own renewal while also speaking out for truth and justice? How can mystical and contemplative silence complement the urge for action against injustice? How can we claim and reclaim silence, especially for the vulnerable and subjugated, not as an experience of suppression, nor a means of escapism, nor even a glib solution for healing, but as a grounding and orientation for renewed speech? Most of all, how might mystical and contemplative silence lead us to the divine and enable us to remain in communion with the divine? With these and other questions in mind, the following chapters explore mystical and contemplative silence as a space for reflection and transformation, challenging the dominance of speech and words that define, judge, and marginalize the vulnerable. In this exploration, I aim to resist the allure of immediate meaning, to gracefully acknowledge my limitations, and to embrace the joy found in accepting the uncertainty and unknowability of the divine mystery.

NOTES

1. Stephen H. Sumida, *And the View from the Shore: Literacy Traditions of Hawai'i* (Seattle: University of Washington Press), quoted in Cheung, *Articulate Silences*, 8.
2. Kim, "We Talk, Therefore We Think," 828–42.
3. Brett J. Esaki's *Enfolding Silence* eloquently explores this alternative aspect of silence in Japanese and Japanese American culture.
4. For diverse forms of the practice of silence, see Greene, *Philosophy of Silence*; Dauenhauer, *Silence*; Kurzon, *Discourse of Silence*; Jaworski, *Power of Silence*; and Knapp, Enninger, and Knapp-Potthoff, *Analyzing Intercultural Communication*.
5. Steiner, *Language and Silence*, 36.
6. Ferrari, "Questions of Silence," 123.
7. Gates-Madsen, *Trauma, Taboo, and Truth-Telling*, 8.
8. There have been various attempts to deconstruct such binary positions across disciplines. To name a few: in *Silence* Bernard Dauenhauer presents silence as a phenomenon instead of devoid of sound; in *Saying and Silence* Frank Farmer suggests ways to hear and listen in the classroom and beyond; and Cheryl Glenn offers a new way to understand silence in conversation with feminism and postcolonialism by proposing a strategy moving beyond the dichotomy in *Rhetoric Retold* and *Unspoken*; see also Clair, *Organizing Silence*.

9. Jonathan Haidt, "Why the Past 10 Years of American Life Have Been Uniquely Stupid," *The Atlantic*, April 11, 2022, https://www.theatlantic.com/magazine/archive/2022/05/social-media-democracy-trust-babel/629369/.
10. Paul Celan, speech on receiving Bremen Literature Prize, 1958, quoted in Becca Rothfeld, "The Thousand Darkness of Murderous Speech," *Poetry Foundation*, January 11, 2021, https://www.poetryfoundation.org/articles/155169/the-thousand-darknesses-of-murderous-speech.
11. Celan, "The Meridian," 54.
12. Friedrich Nietzsche, "On Truth and Lying in a Non-Moral Sense," in Nietzsche, *The Birth of Tragedy*, 139–53; Nietzsche, *The Anti-Christ*, 69–152, 153–230; Nietzsche, *Human, All Too Human*; Heidegger, *On the Way to Language*; Picard, *World of Silence*; Wittgenstein, *Tractatus Logico Philosophicus*; Wittgenstein, *Philosophical Investigations*; Foucault, *Archaeology of Knowledge*; Foucault, *Discipline and Punish*; Foucault, *The History of Sexuality: An Introduction*; Foucault, *The History of Sexuality: The Will to Knowledge*; Dauenhauer, "Silence," 229–30; Dauenhauer, "On Silence," 9–27; Derrida, *Of Grammatology*.
13. More of Derrida's work on language includes *Writing and Difference*; *Dissemination*; *Margins of Philosophy*; and *Speech and Phenomena*.
14. Irigaray, *Speculum*; Kristeva, *Revolution in Poetic Language*; Cixous, "Laugh of the Medusa."
15. Spivak, *Spivak Reader*; Minh-ha, *Woman, Native, Other*; Minh-ha, *When the Moon Waxes Red*; Bhabha, *The Location of Culture*.
16. Olsen, *Silences*, 121.
17. Rodriguez, "Un/Masking Identity," 1067–90.
18. Janice Gassam Asare, "Social Media Continues to Amplify White Supremacy and Suppress Anti-Racism," *Forbes*, January 8, 2021, https://www.forbes.com/sites/janicegassam/2021/01/08/social-media-continues-to-amplify-white-supremacy-and-suppress-anti-racism/; Ashanti M. Martin, "Black LinkedIn Is Thriving. Does LinkedIn Have a Problem with That?" *New York Times*, October 8, 2020, https://www.nytimes.com/2020/10/08/business/black-linkedin.html.
19. Quashie, *Sovereignty of Quiet*. See also Quashie, "The Trouble with Publicness," 329–43.
20. Maclear, "Not in So Many Words," 6–11.
21. Synod of Bishops: Special Assembly for Asia, *Lineamenta*, 2 and 3.
22. Holmes, *Joy Unspeakable*, xx.
23. The spiritual writings of Howard Thurman deserve further attention, as do relatively recent literatures such as Paris, *Spirituality of African Peoples*; Pinn, *Varieties of African American Religious Life*; and Chireau, *Black Magic*, all of which enrich the contemplative aspect of the Black Christian experience.
24. Holmes, *Joy Unspeakable*, 40.
25. Lorde, *Your Silence Will Not Protect You*.
26. Notable works on silence in these fields that inspired my book include Malhotra and Carrillo Rowe, *Silence, Feminism, Power*; Lashgari, *Violence, Silence, and Anger*; Rich, *Dream of a Common Language* and *On Lies*; Tannen and Saville-Troike, *Perspectives on Silence*; Foss and Foss, *Women Speak*; Clair, *Organizing Silence*; Ratcliffe, *Rhetorical Listening*; Glenn, *Unspoken*; Basso, "'To Give Up on Words,'" 213–30; Achino-Loeb, *Silence*; Minh-ha, *Woman, Native, Other*; Palmer, *Courage to Teach*; Boseker and Gordon, "What Native Americans Have Taught Us," 20–24.
27. Esaki, *Enfolding Silence*, 23.
28. Prochnik, *In Pursuit of Silence*, 293.

29. Picard, *World of Silence*, 58.
30. Chrétien, "Hospitality of Silence," 47.
31. Chrétien, 53, referencing Johannes Tauler, *Sermons*, tr. Hugueny et al. (Paris, 1991), 13–17.
32. "Space," Dictionary.com, accessed September 17, 2021, https://www.dictionary.com/browse/space.
33. "Spatiality," *Oxford Dictionary of Human Geography* (2013).
34. Esaki, *Enfolding Silence*, 21–22.
35. Carrillo Rowe, "Be Longing," 15–46.
36. Laird, *Sunlit Absence*, 20–22.
37. Meyer, "A Space for Silence," 321, 336.
38. Heber-Percy, "Exploring the Spiritualty," 226.
39. Tenoudji, "Les gestes du silence," 343–64; quote from Meyer, "A Space for Silence," 322. See also Edgar, "Music and Silence," 311–28.
40. Cage, *Silence*, 102–3.
41. Meyer, "A Space for Silence," 333.
42. Prochnik, *In Pursuit of Silence*, 49.
43. Lefebvre, *Production of Space*, 26, 116.
44. Karlsson, "Doing Visual Research," 23.
45. Dauenhauer, "On Silence," 27.
46. Wolfteich, "Practices of 'Unsaying,'" 161–71.
47. Dauenhauer, "On Silence," 27.
48. de Certeau, *Practice of Everyday Life*, 29–36.
49. Nhat Hanh, *Power of Silence*, 20.
50. For more references of silence in the Christian monastic traditions, see Laird, *Into the Silent Land* and *Sunlit Absence*; Williams, *Silence and Honey Cakes*; Davis, *Monastery without Walls*; Arico, *Taste of Silence*; McColman, *Befriending Silence*; Bianco, *Voices of Silence*; Heuertz, *Mindful Silence*.
51. Merton, *Echoing Silence*, 56.
52. Gorman, *Amazing Fact of Quaker Worship*, 38.
53. Merton, *Waters of Silence*, 267.
54. Cooke and Dingli, *Political Silence*.
55. Stuart Sim aptly describes the necessity of paying attention to the potential of silence in politics and various fields (*Manifesto for Silence*).
56. Matt Murphy, "China's Protests: Blank Paper Becomes the Symbol of Rare Demonstrations," *BBC*, November 22, 2022, https://www.bbc.com/news/world-asia-china-63778871.
57. Carrillo Rowe and Malhotra, "Still the Silence," 1–2.
58. Dreyer and Burrows, "Preface," xv.
59. Rolheiser, *Holy Longing*, 11.
60. McGinn, "Letter and the Spirit," 25–41; and Schneiders, "Approaches to the Study," 15–34.
61. Schneiders, "Religion and Spirituality," 4, 6.
62. Prevot, "Divine Opacity," 166.
63. Schneiders, "Approaches," 20–21; Sheldrake, *Spirituality and History*, 17–37.
64. Haraway, "Situated Knowledge," 575–99.

65. Rowan Williams, *Christian Spirituality* (Atlanta: John Knox, 1979), 1, quoted in McGinn, "Letter and the Spirit," 35–36.
66. Dønen, "Christian Migrant Communities," 222.
67. Orsi, "Everyday Miracles," 11.
68. Lewis, *Cultural Studies*, 437, 420.
69. Michel Foucault, "The Confession of the Flesh," in *Power/Knowledge: Selected Interviews and Other Writings*, ed. Colin Gordon (1980), 194–228, quoted in "What Is the *Dispositif*?" Foucault Blog, modified April 1, 2007, https://foucaultblog.wordpress.com/2007/04/01/what-is-the-dispositif/.
70. Foucault, *History of Sexuality*, 27.
71. Schneiders, "A Hermeneutical Approach," 56–58.
72. Sheldrake, *Spirituality and Theology*, 3.
73. McGinn, "Letter and the Spirit," 31.
74. Wyman, "Constructive Theology," 10.
75. Copeland, "Theology at the Crossroads," 103.
76. Sheldrake, *Exploration in Christian Spirituality*, 94.
77. McIntosh, *Mystical Theology*, 5.
78. Traci C. West, "Defiant Spirituality," in West, *Solidarity and Defiant Spirituality*, 195.
79. McGrath, *Christian Spirituality*, 5–6.
80. Sheldrake, *Exploration in Christian Spirituality*, 107.
81. Rahner, *Mystical Way in Everyday Life*, 173.
82. Sölle, *Silent Cry*.
83. Yore, *Mystic Way in Postmodernity*, 20.
84. Sheldrake, *Exploration in Christian Spirituality*, 114.
85. Kerr, "The 'Essence' of Christianity," 556.
86. *Catechism of the Catholic Church*, 2721.
87. Richard St. Victor, *Collected Works*, 92.
88. Farley, *Beguiled by Beauty*, 14, 18, 77–78.
89. Merton, *New Seeds of Contemplation*, 5.
90. Meister Eckhart, *Qui Audit Me*, sermon on Sirach 24:30, quoted in Walshe, *Complete Mystical Works*, 298.
91. Frohlich, "Contemplation," 67, 68.

2

TO DWELL AND TO FLOW OUT WITH LOVE

Silence in Scripture, Liturgy, and Christian Mystical Traditions

Let stillness be the criterion for assessing everything.
—Evagrius Ponticus, *Philokalia*, VI

Since God's holiness has caused me to keep silence, I have heard many things. And since I have heard many things, why have I retained them?
—Hadewijch of Antwerp, Letter 28

Silence is sought fervently as a spiritual practice in our time, both inside and outside religious settings. Many faith traditions encourage members to pray in silence. Silent meditation in the workplace allows for a pause from frantic schedules. A moment of silence in a school setting aids the young mind's relaxation and mental preparation for the day's activities. Such popular practices of silence are valuable in and of themselves and are immensely useful for coping with the anxiety and stress of daily living. Many of these practices, however, see silence simply as a momentary escape from the realities of pain and loss that surround us. This type of detached silence is indifferent to the suffering of the world and cares very little about the systematic violence that silences vulnerable groups and individuals. Those practices also fail to acknowledge their connection to spiritual traditions where the practice of silence is rich with meaning and has developed as a form of spiritual discipline. As one of my students observed, "the detoxication through silence as a practice becomes a cliché without a rigorous attempt to be accountable to the cause that intoxicates the world." It may sound blunt, but the quest for silence these days has grown into a luxury for the wealthy, who can afford the time and space it requires.

Such a soft approach to silence presents a dilemma for those of us who are aware of its value but still desire to take an active role in alleviating suffering. In both the activist and academic circles in which I am involved, questions are often asked about how to find balance between the need for silent solitude and for impassioned participation with the world. This concern also reflects the desire to balance self-reflection with proactive involvement in social issues. Can we be both deeply connected to the world and committed to the need for introspection? Might the practice of silence encourage us to strive fervently for change while also preventing us from being fixated on only our own voice and personal perspectives? How can we learn to listen to others without being preoccupied with our own problems? How do we determine when it is appropriate to refrain from speaking and when to create space for others to speak while attentively interacting with them?

This chapter deals with these questions by exploring the concept and practice of silence in the Christian mystical tradition. Given that Christian spiritual practice is oriented toward a god who suffered and died for Creation, the pursuit and practice of silence for Christians must not lose its connection to the painful reality of the violent world. The silence taught and pursued in the Christian mystical traditions is more than merely seeking safe haven from the distressing and harsh world. The mystics believed that the God they loved so much cared not only about their interior lives but also about the existence of human and nonhuman beings in the world. The silence the mystics pursued in their yearning for God did not "fall outside the historical world in an allegedly pure encounter of God and the individual soul."[1] These mystics did not consider silence to be only a technique for regaining control of one's time, a means of disengaging oneself from the influence of outside stimuli, or a psychological need to reduce anxiety, as most do in modernity.

Furthermore, many mystics in the tradition encountered silence in its various manifestations beyond speech. They were silenced for their love for God, and yet they also voluntarily remained silent before the mystery of God. They were rendered speechless by their penetrating awareness of helpfulness in face of the harsh reality of the world, and yet they also knew that silence would heal and rekindle their minds and draw them to the ineffable beauty of God. For the mystics, silence was, above all, a love language to communicate with God. Silence directed their highest attention to restore their most intimate relationship with their Beloved. They also used silence to establish a sense of wholeness of Creation in relation to God, who cared deeply about the brokenness of Creation. In the vastly open space of silence, they listened to the God whose Word came to the silenced members of Creation and gave voice to them, as Saint John of the Cross says: "The Father spoke one Word, which was his Son, and this Word he speaks always in eternal silence, and in silence must be heard by the soul."[2] Thus, silence for the mystics was both the place of God to reside in and a threshold to renew their heart to reconnect with others in the world. Their insight may help us understand silence as a resource to come closer to divine love and listen to the suffering of Creation through fully embracing the silence of God.

In regard to describing the rich theological and practical significance of silence in the Christian mystical tradition, I find the writings of two mystics particularly helpful: Evagrius Ponticus, a monk from the Egyptian desert in the fourth century; and Hadewijch of Antwerp, a Beguine from the Low Countries of Europe in the thirteenth century. While the theme of silence is at the core of both of their writings, they each used silence to find their own way to rebuild their relationship with God and with the world. Their writings reveal their desire to strike a balance between the pursuit of silence for union with God and the quest for accountability to the world. Engaging with their writings, this chapter discusses the two interrelated aspects of the spirituality of silence: the mystical and the contemplative. I describe mystical silence as an invitation and practice toward the transcendental, and contemplative silence as the disposition and ultimate state of perfection. While contemplative silence is the state of the soul in union with God and the love language between God and the soul, mystical silence is generative, extending the soul to communion with other human beings while also returning the soul to union with God. Mystical silence creates pure possibility of words and images in its connection to union with God, where contemplative silence orients the soul to continue the journey toward divine love.

I begin with describing the manifestations of the silence of God in the biblical tradition as well as Jesus's silence in the New Testament. Then I address the significance of silence in Christian liturgy, where the silence of the spiritual tradition and the silence of our everyday experience encounter one another. I place greater emphasis through the chapter on my reading of Evagrius and Hadewijch with regard to the concepts of mystical silence and contemplative silence. The two mystics' works motivate us to discuss silence as both a discipline and a goal in the context of human suffering, particularly for those who confront forced and imposed silence that suppresses vulnerable groups and individuals and hinders our ability to listen to and communicate with others with integrity.

THE SILENT GOD AND THE SILENCED IN BIBLICAL STORIES AND CHRISTIAN LITURGY

The God of the Abrahamic traditions is a god who speaks. Yahweh communicates with people via words. The two creation stories in the Hebrew Bible describe how Yahweh's act of Creation began with speech: "And God said, 'Let there be light'" (Gen. 1:3). God repeatedly uses words to bring the void into existence, the earth into being. Yahweh also speaks with the first two human beings and continues to speak with their descendants. However, although speech is at the center of the communication between Yahweh and the Israelites, silence is also an explicit theme in their relationship. God keeps silent in response to their ongoing transgressions and shows the divine presence through nonverbal means. "I have kept still and restrained myself; now I will cry out like a woman in labor, I will gasp and pant" (Isa. 42:14). The silence of God evokes the silence of the Israelites, who are perplexed, frustrated, and humbled by divine silence. Job cries, "When He is quiet, who can condemn? When He hides His face, who then can behold Him?" (Job 34:29). The Israelites perceived that silence was the only means, at the end, to speak about God because God was ineffable, invisible, and incomprehensible. They confessed, therefore, "We could say more but could never say enough; let the final word be: 'He is the all'" (Sir. 43:27).

The silence of God was not just an epistemological principle for the Israelites in their attempt to know and speak about God. Silence reflected the Israelites' experience of suffering. While in many cases God's silence is interpreted as an expression of God's anger at the misconduct of the Israelites, it can also be seen as a unique way for God to show compassion and move their hearts without words. God chose silence as a means to respond to and communicate with them in times of suffering. The silent God in biblical contexts does not mean *Deus absconditus*, the absence of God. The Hebrew Bible includes stories of theophany accompanied by silence, particularly in association with the affliction of people.

The most well-known example of silence as God's way of revealing the divine presence is the story of the prophet Elijah's vision, a crucial moment in the history of the Israelites. The prophet stood at the mountain after his confrontation with the prophets of Baal, and he desperately waited for God's response to his prayer. After a strong wind, earthquake, and fire, the prophet encountered Yahweh in קול דממה דקה (1 Kgs. 19:9–12). The Revised Standard Version translates this phrase as "the sound of sheer silence." It is noteworthy that silence in this passage does not mean the muteness of sound. The word דְּמָמָה means moaning and murmuring as a dejected person or animal grieves and groans, forcibly holding back crying. It could be the sound of a mother dog quietly whining over her lost pups. It could be the sound of a person who suppresses her voice from bursting, with trembling shoulders, and weeps in the face of devastating sadness.[3] Elijah *hears* God's moan in silence. Though the aging prophet does not understand immediately what it means, he eventually changes his course of action after hearing God's silence. He has struggled all by himself laying the future of Israel on his shoulders and crying out to God, "I am left alone"; but now he sets out on the road and establishes Elisha, a new prophet, to share his mission and authority.

This God, who communicates with the Israelites through silence, also listens to their cries through silence. Not only does God harness silence to communicate a message to people, but God also embraces it to listen to those who are unable to speak. In Genesis 4:1–16, after Cain murders his brother out of anger and jealousy, God asks Cain what happened, and Cain lies about killing his brother. God says, "Listen; your brother's blood is crying out to me from the ground!" (4:10). Abel has never spoken in his brief life as depicted in Genesis, and yet his inanimate blood now has a voice. Upon hearing the cries of his blood, God becomes a witness against Abel's murderous brother. In this instance, God decreases the volume of all the sounds of heaven and earth and even pauses God's own voice in order to make the voice of the lonely and mortified Abel blare loudly in the universe. In his reading of the story of Cain and Abel, the Korean minjung theologian Ahn Byung-Mu writes that, while one may conclude that God seemed to play no role when Abel died, in fact, God challenges Cain's power by letting the earth resound with the silent cries of Abel's blood, serving as a powerful testament to Cain's wrongdoing.[4] This ominous silence eventually penetrates Cain's conscience and lets him face the monster within himself. Some biblical scholars also notice that the term "blood" (דָּם) used in this passage in the original Hebrew text is plural (דְּמֵי), meaning "streams of blood," and the verb "crying" (צֹעֲקִים) is in present tense, meaning that the cries of Abel's blood have never stopped.[5] The silent cries of Abel are a tangible example of the ongoing cries of the vulnerable anonymous—those who suffer and are silenced at the hands of the wicked—being heard and acknowledged. God listens to the inaudible voices of the suffering and speaks silence into the consciences of those who commit unjust crimes, raising compound guilt that rests upon them. The story of Cain and Abel demonstrates that silence is one way God repairs injustice and inequity.

The silent God in the story of Cain and Abel is also reminiscent of the God in the story of Hagar and Ishmael in Genesis 21, where the subversive nature of silence challenges conventional logic and morality. Until recently, when feminist and womanist readers, particularly Delores Williams, brought attention to Hagar and Ishmael and presented them as the main characters in Genesis 16 and 21, the two figures had remained silent to readers who were accustomed to Judeo-Christian biases that prioritize the lineage of Isaac, Abraham's second son.[6] The story is, indeed, one of rejection and abandonment. Yet an attentive reading of the story exposes another meaning that can be reassuring for the vulnerable. After the mistress Sarai gave birth to Isaac, the dejected mother, Hagar, and her son were cast into the Desert of Beersheba. When Hagar's flask of water was gone, she put the boy under a bush and went off, thinking "I cannot watch the boy die." Then she sat and sobbed. A seemingly indifferent God shows up and asks the weeping mother a rhetorical question: "What troubles you, Hagar?" Hagar is left silent in the text, which may have been an accurate portrayal of a mother who was devastated by the possibility of losing her son in the desert. Yet, God heard *the boy crying* (Gen. 21:16–17). The Torah says "God heard [וַיִּשְׁמַע] the voice of the boy" twice, even though there is no indication that he cried out.[7] This sound was perhaps inaudible to other human beings, but it must have preoccupied Hagar's heart. Ironically, the name God bestowed on Ishmael (ישמעאל) literally means "God hears" (Gen. 16:11b), while Ishmael remains nameless throughout Genesis 21, simply appearing as "the son of the slave girl" or "the boy." The phrase "God hears" thus is God's recognition not just of Ishmael's vulnerable state of being but also of the divine promise made upon his birth.

Native American biblical scholar Linzie M. Treadway offers a compelling argument about this story. According to Treadway, although this story can be unsatisfactory and objectionable to marginalized readers like Native Americans, it can alternatively be read as a story of assurance showing that God works differently than conventional justice. God acknowledges that Hagar and Ishmael deserve to have a "renewed sense of community with their kinsmen, apart from the exploitation and rejection of the Israelite community, to which they do not fully belong." The wilderness is a place of danger and terror, but it is also a "place of refuge and safety (Jeremiah 48:6)."[8] Even though Hagar and Ishmael never expressed their need to God in words, and may not even have found God's provision to meet their requirements at the time, God knew what they needed. The verb שָׁמַע in Hebrew means "a careful hearing of someone or something as well as responding appropriately in obedience or action."[9] God freed them from the control of those who would never understand their words nor listen to the cries of their hearts.

The theme of silence in the Hebrew Bible appears dramatically again in the songs of the suffering servant from deutero-Isaiah, the second prophetic book of Isaiah (Isa. 42:1–4, 49:1–6, 50:4–11, 52:13–53:12): "He was oppressed, and he was afflicted, yet he did not open his mouth; like a lamb that is led to the slaughter, and like a sheep that before its shearers is silent, so he did not open his mouth" (Isa. 53:7). Writing after the Persian king allowed the Babylonian exiles to return to Jerusalem, deutero-Isaiah delivers a message for the returned Israelites as they restore the temple and recover from the trauma of defeat and exile. The image of the suffering servant reflects the experience of the Israelites and expresses their hope and trust in Yahweh's purpose as well. The suffering servant, though he understands that God has rejected his favor, believes he is suffering alongside God. The silence of the suffering servant is an expression of renunciation of any guarantee for stable presence in the present moment and at the same time a complete trust in the will of God, who remains silent.

The silence of the suffering servant became a crucial marker for Christians, revealing the identity of Jesus the Christ as the Passover lamb. Matthew's presentation of the Passion of Jesus shows that, just like the suffering servant in Isaiah, Jesus remains silent in his confrontation with the Jewish and Roman authorities. Surrounded by the high priest Caiaphas, the scribes, and elders, Jesus was falsely accused of blasphemy, but he chose silence as his response to them (Matt. 26:63). He stands before Pilate, and once again is accused by the chief priests and elders; he does not answer (27:12). Pilate asks him, "Do you not hear how many accusations they make against you?" Jesus gives him "no answer, not even to a single charge" (27:14), which surprises the governor. Being led to Golgotha, Jesus continues to be silent amid more clamors, angry shouts, and jeering. Without a word of complaint, Jesus is moved to the cross where he is again targeted by mockery and humiliation. Finally, Jesus breaks his long and painful silence with a loud cry, uttering not his own words but a phrase in Psalm 22: "My God, my God, why have you forsaken me?" (Matt. 27:46). He receives no answer.

In his reading of the Passion narrative in Matthew, Canadian philosopher Paul W. Gooch observes both the silence *of* Jesus and the silence *in* Jesus. By remaining silent in response to such violence, the silence *of* Jesus discloses the immorality and senselessness of the very attempt. Jesus's decision to remain silent in the face of collective deception and malice is in itself an accusation, a powerful indictment of the sinister motives and wrongful intentions of those around him. Jesus does not "take up the weapon of words in self-defense" nor "participate in a community of corrupted discourse." Meanwhile, the silence *in* Jesus, according to Gooch, is due to his faith in

God's will, which prevented him from speaking because "there are neither words nor understanding." His trust in God breaks the law of economy and allows no logical explanation because it surpasses the limit of human understanding. It is a radical silence, and an attempt to articulate may create "false expectations about our abilities."[10] Because of his deep trust in divine love, Jesus knew that his entire being was to remain in tune with the will of God, and thus to express that love would fulfill love. The silences *of* Jesus and *in* Jesus reveal the fundamental characteristics of contemplation in which one is positioned away from the disruptive and destructive forces of the world and toward the divine.

The Passion narrative is not the only place in the Gospels showing the significance of both the silence *of* Jesus and the silence *in* Jesus throughout his life and ministry. The Gospels repeatedly present Jesus's silence whenever he carries on his internal struggles. The temptation narrative exemplifies the silence *of* Jesus. Before Jesus started his public ministry, he went to the wilderness of Judea to be alone and prepare for his mission (Mark 1:12; Matt. 4:1–11; Luke 4:1–13). He was there for forty days, tempted by Satan. While Mark, who features silence most significantly among the evangelists, keeps Jesus's wilderness experience in silence without commentary, Matthew and Luke interrupt his silence by voicing his internal dialogue with Satan, presenting specific moral and theological tests he must face. But even in their depictions, Jesus hardly engages in conversation with Satan. Instead, he stops the dialogue by simply replying to each of Satan's questions with a short quotation from the Tanakh.[11]

The silence *in* Jesus, too, frequently appears in the Gospels. All four Gospels hinge on a Jesus agonizing in solitary prayer and remaining in God through silence.[12] He retreats from people to a solitary place seeking silence whenever needed. One of the most striking examples of silence *in* Jesus is his prayer in the Garden of Gethsemane before being arrested (Mark 14:32–42; Matt. 26:36–46; Luke 22:39–46). Approaching the last hours before Crucifixion, Jesus takes his disciples with him (Peter, James, and John in Mark, and his disciples as a whole in Luke) to the garden and tells them: "I am deeply grieved, even to death; remain here, and stay awake with me" (Matt. 26:38). He continues to move "a little further" away from them so that he can pray alone with God, allowing the three to join him at a distance. Mark provides his prayer: "Abba, Father, for you all things are possible; remove this cup from me; yet, not what I want, but what you want" (Mark 14:36). Matthew and Luke also do so despite slightly different wording (Matt. 26:39; Luke 22:42). Jesus prays the same prayer three times in anguish, and "his sweat became like great drops of blood falling down on the ground" (Luke 22:44).

In the descriptions provided by the three synoptic Gospels for the entirety of Jesus's prayer, God remains silent. And Jesus neither argues with God nor adds more words to the prayer of his agony. The evangelists avoid verbalizing the silence in Jesus and yet portray Jesus as listening to God's incomprehensible will and consciously following it. Jesus's silence as depicted in the Gospels allows us to reflect on how his will transformed into unhindered freedom to carry out God's will without losing any of the intensity or integrity of his struggle.

The themes of Jesus's silence in the Gospel narratives eventually converge into the greatest silence of all: the event of his empty tomb, the vanishing of the Word of God before his Resurrection. Christian liturgy and prayer are the space in which Jesus's silence is eloquently expressed in *imitatio Christi*, the imitation of Christ.

SPATIALIZATION OF SILENCE IN LITURGY AND PRAYER

Silence remains integral to Christian liturgy across different traditions. Even though the origin of the term "liturgy" in Greek, λειτουργία, means "public service," the elements of the apophatic cannot be separated from the cataphatic in Christian liturgy.[13] The apophatic, *via negativa*, means to refrain from using words to describe God or to negate all the attributes ascribed to God since God is ineffable. On the other hand, the cataphatic, *via positiva*, refers to sacramental participation in the divine that occurs when we affirm and celebrate the abundance of divine beauty through words and images.[14] The intertwining of silence and sound in liturgy indicates that the apophatic and the cataphatic are complementary and do not oppose one another. Silence is as vital as words and songs because the purpose of Christian liturgy is to remember, celebrate, and serve the work of Christ, through whom believers participate in the mystery of the triune God that is ultimately ineffable.[15] The apophatic element is woven into the liturgy as it is directed to the divine in the manner of "the visible likewise to the invisible, action to contemplation, and this present world to that city yet to come."[16] In proclaiming the Incarnate Word, the church must fall silent before the mystery. "To speak of Christ means to keep silent; to be silent about Christ means to speak," says Dietrich Bonhoeffer.[17] Silence always lies behind the words, supports the rituals, and invites participants into the encounter with mystery that words cannot fully express.

Silence in liturgy is not simply a pause.[18] From the Roman Catholic tradition, the *General Instruction of the Roman Missal* indicates specific roles of silence in liturgy to prepare the participants for "the devout disposition" toward God, to recollect themselves, meditate upon the Word of God, and praise God in their hearts.[19] In Quaker worship, the belief that God communicates with each one of the spirits through "a direct and living in-breathing" of the divine life underpins all speech and actions, with silence serving as the cornerstone of this practice.[20] To hear the divine voice speaking to us, one needs to be still.[21] The purpose of silence in Christian liturgy is to listen to God, who speaks in silence—or, more specifically, to listen to "What no eyes has seen, nor ear heard, nor the human heart conceived, what God has prepared for those who love him," as Apostle Paul writes in his first letter to the Corinthians (1 Cor. 2:7–16).

Above all, silence in Christian liturgy orients participants to the meditation of the life, death, and Resurrection of Jesus. The liturgy of Tenebrae may offer a tangible example of how one experiences the paschal mystery of Jesus through silence. Latin for "darkness," "shadows," or "gloom," Tenebrae is the name for three prayer services in the last three days of Holy Week. Before the Tenebrae service begins, the reading of the Passion narrative allows the participants to engage in the liturgical drama of the Triduum, witnessing the unjust and unlawful trial of Jesus and joining his silent protest against the force of evil. Following the unbearable cacophonies of the collective wrongs recorded in the Passion narrative, the Tenebrae liturgy begins with words taken from Saint Epiphanius's sermon for Holy Saturday, recognizing the mystery of the silence of the night Jesus was buried: "Something strange is happening—there is a great silence on earth today, a great silence and stillness. The whole earth keeps silent because the King is asleep."[22] Then the service proceeds with the mournful psalms and the chanted lamentation of Jeremiah, and the diminishment of candles one by one until a single candle remains to symbolize Christ. At the end of the service, a loud noise peals in the space in darkness, emblematizing the earthquake before Jesus died, and the last candle is hidden. Then everyone departs in silence as the silence fuses with the darkness and becomes indistinguishable from it.

The silence in the Tenebrae liturgy manifests how silence emulates the life, death, and Resurrection of Jesus when we observe it in relation to the words and music. The liturgy therefore epitomizes the interplay between the cataphatic and the apophatic that is characteristically revealed in the paschal mystery. Silence in the liturgy is by no means a simple absence of words or the opposite of music. In the liturgy, we witness the simultaneous intensification of sound and silence, culminating in a reflection on the meaning of the cross. When the chant breaks the silence, and the silence soothes the chant, the two engage in a mutual relationship with no hierarchical distinction. The weakening of the sounds of words and music is "received into a deepening of silence" and the deepening of silence paves a path for the modest rise of the sound.[23] Silence creates the condition for the words and music to permeate the minds and hearts of the participants just as darkness was both the fathomless ground and the source of light during the Creation described in Genesis. In turn, the words and music exhaust themselves to the farthest extent in the mode of imitating the God who emptied divine self and died on the cross. Paradoxically, the less the words and music sound, the closer they reach the mystery and the more continuous they become. The silence then gives rebirth to words and music that humbly honor the mystery beyond their capabilities to comprehend. Words and music in liturgy must acknowledge that their roles are to evoke wonder and awe, instead of conquering and dominating the mind.

At the end of the Tenebrae liturgy, words and music rest in silence, making themselves part of the tacit and ongoing whole. Resolving the remaining tension between the cataphatic and apophatic, silence at last becomes a spatial whole that is radically open for us to participate in the divine mystery. In this context, wholeness is not simply a universal structure that encompasses all relationships within the existing order but rather the very foundation upon which all relationships are built. By breaking open the limitations of the existing order, wholeness enables the possibility of relationships that transcend boundaries.

The liturgy provides us with a space to listen to the silence of God and makes us a part of it, both externally in the sanctuary and internally in our hearts. The external silence is a condition for internal silence, which goes deeper into stopping internal noise created by our egos and discriminating impulses. Even while the internal silence is a personal and solitary space for each participant entering the divine mystery, it is also connected to others. Silence trains our ears and mind to rearrange our relation to the whole by offering a heightened awareness of the spatial whole as well as of the subtle things that otherwise remain unseen and unheard by our sensory organs. By participating in silence with the quiet presence of others in liturgy, we learn that silence is hardly pursued by a single person's effort. Silence requires that we be companions and engage in each other's struggle as we wade through the deep and challenging space of internal silence. Through the refrain of staying for the sake of the silent whole, we learn to let go of the noise within. In the temporal and spatial whole, the communion for which humankind was created can be remembered and brought together beyond the sum of individual participants who compose the silence. Eventually, the silence in liturgy awakens us to the abysmal depth of divine mystery contained in the organic whole of Creation.

Liturgical silence also illuminates and expands the patristic adage *Lex orandi est lex credendi*—"the way we pray determines the way we believe."[24] Derived from the fifth-century letter attributed to Prosper of Aquitaine, a disciple of Augustine of Hippo, *Lex orandi est lex credendi* underscores the force of liturgy to affect belief.[25] Nonetheless, as Orthodox theologian Alexander Schmemann laments, the organic connection between liturgy and theology is severed in both the Christian West and the East. This disconnection results in the isolation of *theo-logy*, the speech about God, from the liturgy of worship, thus giving speaking about God an independent, rational status.[26] Schmemann understands liturgy as the primary theological event and the source of theological reflection. In liturgy, Christians gather as a community, encounter the living God, and become enabled to speak about God and put their experience of God into words.[27] The theology of believers is continually shaped by liturgy, and liturgy in turn is shaped through the theology of the participants. While many scholars support Schmemann's emphasis on the intrinsic connection between liturgy and theology, some have expressed reservations about a possible tendency to identify theology with liturgy. The liturgical experience of God is unfathomable, and our human capacity to grasp it is incommensurate. Liturgy thus has limitations—it is "not a symbol to be 'read,'" and the liturgical experience cannot always be translated into words and images.[28] When there is no recognition of the limitation of signs to reveal the mystery, the Christian life is reduced to the act of communal services. This changes the liturgical celebration into a mere transaction, going through the motions to get a reward that will be granted in the future. Theologian Peter Phan provides a convincing case for the true meaning of *Sacrosanctum Concilium*: the glory of God and salvation are the goal and destiny of the liturgical cycle, not the liturgy itself.[29]

The observance of silence in liturgy can respond to this dilemma. Silence serves to balance and complement the characteristics of signs and gestures found in liturgy. It underpins the pacing of liturgy by imbuing intervals with significance or refreshing a predetermined meaning. It sharpens participants' focus on the incomprehensible mystery and heightens their receptivity to the Spirit that has touched their hearts. Silence serves as a reminder that the numinous, which is central to liturgy, cannot be managed or controlled. Inviting mystery into their lives through liturgy is a key way believers build relationship with God and grow closer to God. The act of listening demonstrates the qualities of attentiveness and care, and these are foundational to any relationship, including one with God. One must set aside their own agenda and needs in order to give God their undivided attention. The observance of silence exemplifies that the ways in which one prays defines one's faith. When we choose to pray through the method of silence, then faith becomes first and foremost about listening. Prayer and belief become inextricably linked as a result of the practice of listening to God in silence. We cannot believe it until we listen. We cannot fully listen unless we believe. Through leading a life of contemplation, we strive to emulate Christ, who humbled himself in silence to glorify God. The gift of silence in liturgy is then that the invisible constancy of the Spirit, who is always present and shapes our belief and practice, is revealed and felt. Therefore, the unity, continuity, and commensurability of *lex orandi est lex credendi* reach their zenith in silence in liturgy.

The maxim *lex orandi est lex credendi* is not limited to the Christian activity within liturgy. Liturgy must be organically connected to the spirituality of everyday life, internalizing the liturgical experience into the attitudes or values of the believer and at the same time manifesting them in space outside the church.[30] The observance of silence in liturgy, which allows participants to relinquish the impulse to control their lives in the face of mystery, also invites them to reflect upon the layers of uncertainty and ambiguity that remain unsolvable, irrelevant, and obtrusive in everyday life. Not only does liturgy herald the splendor of God, but it also reminds us of the brutality of the cross, which echoes the terrors of life's margin, where death is contained and accountability is demanded.

Theologian William T. Cavanaugh points to liturgy as an antidote to the ills of modern politics. According to Cavanaugh, the church has a responsibility to act as a public institution because Christians view God as redeeming history. He claims that Christians express political witness in liturgical practice and that these practices may help Christians make an informed decision about how to participate in politics. Liturgical practice runs counter to the secular modern concept of individuals as rational, self-sufficient, and fragmented entities who interact with each other only when it benefits them.[31] Silence, provided it is neither deliberate ignorance nor avoidance, does not conceal an unsettling uncertainty and inexplicable ambiguity; rather, it elicits reflection and understanding. In other words, silence in liturgy can help us recognize the inexplicable component of life experiences before we react rashly or allow those experiences to be written over by ideologies of dominance and abrasive political agendas. In this regard, silence may serve as both an ongoing critique of the voices of authority and a conduit for hearing the voices of the weak and vulnerable. The maxim *lex orandi est lex credendi* is then enlarged to include *lex vivendi*—how one lives.

While liturgical silence epitomizes how silence in Christian tradition permeates and shapes Christian practice and theology, questions persist. Within the framework of the Christian tradition of apophasis, silence does not just function as a method of discipline or means for resistance. To the mystics and contemplatives, silence was more than a habit to keep oneself from the destructive forces of the world. It was also prayer par excellence, the pinnacle of contemplation, and an indication of one's mystical union with God. Silence led them into the state of oneness with God as they became part of silence, which was God's being and doing. In other words, the mystics on the one hand learned from the silence *of* Jesus and made it a practice to confront against toxic influences of the world; on the other hand, they joined the silence *in* Jesus, surrendering themselves to God, who transcends reason and comprehension. Further discussion is warranted given the comparable yet distinct attributes of the two silences. I name the silence *of* Jesus mystical silence, experience that inspires, orients, and prepares the mind for union with God.[32] I name that silence *in* Jesus contemplative silence, a disposition toward God and the stillness of the mind that remains in union with God. These two interrelated aspects of silence invite a question: How may we approach contemplative silence in the beyond while remaining accountable for the mystical silence in the mundane, which cannot be separated from the semantic dynamics of everyday reality? I examine this question by exploring models of silence drawn from the writings of Evagrius Ponticus and Hadewijch of Antwerp. I first turn to Evagrius and his fellow monks and nuns who sought solace and faced challenges in silence in the desert of early Christianity.

MYSTICAL AND CONTEMPLATIVE SILENCE FOR EVAGRIUS

When Saint Anthony the Great entered the desert and joined unknown ascetic hermits in AD 270, he introduced the spirituality of silence into the Christian tradition. As he gazed upon the vast wilderness, he experienced an awakening of his heart, realizing that this expansive and solitary place was where his deep longing could find its response.[33] He recognized that the desert provided a silence that he hoped would restore his vision of the world through God's perspective. Anthony died in AD 356, leaving thousands of monks and nuns to follow in his footsteps and devote their lives to silent prayer in the desert. A life of intimacy with God in silence was for Saint

Anthony and his followers both "the fruit and the course of renewed style of living together" in prayer.[34] The Desert Fathers and Mothers established the Jesus Prayer, a form of silent prayer that focuses on humility and the opening of one's heart to divine grace. By quietly repeating the phrase "Jesus Christ, Son of God, have mercy on me, a sinner" (Lk. 18:10–14), they were led to a continuous and internal form of prayer. This tradition of silent prayer evolved into hesychasm, or "the practice of silence," an enduring approach within the Christian Orthodox tradition that emphasizes a contemplative prayer experience.[35] The word "hesychasm" originated from the Greek word *hesychasmos* (ἡσυχασμός), meaning stillness, rest, quiet, and silence.[36] The hesychast interprets Jesus's instruction to "go into your closet to pray" (Matt. 6:6) to mean that one must retreat from the world in order to acquire stillness through which one enters union with God.

Because hesychasm was a practice of retreating from external distractions to the tranquility of the mind, a quiet place was vital. Within the practice of silence, the monks and the nuns of the tradition wanted to be left alone, minimizing interactions with others.[37] The atrocity of the late Roman empire impoverished the perspective of all Christian communities and tore the fabric of their world apart. While some may view this isolation as a "fleeing" from the noisy world, the poignant call of hesychast spirituality was to pursue life in the desert not as a means to break free from harsh reality but rather to rebuild the broken world.[38] They were skeptical that Christendom under the empire could provide any clarity on what Christian life should be like. Theologian Rowan Williams offers a perspective to interpret the desert tradition's pattern of fleeing from the world: the desert monks and nuns withdrew from the corrupt "social systems . . . [and from] conformity and religious mediocrity," but they were not escaping from responsibility or a relationship.[39] Rather, they believed that by entering the desert they would assume an even more intense level of responsibility for their own sins and of others in the world. Their sense of interdependency among human company was intrinsic to their understanding of their vocation.

What the desert monks and nuns sought in the silent cell was, therefore, not some esoteric technique for uniting with the divine but a holistic Christian life. The desert allowed them to be keenly aware of the source of strife and fragmentation inside themselves and in the world. By retreating into silence, they endeavored to heighten the sense of intimacy with their neighbors and with the divine. To put it another way, they wanted to maintain a "critical edge in awareness" of their words and actions, as well as a "reverent distance from the intimate places of the others' heart or conscience," which affected their relationship with God.[40] The pursuit of silence in the desert was firmly rooted in the biblical precept to love God and to love our neighbors; as Anthony said, "Our life and our death are with our neighbor. If we win our brother, we win God. If we cause our brother to stumble, we have sinned against Christ."[41]

The importance of silence in hesychasm is not limited to the external and physical. Silence in a physical place allows for an increased depth of prayer, which eventually creates internal space for the mind to dwell and stay with God. *Logismoi* (λογίσμοι), the chains of evil thoughts such as gluttony, impurity, avarice, sadness, anger, *akedia*, vainglory, and pride, desensitize the soul and stir up passions.[42] By cultivating inward stillness free from *logismoi*, hesychasts pursued a state of deep silence that they believed allowed for union with God. In this inward silence, hesychasts were convinced that the presence of the divine could be attained like "a still pool of water capable of reflecting the sun."[43] Yet this silence was not a carefree haven or a transient feeling of serenity and calm. The desert monks and nuns found their true selves in silence by becoming one with God who mourned the brokenness of Creation. In other words, not only did they listen to God, who spoke from their hearts in silence, but they also listened to the silent cries of Creation that God voiced in silence.

The hesychast tradition's pursuit of silence sheds light on my description of the relationship between mystical and contemplative silence. Evagrius Ponticus, an Egyptian monk and spiritual writer of the Christian East who continues to have an impact in the West as well, aptly expresses the two levels of silence. Evagrius was born around 345 at Ibora, Pontus, near Arnesi, where Basil the Great (330–379), Gregory of Nazianzus (329–390), and Macrina (327–379) established a model for monastic life along the Iris River. The brilliant and ambitious young Evagrius rose to prominence by his active engagement with the various theological debates that were taking place at the time. In spite of this, a failed love affair drove him to escape Constantinople for Jerusalem, and he eventually chose to pursue a monastic life in the cells of Nitrus and Egypt.[44] Evagrius authored some of the earliest philosophical and theological expositions on hesychasm. Among them, *Chapters on Prayer*, *Reflections*, and *On Thoughts* were particularly influential in the transmission of the hesychastic tradition's voluminous vocabulary and a vision of the spiritual life rooted in prayer.[45]

What I find remarkable in Evagrius's treatises on prayer is his description of the relational character of prayer. Based on his trinitarian understanding of God, Evagrius perceives that prayer is intrinsically relational, because it is a "continual intercourse of the spirit with God," who is radically relational.[46] First and foremost, prayer is "the mind's conversation with God," who loves creatures and communicates with them.⁴⁷ This conversation must be initiated by the grace of God, and the mind in the conversation responds to God with thanksgiving. The mind, in turn, is required to have an attitude of attentive openness toward God. Although physical steadiness is ideal, stillness of the mind is essential for this conversation because mental distractions inhibit the relational flow between God and the mind. The mind constructs distracting images based on its attachment to rational things that stir passions and thus disturb the mind's concentration on the conversation with God.

While prayer must be free from passionate distraction, the experience is not a condition of apathy in the modern sense. Evagrius cautions against the vice of insensitivity or hard-heartedness as much as he warns against passion.⁴⁸ The relational nature of prayer causes particular emotions, or more precisely, transfigured emotions, leading one to *apatheia*. A simple translation of *apatheia* is the state of love. Unlike the English word "apathy," *apatheia* is a profoundly relational term expressing "the full and harmonious integration of emotional life under the influence of love."⁴⁹ When the monks and nuns experienced the state of *apatheia*, they were not expected to remove all human emotions and show an equal degree of indifference toward all. To the contrary, they learned to love all, to keep harmonious relationships with their siblings, and to be sensible to the wholeness of Creation. The emotions Evagrius considers in this context are different from passions that agitate the mind. The passions of distraction are the construction and the claim of the mind, while the emotions during prayer are an indication of the mind becoming close to divine love. Passions make the mind feel further from God as they falsify love, but the emotions of prayer allow the soul to access divine compassion. Evagrius does not hesitate to adopt emotive terms—"compunction" and "joy" in particular—in describing this relational nature of prayer.

According to Evagrius, compunction, κατανύξεως in Greek, entails a profound sense of humility, repentance, and a "piercing and puncturing of the soul with tears."⁵⁰ Unlike passion, compunction is a "peaceful" state of mind, sprouting from "natural" seeds that are the potential of nature given by God in Creation.⁵¹ What anchors compunction is an unending yearning for the divine, and it reconnects the soul to divine love. It serves as a reminder to the soul of its mortality and fragile existence as a result of its estrangement from divine love. Theologian Douglas Christie writes that compunction is a "sustained process of self-reflection, opening oneself to the possibility of change and renewal, a transformation of one's entire relationship with the world."⁵² Compunction is not a fleeting review of one's life. It requires a rigorous practice of looking into the deeper roots of one's sacred desires.

For the mind to immerse in compunction, the practice of silence is essential. The mind must guard itself from distractive thoughts in order to open itself to compunction. Silence softens the mind by helping it to see its true nature in relation to God. It also assists one to form a communion with others who gather in silence and share sensitivity to helplessness and awareness of brokenness in hope of change and renewal. A monk is one who "esteems himself as one with all people because he ever believes he sees himself in each person," says Evagrius.[53] The Holy Spirit is not only present with the monks and the nuns who feel compunction during silent prayer, but also feels it with them: "The Holy Spirit, sympathizing with our weakness, regularly visits us."[54] On the whole, silence provides a mental space in which one can experience compunction and become receptive to the power of love. It prepares one to be filled with a "new way of seeing and speaking" with an awareness of one's intrinsic connection to God and to Creation.[55] Silence in this context remains in a mystical dimension as it creates a threshold or an in-between phase that can hold open space for many possibilities. The liminality of mystical silence thus allows for a quality of ambiguity and uncertainty through which one is compelled to examine their words, emotions, thoughts, and deeds with deep trust in divine love.

Other than compunction, Evagrius also highlights joy, which demonstrates the aspect of contemplative silence. Evagrius concludes *Chapters on Prayer* by describing prayer as the fruit that ripens when joy transcends all: "When you give yourself to prayer, rise above every other joy—then you will find true prayer."[56] Praying is intense joying, and intense joying is praying. To Evagrius, joy is not delight or pleasure. Joy is more of a disposition than a "feeling," in the same way that true prayer is more of a state than a practice. Theologian Virginia Burrus's reading of Evagrius's *Chapters on Prayer* offers insights into understanding what Evagrius means by prayer as sublime joy. Quoting French philosopher Jean-Luc Nancy's essay "Shattered Love," Burrus explains that the nature of joy for Evagrius is a state in which the soul is transformed by and into the radical relationality of divine love. Divine love here works as both a facilitator (*eros*) and the final destination (*agape*). In true prayer, one attains the sublime joy that is a mark of divine love at work. Divine love cuts across one by "breaking" her heart, "that constitutes [her] 'heart' as such in its very bearing—and thus exposes [her] to joy." In other words, joy encompasses the senses with an invitation both to rejoice and to become. It drives one to realize that, apart from God, there is no such thing as an independent self or a basis for one's existence. To feel joy is to feel the dissolving of the falsified state of being estranged from God. Divine love keeps one open and allows the flow of love—to love and to be loved—to continue.[57]

By surrendering oneself to the work of love that is radically relational and the source of all intimacy, one can release the falsified construction of estrangement and return to the state of union with the divine. Evagrius says, "when minds flow back to [God] like the torrents into the sea, [God] changes them all completely into [God's] own nature, color, and taste."[58] God is the ground of all relationships. The union with God is the relationship that underpins and gives rise to all other relationships. In this deepest relationship with God, one remains silent because one has no need for words, just as moments of contented peace arise in the relational space between silent lovers. It is important to affirm that silence in this state is never the consequence of being silenced against one's will, but rather the consent to relinquish the urge to fill silence with words. In this state of joyful prayer, nothing arises as an object of thinking, willing, or speaking independent of God. One sees, hears, and feels everything in and through God. This is what I call contemplative silence, the goal of the spirituality of silence.

The descriptions of compunction and joy, the two emotions arising as the result of the presence of divine love during silent prayer, illuminate the respective functions and defining features of mystical and contemplative silence. Mystical silence serves as a restorative awakening, wherein the Spirit-inspired mind vigilantly counters the illusion of separation from God, thereby reinstating a relational wholeness with the divine. Meanwhile, contemplative silence is the state of mind enthralled by fundamentally ineffable divine love. Contemplative silence is therefore not a practice but the sign of pure prayer, which is joying exuberantly with God and in God to the extent one loses themselves in God. Contemplative silence, then, is to be approached through the practice of mystical silence that strips all mental constructions that obstruct the work of divine love. While contemplative silence is grounded upon one's communion with God, mystical silence is creative, extending the communion toward others as well as bringing it back to God.

Evagrius provides spatial metaphors for pure prayer that further clarify the interdependent nature of mystical silence and contemplative silence. In his depiction of the mind during prayer ascending to and uniting with God, Evagrius names pure prayer as the "place of God" or "the temple of God," drawing on the biblical imagery of Exodus 24:9–11: "When the mind has put off the old self and shall put on the one born of grace, then it will see its own state in the time of prayer resembling sapphire or the color of heaven; this state scripture calls the place of God that was seen by the elders on Mount Sinai."[59]

Evagrius warns that the "place of God" that the mind attains during prayer must not be confused with the idea that God has a physical dwelling place or is only accessible in an imagined realm that one might experience in trance. He considers this thought to be one of "the traps" that leads to the false belief that "God is actually situated there as in a place." Instead, for Evagrius God is "without quantity and without all outward forms."[60] The "perfect place of God" is of silent emptiness, open and accessible to the mind that has suspended its perception and imagination. One cannot comprehend, grasp, furnish, or claim this space, they can only dwell in the state of the mind where union with the life of God is the pinnacle of contemplation.

In looking closer, I want to bring our attention to the line in which Evagrius presents his most illuminating spatial metaphor of the "sapphire or the color of heaven" as the "place of God." He writes that during prayer the mind will see its own state that resembles the "sapphire" or "sky-blue" that shines in the soul. This state of mind allows the heart to see and experience "the place of God." In other words, the mind corresponds with the vision of God during true prayer, and then mind itself becomes the place of God by manifesting God through itself like a mirror or perfect, still water. The vision of God for Evagrius is not knowledge that can be gained. Rather, it is the transformation of the soul to become the actual place of God by losing attachment to the fabricated construction of self sans God. The way one sees becomes identical with the way one exists.[61]

In summation, in the journey of the soul, silence is both the departure point and final destination. The openness toward mystical silence allows for divine love to be heard and felt. It paves the way for the soul to unlearn and feeds the longing to return to God who is the whole. Contemplative silence is to listen *in* God and to be silent in God's place. It is the contemplative silence in union with God that traces back before Creation, to a profound stillness that gives birth to all words and draws back to itself. By opening up and spacing itself out, contemplative silence orients mystical silence to the divine. Mystical silence, meanwhile, promotes our ability to unlearn by clearing out space to experience the place of God given to us at Creation. It awakens compunction in our hearts, leaving us vulnerable to the arrival of love and eventually inviting us into the joy of letting go of our ego and returning to God. Through this abiding sense of wholeness in silence that also draws and enraptures, the soul knows that God is the supreme relationality that grounds, integrates, and nourishes all relationship.

To Evagrius, the wholeness that finds in the place of God is a sense of interconnectedness not only with God but also with the living world God created. By virtue of God's intimate relationship with Creation, one forms a radical unity with God and renews their relation with Creation. In this place, one relinquishes belief in non-sentient detail and instead connects with everything in unity through detachment from fabricated perceptions and imaginations. Hence Evagrius says, "Let stillness be the criterion for assessing everything."[62] Experiencing silence in the place of God amplifies our sensitivity to God's Creation because we listen more by quelling the noise within and outside. By allowing ourselves to be open and receptive to God, we cultivate the ability to hear what can only be heard when the volume of our own voice is lowered. Just like Evagrius and his fellow monks and nuns in the desert, we grow to take on the responsibility of clarifying for those who were engrossed in matters apart from God. We join the silence in Jesus, who surrendered his own will to the work of love. Eventually, we are enabled to listen in "sheer silence" to the God who honored the silence of Abel, Hagar, and Ishmael. Thus, the seemingly self-contradictory statement of contemporary mystic Thomas Merton makes sense for us: "My solitude, however, is not my own, for I see now how much it belongs to them—and I have a responsibility for it in their regard, not just in my own. It is because I am one with them that I owe it to them to be alone, and when I am alone, they are not 'they' but my own self. There are no strangers!"[63]

Merton's epiphany directs us toward our next discussion, in which I must ponder questions that relentlessly disturb me. Most notably: if the desert provided the monks and nuns with external and internal space for silence so that they could devote their lives to contemplation, what can we do as we pursue contemplation in the mundane of modernity, where we are inevitably confronted by forces that disrupt our minds' stillness? Is silence an appropriate response to the experience of suffering and loss in the world that urges us to bear witness? The Fifth Ecumenical Council's identification of Evagrius as an Origenist in 553 cast a shadow over his legacy. This heresy accusation overshadowed his contributions, dimming the light of his profound theological insights and constraining scholarly engagement with his work. Ironically, while his contemplative teachings deeply resonate with the silenced, they could not spare his own voice from being silenced.[64] In what way can we practice mystical silence and abide in contemplative silence when we must speak for ourselves and engage in the protest of the defenseless, whose tongues have been severed and who have no one to listen to them? How can we make silence our goal when it exists alongside the loud cacophonies of a violent world that would prefer to silence the vulnerable?

In what follows, I delve into these questions by reading the works of Hadewijch of Antwerp, a mystic and poet from the thirteenth century. Hadewijch's life context reveals the difficulties of navigating a world that does not permit us to remain numb in facing the reality of suffering and loss. However, she teaches us that following the lead of love can serve as both a means and an end goal for a contemplative life while actively being accountable to the world.

MYSTICAL AND CONTEMPLATIVE SILENCE FOR HADEWIJCH

Hadewijch was a mystic, poet, and writer who belonged to a community of Beguines. Beguines were Christian lay religious orders for women that were active in the Low Countries in medieval Europe.[65] Along with their male counterparts, Beghards, Beguines were part of a larger spiritual revival movement that took place in Western Europe during the thirteenth century. This movement emphasized the imitation of the life of Jesus through voluntary poverty, care for the impoverished and sick, and religious devotion. Beguines lived in semimonastic communities without taking formal religious vows, which granted them relative independence from the institutional church yet placed them in precarious circumstances for the same reason.

Hadewijch's writing vividly depicts her own and a Beguine's life context. Hadewijch left behind a body of work that includes *Visions, Poems in Stanzas, Poems in Couplets*, and letter-treatises that show a remarkable intellectual originality and poetic beauty. Although little is known about her life, we know from her writing that her life was marked by some adversities. There is some evidence that she may have spent a part of her life living in exile after being expelled from her community. Though it is difficult to pinpoint the exact cause of her exile, we can suspect that she was intensely concerned about it, and that it caused her to feel upheaval and disorientation so profound that the very idea of ever knowing God or finding peace in her mind seemed improbable. Not only the contents but the genre and style of her writing reveal the challenging circumstances she faced. She wrote her theological treatises in the tradition of bridal mysticism, but, instead of replicating it, she mixed it with the style and expressions of the vernacular courtly genre Minnesang.[66] While bridal mysticism is characterized by the purely spiritual and faithful relationship between Christ and the soul, Hadewijch attires it with the stories of chivalric adventure developed in Minnesang, in which the relationship between two lovers is not protected by the security and stability of marriage. The soul in her writing is not a bride who sealed her relationship with her beloved in wedlock and who patiently waits for his return but rather a "knight" who never gives up his unwavering desire to pursue his beloved. This may reflect Hadewijch's own experience pleading for the power of love while she was exiled.

Hadewijch's Christology, central to her mysticism, articulates a profound paradox: to be divine, one must fully embrace humanity, as Christ did. Her belief that one must love God and human beings advocates for a divine identity that does not forsake human nature. In her letters and poetry, she explores the union with God, equating it with the soul's union with Christ, especially through the Eucharist.[67] This union is described as an intimate, almost physical communion, leading to a blissful yet painful experience. Hadewijch perceives this union in two stages: the joy of Christ's presence during the Eucharist and the sorrow of His absence afterward. These stages, termed "fruition" (*ghebruken*) and "non-fruition" (*ghebreken*), signify the soul's fluctuating states between enjoying Christ's presence and suffering from His absence.[68] In Hadewijch's writing, the two are complementary and reciprocally interconnected. Theologian and renowned Hadewijch scholar Paul Mommaers adds:

> However strong and permanent the contrast between *ghebruken* and *ghebreken*, they complement each other intrinsically. Far from indicating a succession of exaltation and depression, or a construction made up of loose component elements, these opposites appear as interacting elements of an organic unity. For Hadewijch there can be no "enjoying" independent of "failing," and "failing" is essentially connected with "enjoying." Moreover, these two contrary feelings intensify each other within the mystic's single experience of the being-one.[69]

The Eucharist becomes a moment of intense spiritual and physical union in which the soul and Christ share an inseparable bond, leading to both joy and pain. Hadewijch's Christological perspective underlines the necessity of deeply experiencing Christ's humanity, while also acknowledging the unattainable nature of such an experience, transforming it into a perpetual and insatiable longing for him. The union with Christ is not just a spiritual elevation but involves a tangible experience, akin to sharing bodies in the Eucharist. Longing for this union with both Christ's humanity and divinity, characterized by both utmost intimacy and impossibility, is essential for spiritual growth and understanding.

Hadewijch adopts a spatial and topographical metaphor for the description of both "the place of Christ" and her spiritual journey to reach such a place. Just like Evagrius's place of God, Hadewijch's place of Christ is where she "desire[s] to be one with [Christ] in fruition" and communes with God deeply.[70] She frequently refers to the place by another name: "the abyss." The imagery of abyss in Hadewijch's writing displays her understanding of "the common abyssal nature of the soul and the divine," "the place where the soul meets God," and "the mutuality of the relationship between God and the soul."[71] In this bottomless place, the soul becomes one with her beloved Christ both "in spiritual understanding and feeling" and joyfully remains in a "blissful silence."[72] Like Evagrius's soul in silence that dissolves all boundaries of estrangement from God, Hadewijch's soul finds herself in the abyss transcending the need for words, concepts, and images. It is noteworthy that, both for Evagrius and Hadewijch, the only medium for the communication between God and the soul in the ultimate place is silence.

Hadewijch's spatial metaphor in her portrayal of "the Land of (Lady) Love" adds a description of the challenging path that takes the soul to union with God. This metaphor illustrates an entirely different facet of the loving relationship between God and the soul. In Middle Dutch, Love (*Minne*) is both a noun and a verb describing the nature of the relationship between two lovers and also their performance in the relationship.[73] The Lady Love in Hadewijch's writing represents at least one powerful aspect of the divine and of the relationship between Christ and the soul.[74] The Land of Love, however, is not a tranquil and well-paved place to walk or dwell. It leads the soul to a "cruel desert" and "deep wildernesses" that stretch on forever. The imagery of the Land of Love reflects Hadewijch's impression of the geographic road conditions in the thirteenth-century Low Countries.[75] Yet the mystic employs the metaphor to describe her journey in the service of Love, especially the external challenges and inner conflict through which she feels as if God is absent. While the landscape itself is onerous and dreary, the soul also encounters various threats along the road, including a tormenting "winter," severe "storms," and "the thieves." Love beckons the soul to take a journey responding to her, but at the same time, the soul may also find herself lost and exiled, barred from all that is familiar. A blissful moment tasting the sweet consolation of Love is immediately followed by bitter and lonely desolation. The soul grows restless and anxious. For Hadewijch, neither resorting to rest nor pursuing clear direction gives solace to the soul. She "piteously laments" in her exile. Nonetheless, she continues her journey because she cannot stop desiring Love. For she knows that in Love alone can she reside.[76] The road ahead of the soul is tough, but Hadewijch illustrates that one does not travel it alone.

Hadewijch's description of the hardships she encountered on her journey to the Land of Love not only chronicles her personal effort to incorporate difficult experiences into her spiritual growth but also speaks to the struggles we face in today's tumultuous world. Her determined pursuit of the union with Love, the place of contemplative silence despite the obstacles she encountered along the way, then, may serve as an inspiration for us to consider the role of mystical silence both as means of resistance and of spiritual practice in our own life. Simply put, can silence become a resource and remedy for the reality of pain and loss? Does Hadewijch offer any guidance on this matter? The answer is a gentle, resounding yes.

Hadewijch's response begins with an acknowledgment of the difficulties involved in following Love's lead and the potential repercussions of doing so that keeps her crying out; in other words, she recognizes that the obstacles of life prevent us from ever attaining complete peace in this world:

> How can life horrify and grieve
> One who has given [her] all for all
> And in the darkness is driven the wrong way
> To a distance from which [one] envisages no return,
> And in a storm of despair is wholly crushed?[77]

The soul desires Love devastatingly in the midst of those serious challenges, but Love seems hopelessly tough and complicated. Love is "sweet" and yet "tempestuous"; "her great wealth bestows pauperism"; "her tender care enlarges our wounds."[78] Although Love may accompany the soul on the journey, she may also lead the soul into a state of exile, with no assurance of return. In response, the soul suffers, becomes resentful, and bitterly laments. While this paradoxical claim of pain and pleasure is Hadewijch's most persistent portrait of Love, she commits that the soul cannot stop the pursuit of Love since nothing else fulfills her like Love. Hadewijch captures the soul's ambivalent journey in its pursuit of Love, using the contradictory yet complementary terms "fruition" (*ghebruken*) and "non-fruition" (*ghebreken*), mirroring her experiences in the Eucharist. Along the course of her journey, her soul experiences an unhindered sense of the presence of God (*ghebruken*) and at the same time the painful feeling of the loss of God (*ghebreken*). And yet the experience of loss instantly rewards a blissful moment of residing in God's presence. Love "lifts her up into fruition [*ghebruken*] only to strike her down again into wanting [*ghebreken*]."[79] The soul's journey is a recurrent wandering between the presence of God and the absence of God, between the fullness of joy and dreadful loneliness, between perfect communion that requires no words to express it and a perpetual pleading and painful cry for love.

Hadewijch's journey for Love provides us with an impossible itinerary and an absurd guide, yet provides meaningful insight into how the mystic coped with her exterior and interior struggles in pursuit of being one with God. Interestingly, what drives Hadewijch to continue this oscillating journey is not the "fidelity or faith" (*trouwe*) in Love but the "unfaith" (*ontrouwe*) in Love. As Hadewijch puts it: "This unfaith is higher than any fidelity that is not abysmal, I mean, than a fidelity that allows itself to rest peacefully without the full possession of Love, or than a fidelity that takes pleasure in what it has in the hand. This noble unfaith greatly enlarges consciousness."[80]

The mystic's gift is the persistent awareness of her deepest desire to abide in the place of Love, where she can finally find rest. In contrast to popular modern opinion, unwavering faith prevents the soul from giving what Love demands, which is nothing less than everything. In her book *Longing and Letting Go: Christian and Hindu Practices of Passionate Non-attachment*, theologian Holly Hillgardner offers an astute reading of Hadewijch's notion of "noble unfaith." According to Hillgardner, for Hadewijch, faith problematically discourages seeking and proposes contentment in the status quo, where unfaith does not tolerate "letting desire be satisfied." To put it another way, faith prevents Hadewijch's soul from yearning for Love by allowing desire to be satisfied before communing with Love.[81] In contrast, unfaith expands Hadewijch's reach, bringing her closer to the abyss, where she communes with God. Only in the abyss does the soul feel that the journey is complete, and because the final goal is to become one with Love, in an ideal way "everything is lost in love."[82] Her unfaith and her intense desire for Love enable her to use her experiences of loss and suffering as a catalyst for even stronger longing, rather than allowing these feelings to become destructive.[83]

Hillgardner links Hadewijch's idea of unfaith with American philosopher Judith Butler's notion of dispossession. Butler's dispossession refers to being moved "outside of the self" in ardent desire as well as to being "beside oneself" in grief or rage. Butler argues that desire and grief disrupt the illusion of a self that is protected by invulnerable autonomy and self-sufficiency. For Butler, the experience of being "beside oneself" is an ecstatic movement where one understands that they cannot exist apart from their relations with others in the world. Dispossession thus entails its necessary state of unlearning, or "undoing" of the self as a given, fixed, and foundational entity.[84] According to Hillgardner's Butlerian reading, Hadewijch's unfaith can be viewed as a form of liberative dispossession. Oscillating between fierce yearning and intense grief, she becomes aware that her struggles to maintain a sense of an independent and autonomous self is misleading. She is "beside herself" in pain, and she is aware that allowing herself to become self-satisfied in the safety that faith provides will distance her from Love. In unfaith or dispossession brought by both her desire and loss, Hadewijch realizes she can never be whole and complete outside of her connection with Love. In this undone, unknown, and unlearned state of unfaith or dispossession, she bravely chose to follow the lead of Love.

Through the Butlerian lens, Hadewijch's mysticism reveals the profound potential for offering a perspective on the connection between contemplative silence and mystical silence. First, Hadewijch maintains that for the soul in union with Love, the richest and most appropriate language is silence, not only because she finds God ineffable, but also because she has no need for words in her communication with God. Silence is the perfect language of love for the mystic and the abyss is the place of contemplative silence. The soul in the abyss, the ultimate place of Love, is "unable to find any comparison or metaphor" for "the unspeakable beauty and the sweetest sweetness of her lover."[85] And when she "feels with God in God," the soul also desires no language, because she knows "nothing separates [her] more from [her lover] than having to speak."[86] In this most intimate relationship—the coming together of the two silent lovers, God and the soul—silence is not a sign of diminishing or destroying Hadewijch's soul but of widening and deepening her relationship to the whole that Love gives the soul.

One may notice the remarkable resemblance between Evagrius and Hadewijch in their yearning for silence in the contemplative dimension. Like Evagrius's soul in silence that dissolves all boundaries of estrangement from God, Hadewijch's soul finds herself in the abyss of Love, transcending the need for words, concepts, and images that separate her from God. For both of them, contemplative silence is the state of soul captivated by divine love that is inherently unspeakable. It offers the soul the foundation of all intimate relationships in which the soul can happily let go of the urge to speak. Hadewijch experiences the same freedom from thinking, wanting, or speaking separate from God in contemplative silence as Evagrius, and she too feels no need to communicate with words since Love in the abyss fully hears and accepts her. For both of them silence is the language of Love. The sublime joy and the incomparable sweetness in Love go beyond the reach of language, and both mystics feel a complete sense of fulfillment in silence. For them, the state of contemplative silence is a gift from God. Yet both mystics understand that in order to attain contemplative silence, one must devote themselves to the rigorous practices of surrendering themselves to God, by letting go of their attachment to the fabricated constructions of the world and themselves. In other words, attaining contemplative silence necessitates a continual exposure and practice of mystical silence.

The two mystics' differing circumstances, nonetheless, permitted them to pursue distinct vocations and engage in mystical silence in ways unique to them. Evagrius, the desert monk, was gifted to cultivate sheer sensitivity to the internal struggles that silence allowed him to listen to and that urged him to develop a sense of wholeness in solitude. In contrast, Hadewijch, the Beguine, walked toward the challenges of the world in her yearning for Love. She renewed and refreshed her language in order to express the mystery of the human condition and honor the hunger to reach beyond life's obstacles for the ineffable Love. The gift of Hadewijch is for the poet. She sees herself as a summoner. She is aware that in the place of God, she does not need speech, but she also understands that the place of God is where Love gives birth to the Word of God. Hadewijch's poetic talent prompts her to proceed in two directions while employing the mode of mystical silence: On the one hand, she dispossesses her language, undoes her action, and unlearns herself in order to commune with her lover through silence.[87] On the other hand, her "unfaith" in the pursuit of Love does not allow her to plateau in "faith," which is the state where she is simply to conform and comply, not of the state of contemplative silence where she perfectly belongs. It is her "unfaith" that exposes her to mystical silence and drives her in the perpetual mode of search and broadens her horizons for the deepest form of communion. Hadewijch's poetic gift ties her more closely with others in the world, as she expresses it to be "flowing into his goodness and flowing out again in all good."[88] Hadewijch speaks of this paradox clearly:

> Since God's holiness has caused me to keep silence, I have heard many things. And since I have heard many things, why have I retained them? Not in folly did I retain what I retained. I retained everything before and after. So I kept silence then and reposed in God, until the time when God bade me speak... until the time when someone will come with such discernment as to ask me what I mean.... Thus spoke a soul in the liberty of God.[89]

Hadewijch, as poet, is broadened by her communion with God through silence, and unceasingly seeks new language to connect with other yearning souls. She cannot rest because she always emulates her lover, Christ, and she knows that there is always more to love. She constantly searches, moves, and grows toward Love until she is "wholly devoured and engulfed in [Love's] unfathomable essence."[90] For her, the journey *toward* Love and the journey *within* Love are synonymous, because "the whole universe belongs to Love."[91] Here, mystical silence preserves both the ability for renewal as well as maintains the sense of whole in its connection to contemplative silence. The abyss, the place of contemplative silence, serves as both a fertile ground for the poet's words as well as a vanishing point beyond the grasp of her language. In the words of Pseudo-Dionysius, the abyss is "always proceeding, always remaining, and always being restored to itself."[92] Grounded in the contemplative silence of the abyss and guided by mystical silence in navigating the mundane, the poet recognizes the limitation of her language. She is aware that her words have the potential to either hurt or help people. The poet assumes a "posture of vulnerability" toward that which lies beyond her comprehension.[93] Thus, contemplative silence for Hadewijch the poet is a radical opening as well as an unbounded dwelling. Mystical silence sensitizes her for ever-renewing words. The poet, aligning with Chrétien's reflections on modern discourse, understands that "Without this silent gestation of speech, we would have to content ourselves with 'the established language' . . . if the silence by which [we] listen to silence did not condemn [us] to speech, did not wound [us] with a burden of speech, if it remained a permanent muteness, [we] would cease to listen, and [we] would become empty, even if this emptiness were to be thought of as ecstatic."[94] By engaging with the interplay of these two dimensions of silence, Hadewijch's words return gladly to silence when they have exhausted themselves in service to Love. By searching for the space into and out of Love that speaks in silence, Hadewijch demonstrates that embracing and maintaining both mystical and contemplative silence is not only feasible but also essential for life in the mundane world.

RESPONDING TO THE REALITY OF SUFFERING

Even though the worlds of a monk in the fourth century and a Beguine in the thirteenth century are vastly different from the world we live in today, both Evagrius's and Hadewijch's struggles ring true for those of us who value silence but also want to be involved in a world full of pain. They teach us that we need to consider the mysticism of silence not merely in the realm of private and subjective experience but also in public and political life, where we must confront the forces that silence the vulnerable and listen to the silence of God that voices those who are silenced. The depictions of silence in both the Hebrew Bible and the New Testament enrich this insight that silence in the Christian tradition is intrinsically rooted in Jesus, who protested against the violence of the world with silence as well as surrendered his word to the mystery of the silent God. Our participation in liturgy may also provide us with a perspective on the value of embracing silence as a remedy against the noise and chaos of modern politics, all the while being mindful of the obscurity and ambiguity that permeate everyday life. The Christian mystical tradition commands that silence is the language that God and the soul share in their most intimate relationship. Thus, we keep our journey toward divine love through and in silence, despite the internal and external challenges. To be more specific, making time and space to open ourselves to mystical silence in the midst of life's adversities is necessary to strike a balance between authentic engagement with the challenging world and our need for self-reflective prayer in anticipation of the contemplative silence in which we remain in communion with divine love.

The teaching and practice of silence in the Christian mystical tradition, bearing uncertainty and rupture, challenge the predisposition of modernity to be captivated with a false certainty of safety. As theologian Inigo Bocken remarks, there is a tendency in our time to be "obsessed by the will to control and to close" the lack of control.[95] In contrast, the spirituality of silence suggests a possibility to endure the lack of control and even find meaning in the rupture. Mystics in the Christian tradition, like Evagrius and Hadewijch, cherished the value of silence in which they turned their sense of losing the certainty of God into their hunger for God, and they endured the hunger in order to let go, to free themselves from any fixity, to surrender their ego to the desire of the heart, and to attune themselves to what is always beyond and beloved. Silence helped them to be more attuned to their inexhaustible desire for God and journey with love, instead of defining the voice of God. Desire forms the life of mystical and contemplative silence, and the practice of silence intensifies the desire that surpasses desolation and offers communion, in spite of the inevitable temptation and the consequent slippage to fall out of tune with the ultimate place of the silent God.

How, then, can we transfer the teaching of the Christian mystical tradition into theology and spirituality for the contemporary world, which veers from one extreme to another, from opulence to abject poverty, from the ravenous hunger to conquer and control others to the hopeless emptiness of giving up a reason to live? This question turns us to the following chapters, where I discuss the significance of silence in our contemporary experience of violence in parallel with the silence that the disciples of Jesus experienced as they encountered his empty tomb. The loss and rupture Jesus's disciples faced in his empty tomb, the place where the Incarnate Word disappeared, may guide us to ponder silence both as an instrument and goal for our active contemplation in the world.

NOTES

Part of Chapter 2 will be published in a different form in the tentatively titled *Contemplation and Christian Freedom: The Power of Spiritual Practice to Transform Resistance to Evil*, edited by Mary Frohlich, RSCJ, and Benedict Shoup (Wipf and Stock, forthcoming).

1. Sölle, *Silent Cry*, 146.
2. John of the Cross, "Maxims on Love, 21," 675.
3. Burney, *Notes on the Hebrew Text*, 21.
4. Byung-Mu, "The Story of Cain and Abel."
5. Byron, "Abel's Blood," 74.
6. Williams, *Sisters in the Wilderness*.
7. Aharon Yaakov Greenberg, *Torah Gems*, vol. 1 (Tel Aviv: Y. Orenstein, Yavneh, 1992), 168, quoted in Laurence P. Malinger, "Hearing the Silent, Seeing the Invisible: Vayeira, Genesis 18:1–22:24," Union for Reform Judaism, November 2006, https://reformjudaism.org/learning/torah-study/torah-commentary/hearing-silent-seeing-invisible.
8. Treadway, "Freedom in the Wilderness," 126–30.
9. "שמע," *Old Testament Hebrew Lexical Dictionary*, accessed July 23, 2022, https://www.studylight.org/lexicons/eng/hebrew/8085.html.
10. Gooch, *Reflections on Jesus and Socrates*, 57, 59, 78, 79.
11. MacCulloch, *Silence*, 37.
12. The Gospel verses indicating Jesus's silence include Mark 1:12, 35, 45; 2:13, 23; 3:7, 13; 4:1; 6:31–32, 45–46; 7:24, 8:27; 9:2; 14:32; 15:25, 33; Luke 6:12–13; 9:18; 11:1; 22:39; 23:46; Matthew 5:1; 13:1–3; 14:22–23; 15:29; John 7:10; 8:1–2; 10:39–41.
13. The Greek term means an action through which people come together to become something corporately which they were not as separate individuals. In other words, it is a gathering whose unifying purpose is to serve the world on behalf of God. Guroian, "Seeing Worship as Ethics," 334.
14. Cataphatic spirituality emphasizes the similarity between God and Creation that emanates from God's self more than its dissimilarity. Although Creation is not identical with God, Creation exists within God's being, and thus human persons may mystically experience the presence of God in and through Creation and incarnation. The transformed and purified consciousness of the cataphatic mystic discovers God in all things and all things in God, although God is recognized to be always more than any single manifestation of mediation on God's presence to the mystic. Sheldrake, *New Westminster Dictionary*, 393.
15. Paul VI, *Sacrosanctum Concilium*, 14. Here I adopt the definition of the apophatic in liturgy offered by Kieran Flanagan ("Liturgy, Ambiguity and Silence," 196): "In theological terms, the apophatic is defined as a negative means of the knowing of God; in liturgical terms we use it as a means of seeing how what is incomplete in the form of the action is rendered complete in its contact with silence."
16. Paul VI, *Sacrosanctum Concilium*, 2.
17. Bonhoeffer, *Dietrich Bonhoeffer*, vol. 12, 300.
18. Ratzinger, *Spirit of the Liturgy*, 209.
19. The *General Instruction of the Roman Missal* mentions four moments of silences: the sacristy before Mass, the Penitential Act and the period after *Oremus*, meditation after the homily, and post-communion. *General Instruction of the Roman Missal*, paragraphs 45, 51, 54, 56, 164, 165, 271.

20. Jones, "Rethinking Quaker Principles," 179–82.
21. Bronx, *Silence*, 20.
22. Epiphanius, "An Ancient Homily for Holy Saturday," 11.
23. Flanagan, "Liturgy, Ambiguity, and Silence," 217.
24. McGrath, *Christian Theology*, 142.
25. Wainwright, *Doxology*, 225–26.
26. Schmemann, *Liturgy and Tradition*, 13.
27. Lloyd, "Liturgy in the Broadest Sense," 77.
28. Cavanaugh, *Theopolitical Imagination*, 92–93.
29. Phan, "Liturgy of Life," 8–9.
30. Cavanaugh, *Theopolitical Imagination*, 92–93.
31. For more information, see Cavanaugh's *Theopolitical Imagination* and *Torture and the Eucharist*.
32. As I define the notions of mystical and contemplative silences, I was inspired by the notion of liminal silence from the historian of medieval monasticism Burcht Pranger's insight. Pranger argues that some particular types of silence contain both silence and vigilance. Using the term "liminality," coined by anthropologist Victor Turner, Pranger claims liminality in this context as "a realm of pure possibility" in practice and distinguishes it from mystical silence that is an experience of transcendence. Pranger's article helped me describe the liminal dimension of mystical silence. See Pranger, "*Dimida Hora*," 229–45.
33. Williams, *Silence and Honey Cakes*, 15. While Saint Antony is still widely considered the founder of monasticism, it is worth noting that scholars are increasingly questioning the historical accuracy of Athanasius's portrayal of Anthony as the sole founder of monasticism. While Athanasius's "The Life of Antony" significantly influenced the perception of Anthony's pioneering role, recent research suggests a more complex and collective development of monastic practices, involving various figures and communities. See Barnard, "Did Athanasius Know Antony?" 139–49.
34. Williams, *Silence and Honey Cakes*, 22.
35. Ugolnik, "Internal Liturgy," 99–133. See also Chariton, *Art of Prayer*.
36. MacCulloch, *Silence*, 185.
37. Leloup, *Being Still*, 1–28.
38. Williams, *Silence and Honey Cakes*, 25.
39. Williams, *Where God Happens*, 70.
40. Williams, 63–64.
41. Saint Anthony quoted in Williams, *Where God Happens*, 9.
42. Evagrius, *Praktikos and Chapters on Prayer*, 17.
43. Ward, *Wisdom of the Desert Fathers*, xvii.
44. Leloup, *Being Still*, 28–29.
45. McGinn, *Foundations of Mysticism*, 151. Texts used for this essay are Evagrius Ponticus, *Praktikos and Chapters on Prayer*; and Casiday, *Evagrius Ponticus*.
46. Evagrius, *Praktikos*, 56.
47. Evagrius, "On Prayer," in Casiday, *Evagrius Ponticus*, 188.
48. Corrigan and Glazov, "Compunction and Compassion," 68.
49. Bamberger, *Praktikos*, lxxxiv.
50. Corrigan and Glazov, "Compunction and Compassion," 64.
51. Evagrius, *Praktikos*, 32.

52. Christie, *Blue Sapphire*, 77.
53. Evagrius, *Prayer 125*, quoted in Corrigan and Glazov, "Compunction and Compassion," 70.
54. Cf. Rom. 8:26. Evagrius, "On Prayer," 192.
55. Corrigan and Glazov, "Compunction and Compassion," 68.
56. Evagrius, *Praktikos*, 80.
57. Burrus, "Praying Is Joying," 197, 198; Nancy, *Inoperative Community*, 164n6. I revisit the subject of joy in chapter 5.
58. Evagrius's letter to Melania, section 6, quoted in McGinn, "Unio Mystica/Mystical Union," 203.
59. Evagrius, "On Thoughts," in Casiday, *Evagrius Ponticus*, 114.
60. Evagrius, *Praktikos*, 66.
61. For an eloquent description of Evagrius's image, "blue sapphire of mind," see Christie, *Blue Sapphire*, 171–77.
62. Evagrius, *Philokalia*, VI. 33, quoted in Laird, *Sunlit Absence*, 43.
63. Merton, *Conjectures of a Guilty Bystander*, 142.
64. Michelson, "Philoxenos of Mabbug," 175–76.
65. Hadewijch wrote in four genres: visions, poems in stanzas, letters, and poems in couplets (or poems in mixed forms). All Hadewijch quotations are taken from the English translation of Hadewijch's works by Columba Hart, in *Hadewijch: The Complete Works*. For necessary modification, I refer to the original Dutch versions of Hadewijch's works, edited by Jozef van Mierlo, *Hadewijch: Visionen, Hadewijch: Strophische Gedichten, Hadewijch: Brieven*, and *Hadewijch: Mengeldichten*, hereafter cited as *Visions, Poems in Stanzas, Letters*, and *Poems in Couplets*, each by number and line and the page number of Hart's translation, for example: (*Visions*, VII.64:72).
66. The Christian tradition of bridal mysticism derives from the biblical tradition of divine love and the exemplification of Jesus's self-sacrificing love. The tradition is founded on the Song of Songs, which Origen first appropriated as an allegory of the reciprocal love between God and the soul, an intimate relationship with Jesus, and the mystical language of the Johannine Gospel and Epistles.

    "Minnesang" is a term given to the twelfth- and fourteenth-century traditions of lyric poetry and song writing in Germany and Switzerland. The term identifies the theme of love (*minne* means "love" in Middle Dutch) and points to the fact that these were songs (*sang*) intended to be performed to musical accompaniment. "Minnesinger," *Encyclopedia Britannica*, accessed October 2022, www.britannica.com/EBchecked/topic/384329/minnesinger.
67. As with most medieval mystical women writers, Hadewijch makes the Eucharist the center of her religious life. Hadewijch, *Letters*, XXII.285:100. The significance of the Eucharist in Hadewijch's writing has been highlighted by Carolyn Bynum's studies of the relationship between food and medieval women writers. Bynum, *Holy Feast and Holy Fast*; Petroff, *Body and Soul*.
68. *Ghebruken* is a Dutch word translated as "to have fruition," "to enjoy," or to "possess" in Hadewijch's literature. *Ghebreken* contrasts *Ghebruken*, translated as "to fail" or "to fall short," "to miss" or "to lack." See Mommaers, *Hadewijch*.
69. Mommaers, *Riddles of Christian Mystical Experience*, 171–72.
70. Hadewijch, *Hadewijch*, 267.
71. Hillgardner, *Longing and Letting Go*, 80.
72. Hillgardner, 80; Hadewijch, "Letter 28," in *Hadewijch*, 112.

73. *Minne* also implies the dynamics of the triune God. See McGinn, *Flowering of Mysticism*, 201–11; Mommaers, *Riddles of Christian Mystical Experience*, 163–89. See also Newman, *God and the Goddesses*, 175.
74. Hadewijch, *Hadewijch*, 187, 234. The Land of Love is one of Hadewijch's preferred images that appears in her writing. In describing the landscape of Love, the mystic borrows a basic idea and style from the troubadours while constructing a uniquely dynamic tale of a traveling soul in her search for Love (*Minne*). Just like a troubadour travels a difficult road to find his partner, so the soul in Hadewijch's writing also journeys—to the Land of Love, responding to the call of Lady Love. However, unlike the troubadour's partner who is a personification of an ideal lover, Hadewijch's Lady Love is a "real and infinite being" who is the divine. See Newman, *God and the Goddesses*, 175.
75. Guest, *Some Aspects*, 193.
76. Hadewijch, *Hadewijch*, 64, 77–119, 168, 288, 255.
77. Hadewijch, 173.
78. Hadewijch, 344–45.
79. Mommaers, *Riddles of Christian Mystical Experience*, 129.
80. Hadewijch, *Hadewijch*, 60.
81. Hillgardner, *Longing and Letting Go*, 72–73, 337.
82. Hadewijch, *Hadewijch*, 194.
83. Hollywood, "Love Speaks Here," 205.
84. Butler, *Precarious Life*, 24, as quoted in Hillgardner, *Longing and Letting Go*, 113.
85. Hillgardner, *Longing and Letting Go*, 114.
86. Hadewijch, *Hadewijch*, 113.
87. Catherine Keller, "Undoing and Unknowing: Judith Butler in Process," in *Butler on Whitehead: On the Occasion*, ed. Roland Faber, Michael Halewood, and Deena M. Lin (Lanham, MD: Lexington, 2021), as quoted in Hillgardner, *Longing and Letting Go*, 117.
88. Hadewijch, *Hadewijch*, 71.
89. Hadewijch, 113.
90. Hadewijch, 354.
91. Guest, *Some Aspects*, 193.
92. Pseudo-Dionysius, *Complete Works*, 83.
93. Michael Sells, *Mystical Language of Unsaying*, as quoted in Burrows, "Words That Reach into the Silence," 213.
94. Chrétien, "Hospitality of Silence," 57–58.
95. Bocken, "Nomad and Layman," 121.

3

THE SILENCE OF JESUS'S EMPTY TOMB

Listening to Silent Cries amid Suffering

Awake, O Lord! Why do you sleep?
Rouse yourself! Do not reject us forever.
Why do you hide your face and forget our misery and oppression?
—Psalm 44:23–26 (NIV)

Impossible to hold in its totality, ever changing and elusive, the silent story of disappearance asks not for mastery but for a patient listening to its faint call.
—Nancy J. Gates-Madsen, *Trauma, Taboo, and Truth-Telling*

The Look of Silence, a 2014 documentary film directed by American filmmaker Joshua Oppenheimer, features Adi Rukun, an Indonesian optometrist whose brother was brutally murdered in the Indonesian mass killings of 1965–1966.[1] In the film, Adi visits the perpetrators, who remain in power almost fifty years after the massacre. While testing their eyesight, Adi quietly looks at them and asks them to accept responsibility. The embarrassed perpetrators explode into rage, denying and justifying their crime. During its ninety minutes the film is frequently interrupted by long intervals of silence, creating a sharp contrast with the perpetrators' benign, vulgar, loud verbosity.[2] Not only Adi's narrative but his silence powerfully express his visceral pain and testify to the death of his brother and the trauma the whole community had endured since the genocide. Silence strongly bonds Adi, the director, and the audience and invites all to remember the painful history and the numerous deceased, still recognizing the impossibility of "mak[ing] ... whole what has been broken."[3] The film is "a kind of poem made in memoriam to all that's destroyed" before which one should "pause and strain to listen to the silence that follows atrocity," the director said in an interview.[4]

As in the film, silence in times of suffering and trauma has myriad countenances. There is, of course, the silence forced and maintained by unjust systems. There is the silence of the millions of deceased victims, like Adi's brother, whose painful absence lingers endlessly. There is also a dejected silence like those of Adi's parents, who lost the words to grieve their son and cannot even properly mourn this irrecoverable wound. And there is a stoic silence like Adi's, who curbs his emotions in front of murderers in order to fully witness their depravity. The numerous chords of silences express the inarticulable experiences of each person while infinitely reverberating the silent cries of the victims and survivors. Before rushing to speak, one must be immersed in silence "physically, emotionally, spiritually, poetically, sensorially, and in every way" to truly understand the depth of silence.[5]

This chapter builds upon the previous exploration of mystical and contemplative silence and extends it to examine how it can be applied in post-traumatic suffering. In particular, I emphasize the subversive capacity of silence, as it allows us to unlearn and opens us to the unknown and uncertain, especially in the aftermath of violence. Among many challenges during and after experiencing violence, victims and survivors struggle with the inability to make sense of the world and to restore the lives they had before. The memories of traumatic events cannot be removed, nor can they be replaced, no matter how arduous one's attempts are to restore the past or to create a new life. One must live with a huge hole that will perpetually remind them of the lost pieces of their lives. Words are too frail and flimsy to reach the immeasurable depth of the gaping hollow. It is silence, instead of speech, that holds the complexity of memories when healing is delayed. Thus, in the face of profound emotional and cognitive turmoil, I turn toward silence and yet pose questions: Can the practice of silence assist survivors in the complex and often delayed processing of trauma, particularly when language proves to be inadequate? How can we recognize the role of silence in upholding memories? Is it possible to view silence as a distinct form of testimony? How might we harness mystical silence to help survivors endure the uncertainty and atrocity that lie in their journey toward recovery? And above all, how can we leverage the capacity of mystical silence to embrace brokenness and strain our ears to listen to the unsaid and unspeakable?

I begin this chapter by observing the most somber and obfuscating silence in the New Testament—the silence around Jesus's tomb where all speeches about God "[lie] dead in the grave with the Son of God."[6] When we read the Gospels as trauma literature, especially Mark, the stories of the disciples witnessing Jesus's tomb echo the numerous stories of victims and survivors under unjust political realities whose traumatic experiences defy a meaning of life. In the aftermath of Jesus's execution, the disciples had to face his empty tomb. His body, the proof of violence, had vanished, and silence filled the site that held so many untold stories and questions, while inhibiting the disciples from making any sense of Jesus's death. I portray the disciples of Jesus as survivors of a traumatic event of violence and immerse with them into the ominous silence of the Incarnate Word of God in his tomb during Holy Saturday. While conventional readings of the empty tomb account present the silence as a rhetorical device of the Gospel author to highlight the significance of the Resurrection, such a triumphalist reading largely ignores the traumatic experience of the disciples, who were left without even the body of their loved one to mourn. I argue instead that we must recognize the silence of the empty tomb in order to remember and testify truth and seek the mystical and contemplative moment in the silence. This approach will enable us to incorporate the mysticism of silence into our efforts to address the political struggles of our time. How might silence inspire trauma survivors to navigate their suffering and embark on a transformative journey while also holding those who stand by them accountable to remember and testify, as it did to the followers of Jesus?

By recognizing the significance of the silence of the tomb, this chapter presents silence as a spiritual space to engage in remembrance and testimony in the aftermath of traumatic events. While referencing other examples, my primary focus will be on the story of the *Sewol* ferry disaster in South Korea in 2014, which took the lives of 304 people, mostly high school students on a field trip. I bring attention to the advocacy efforts of the trauma survivors, many of whom are the parents of children lost in the tragic event. Specifically, I explore their campaign for a dedicated space to remember the deceased and testify the truth of the event. After the tragedy, the parents of the student victims led protests to preserve the empty classrooms that had been occupied by their children, a symbol of their desire to honor the memories of their loved ones. Drawing an analogy between the empty tomb of Jesus and the empty classrooms of the victims, I will discuss the role of silence in both places—the silence that beckons us to bear witness to the tragedy of life, engage in the practice of unsaying, and remain open to the transcendent, while finding the courage to continue on a path of restoration and connect with others who share grief. Let us first turn our attention to the site of Jesus's empty tomb, where the silence of the Incarnate Word echoes the silences of countless victims of unjust political realities and the inexplicable sorrow that the living must endure.

JESUS'S EMPTY TOMB

None of the Gospel narratives gives us a full story about what exactly the disciples were doing after Jesus's Crucifixion before the first witnesses visited the tomb. Fragmented stories, however, show the urgency of the harrowing night, during which they were filled with fear, guilt, and shame while protecting themselves from the threat of being killed themselves. When Jesus was arrested in Gethsemane, most of his disciples scattered and fled (Mark 14:50; Matt. 26:56). Peter and another disciple stayed in Jerusalem, following Jesus from a distance to the high priest's house (Mark 14:54; Matt. 26:58; Luke 22:54; John 18:15–16). Peter eventually denied that he knew Jesus, and he was left afterward with tormenting guilt, shame, and sorrow (Matt. 26:75; Luke 23:62). Meanwhile, at the time of Jesus's execution, the disciples watched him being crucified from afar (Luke 23:49). John had taken Mary, who had just lost her son through gruesome torture and a humiliating execution, back to his own home (John 19:27) and remained with her overnight. All four Gospels narrate that Joseph of Arimathea—a rich man, esteemed member of council, and "secret" follower of Jesus—assumed responsibility for the burial of Jesus. He dared to ask Pilate for permission to take the dead body of the lone criminal to bury it properly. John's Gospel alone features Nicodemus accompanying Joseph to the site of execution to handle the dead body of Jesus with dignity. The two men took the deceased from the cross and bound him in linen cloths with spices (John 19:39–40). Then they carried the corpse to a sepulchre in a nearby garden that belonged to Joseph. It was a speedy burial since the Sabbath was approaching (Matt. 27:60).

Following the scene of that turbulent night, the story of the empty tomb appears in all four Gospels.[7] The four evangelists report that on the early morning after the Sabbath, about a day and a half after Jesus had been crucified, the women disciples of Jesus went to the place where he was buried and they found the tomb empty. Beyond this entry, each Gospel writer delivers a slightly different story, leaving it open to theological imagination. Despite its abrupt ending, Mark's account of the empty tomb deserves our foremost attention, because it is the primary source for the other Gospels. According to Mark, Mary Magdalene, Mary the mother of James, and Salome visited the tomb to anoint Jesus's body. It was early dawn, and they worried about how to move the large stone from the entrance of the sepulchre (Mark 16:4). Upon their arrival, they saw that the stone was already rolled back, and Jesus's body had vanished. A mysterious youth sitting at the sepulchre announced to the women the news of the Resurrection. They listened to the news; however, they remained silent: "For terror and amazement had seized them; and they said nothing to anyone, for they were afraid" (16:8). The original and earliest manuscript of Mark ends with this strange silence.

Mark's enigmatic final verse has called forth numerous scholarly responses attempting to fill the that the first witnesses experienced. A traditional theological view, proposed by Karl Barth and Walter Kasper, among many others, highlights the presuppositional function of the empty tomb leading to the Easter proclamation. The tomb must be empty, and the first witnesses remain silent in order for the news of the Resurrection to have a sole focus. In this light, the empty tomb is "indispensable if we are to understand what the New Testament seeks to proclaim as the Easter message," because silence is to "obviate all possible misunderstanding."[8] The empty tomb is thus the evangelist's rhetorical device "to attract attention and raise excitement in the minds of those listening" and to reduce doubts and misunderstandings.[9] The silence of the women disciples, according to the traditional view, is assumed at best as an instrument to amplify the triumphant Resurrection or as a demonstration of the failure to speak about the Resurrection.

The conventional perspective dismisses the silence of the tomb in favor of the Resurrection narrative but fails to acknowledge the significance of the emptiness left in the tomb and the emotional turmoil experienced by the first witnesses, who were left without the body to grieve over. In her book *Spirit and Trauma: A Theology of Remaining*, theologian Shelly Rambo challenges the triumphalist reading and offers another view to see the story through by drawing on her compelling analysis on the narratives of Holy Saturday. Rambo argues that the conventional reading of Holy Saturday "can often operate in such a way as to promise a radically new beginning to those who have experienced a devastating event." Although a sense of hope might be necessary for the survivors when they feel as if they are drowning in a bottomless hole in the aftermath of a traumatic event, "it can also gloss off the realities of pain and loss, glorify suffering, and justify violence."[10] Rambo shifts the focus toward the ongoing struggle of trauma survivors living between life and death, where they must learn to live with pain while striving to heal through brokenness.

Reading the account of Jesus's empty tomb through the lens of trauma literature, similar to Rambo's analysis, highlights notable parallels with the experiences of trauma survivors. Mark's narrative shows that the women disciples were not able to grasp the nature of their experience and verbalize, particularly due to the absence of Jesus's body. Following the night of

Jesus's Crucifixion, disciples were confronted with the jarring discovery that his body had disappeared from the tomb. The rabbi and friend with whom they shared their life, values, and hope for the kingdom of God had disappeared without a trace. As Hans Urs von Balthasar comments, "The apostles wait in this emptiness. Or at least in the non-comprehension that there is a Resurrection and what it can be."[11] Throughout this time of terror and injustice God has been silent, and has now left the disciples with a desolate and hollow grave. There was no divine vindication for the unjust death or solace for the survivors, only ominous silence.

Nonetheless, this silence of God is not foreign to the faithful. When we are surrounded by darkness and it seems God does not respond to our cries, the feeling of abandonment and hopelessness is often more severe than the trouble itself. When Job lost everything but his physical and mental suffering, he and his friends desperately yearned for God to break the silence and bring clarity to their bewildered minds. Yet God's mysteries were unfathomable. Despite his unyielding faith that one day he would be vindicated, Job found himself waiting in vain for God's response which he so desperately sought (Job 24:1–2). Job testifies to his anguish in the face of God's silence: "If I go forward, he is not there; or backward, I cannot perceive him; on the left he hides, and I cannot behold him; I turn to the right, but I cannot see him" (23:8–9). His agonies find countless echoes in human experiences.

To make sense out of the silence of God, classical Western theism holds belief in divine providence, which asserts that all events in the world occur under God's control as the creator of heaven and earth.[12] The faithful who desire to live in the world responsibly need conviction in divine providence because it provides a foundation for their hope, purpose, and relationship with God and the rest of Creation, especially in the face of insensible suffering. This belief is built upon the attributes of God as omnipotent, omniscient, and omnibenevolent. It assures that the faithful can trust in God's ability to bring good even in the midst of tormenting pain, and to ultimately bring justice to the unfaithful.

Critiques of classical Western theism pose a challenge to its view of God as a being who wields divine power to direct the course of Creation.[13] These critiques argue that theodicy arises from ontotheology, which defines God as the highest being or the totality of all beings, whose larger narrative engrosses all the narratives of particular beings in the world.[14] This all-encompassing view of God leaves no room for the tragic human experiences that fall outside of the glorious divine triumph. Those who exist on the fringes or outside this overarching narrative may feel silenced and ignored, their experiences of pain and loss dismissed or marginalized.[15] As a response to the shortcomings of theodicy and the God of ontotheology, theologians turned their attention to the mystical tradition of apophasis, focusing on the God who is radically outside the reach of human understanding and language.[16] Drawing on the ultimate simplicity of God and the limits of human language as central principles for their theological framework, these theologians questioned triumphalist rhetoric and explored diverse ways to envision Christian hope, engaging in prayer and mystical life as well as addressing ethical questions.

I resonate with the qualms and apprehensions of the theologians in the tradition of apophasis, acknowledging the limitations of human language and thought in expressing the ineffable mystery of God and the inexplicable nature of suffering. And I focus on the role of silence by integrating it into theological discourse in response to trauma and suffering. The goal of my approach is not to solve all theological puzzles or eliminate suffering but rather to foster empathy and connection and find ways to continue living in the face of irrecoverable wounds while holding memories and seeking for ways to continue testifying. By creating space for openness beyond ordinary horizons, I believe that silence allows for a humble and reflective engagement with both divine mystery and human suffering, the silent God and the silenced, moving beyond facile explanations and easy answers.

The problem of the God of classical Western theism is not only that it leaves no room for voices outside the divine metanarrative, but it also repeals the silence of God because it assumes that all the events in the world must be explained, interpreted, and put into words, fitting into the glorious end. The silence of God in this view is simply a matter of timing, and it will be broken at last in the way the faithful hopes and desires. However, for the first disciples of Jesus, the site of the empty tomb offered no certainty that would guarantee the future, direct the next movement, or dictate the next words. Just as the Welsh poet R. S. Thomas lamented in his poems about Holy Saturday, the disciples struggled with "this great absence / that is like a presence, that compels / [them] to address it without hope of a reply." The empty tomb was a still place in the disciples' narratives, a place where they could not simply bypass the void and move ahead with any clear sense of what is to come. Instead, it was a place of uncertainty and perplexity that demanded patience and reflection. And it is a place where we, too, tremble before "the narrowness that we stare over into the eternal silence that is the repose of God." It is a place of waiting when hope withdraws, thoughts bewilder, and words falter. What resources have we "other than the emptiness without him of [our] whole being, a vacuum he may not abhor?"[17]

This void nevertheless warrants our deeper gaze because it brings us to a fundamental aspect of the human experience of pain and hardship. We live in a world where the problem persists, yet our faith often provides us with a false sense of protection. We witness wrongdoers repeatedly entering and exiting history's ominous gates without being held accountable for their actions.[18] Our attempts to resort to claim certainty prematurely in response to the reality of suffering often bring destructive consequences. The painful realities of the world "cannot be overcome by simple formulas and easy supernatural solutions."[19] The silence of Jesus's empty tomb urges us to be patient with fear, confusion, doubt, and the failure of expectation, even if it means enduring discomfort for a while, for otherwise our theological language about suffering will turn insensitive and irresponsible. The silence is mystical because it "opens a space where God is free to reveal himself as he is, rather than as we would have him be, and to transform without the disruptive clamour of our misshaping words," as theologian Richard McLauchlan writes in his commentary on R. S. Thomas's poetry.[20]

Nonetheless, to linger in the silence of the tomb does not mean one must remain stuck with desolation or pessimism. Rather, one must attune to the divine love that reaches out to the hopeless and lost, even if it appears nebulous and inconsequential. For it reveals the absence of God, whose utter self-diminishment raised the abandoned from darkness. The early Christians believed that on the night of Holy Saturday, when the disciples were full of sorrow, confusion, shame, and fear, the Crucified One left his silent grave with his wounded and scarred body and went to "the dead [νεκροῖς]" to proclaim the Gospel so that "they might live in the spirit as God does" (1 Pet. 4:6). According to liturgical theologian Martin F. Connell, early creeds put emphasis on God's presence with the dead in the lower world. The old liturgy of Holy Saturday illuminates Christ giving his hands to the discarded who were trembling in fear and raised them up, saying: "Sleeper, awake! Rise from the dead, and Christ will shine on you" (Eph. 5:14). This emphasis was attenuated when Christians in the fourth century replaced the formula "descended to the lower world" with "descended into hell," moving the focus away from God's presence with the dead to Christ's offer of victorious salvation to sinners.[21]

In *Mysterium Paschale*, Balthasar provides his interpretation on Christ's descent, highlighting his solidarity with those discarded. In his coming down to the hopeless place, Christ took the whole experience of the unredeemed upon himself. The suffering of Christ was "just like that of the damned who cannot be damned anymore," and thus his solidarity with them is none other than his renunciation that enabled him to connect with them and be present with them. Jesus's extreme self-deprivation is expressed in the silence of his tomb, which caused bewilderment among the living who insist on perceiving him as the glorious embodiment of the Word of God. Yet through the voluntary surrender of his identity as the Word of God to become the silence of the tomb, Christ chose to descend to those who were deprived of strength after they exhausted all the resources of hope.[22] Christ then invites the living to see divine love in the lowest points of our lives and prompts us to attune our ears to the subtle whispers of that love.

According to Balthasar, "hope in the theological sense is a participation in the divine life." To stand in solidarity with Christ on Holy Saturday is, therefore, to share in his self-renunciation manifested in the silence of his tomb, following him at a distance so that we recognize the silence of our own reality—the unheard voices and silent cries with whom Christ remains in solidarity.[23] And at this juncture we may revisit the essential aim of the mysticism of silence, which is to foster our ability to withstand confusion and uncertainty while seeking a renewed way to express love. Should we allow our theological preoccupations and religious impatience to take precedence over silence, we risk stifling the voices of those who are stripped of their vitality as well as ignore some of the most tormenting pain and perplexing questions that we have to face, all because we believe that we already have the answers.[24] We may also fail to recognize the good news that is slowly but unexpectedly coming through silence when it seems there is no answer to our cries or any assurance of eventual resolution. Therefore, I suggest that Jesus's empty tomb is a space of mystical and contemplative silence that beckons us to bear confusion and uncertainty and to remember our pains and losses, instead of hastily seeking glorious victory in the way we anticipate. It enables us to resist "our controlling tendencies, our desire for speedy resolution and instant meaning," so that we can listen to the discarded, grieve properly for irrecoverable wounds, testify forgotten truth, stand in solidarity with lonely souls, and become mindful of the slow and deliberate work of love.[25]

NUMEROUS EMPTY TOMBS

Establishing a parallel between the silence of Jesus's tomb and the silence of the victims of unjust reality, I underscore silence in political struggles as a space for remembrance and testimony, highlighting the role of mystical and contemplative silence in the process. In this section, I recognize the shortcomings of relying solely on speech in political activism and suggest that silence can assist us in navigating intricate political circumstances with greater integrity. Then, I bring together the seemingly disparate practices of silence and political activism to examine how they can enhance one another. The spirituality of silence involves a deep, intuitive awareness of the divine through stillness, allowing us to transcend our egos and perceive the world in a more compassionate and interconnected way. This approach may help us to respond to the aftermath of tragic events, allowing us to mourn and remember the deceased as a part of the lives of living. I propose that, by embracing mystical and contemplative silence, we can cultivate a more sensitive and humane approach to political activism grounded in a deeper understanding of our shared humanity.

Silence and Collective Memory

In his reflection on the war memorials to the missing, American historian Jay Winter says, it is, "literally, an empty tomb, and by announcing its presence as the tomb of no one, this one became the tomb of all who had died in the war." Winter's remark powerfully resonates with our reflection on the silence of Jesus's empty tomb, highlighting its broader significance in representing the lost and forgotten. Just as Winter argues, the anonymity of the missing soldier's tomb is not only a "cry against war" but "an extraordinary statement in abstract language about mass death and the impossibility of triumphalism."[26] So is the silence of Jesus in his empty tomb. When viewed from this angle, the silence of Jesus's empty tomb becomes a poignant symbol for the silent cries of those who have perished or barely endured unjust circumstances, such as genocide, war, and state-sponsored violence in countries like Indonesia, Argentina, Cambodia, Bosnia, South Africa, Vietnam, Myanmar, Xinjiang, South Korea, Ukraine, and Palestine. Echoing with the silence of those victims, the silence of Jesus's empty tomb amplifies their silent cries and inexplicable trauma and encapsulates their pleas for meaning amid the injustice and malevolence that pervade our world. We must pause, wait, and listen to the voiceless victims and survivors along with the divine silence surrounding Jesus's tomb while refusing to verbalize the implication of their death in fake triumphalism or effortless pessimism.

Nonetheless, silence in the aftermath of violence is often associated with oblivion and amnesia, particularly when it comes to collective memory. To remember the past, one recalls and recollects it through words and images. Memory seems to remain in the domain of language, precisely because silence does not address the socially constructed ways in which groups and individuals recount the past.[27] The relationship between silence and memory, however, is more complex and multilayered than it appears. Historian Thongchai Winichakul argues that silence under the control of repressive regimes and after traumatic events cannot simply be dismissed as oblivion or meaninglessness. In his book investigating the collective memory and silence around the October 6, 1976, massacre in Bangkok, Thailand, when police and right-wing paramilitaries and bystanders violently suppressed protesters who had occupied Thammasat University and the adjacent Sanam Luang. Winichakul states that silence in such a context appears to be a "symptom of the inability to remember or forget, the inability to articulate memories in a comprehensible and meaningful fashion, or to depart from the past completely." Silence, in this respect, is a different kind of memory "that is marginalized or unrecognized, suppressed, unvoiced, or unrepresented." It is "the memory we fail to hear or see, located adjacent to the expressed and voiced one." Winichakul terms such silence as "unforgetting." Just as silent notes contribute to the essence of music, "unforgetting" also forms an integral part of the overall landscape of memory. In order to give collective silence a meaningful context, we need to "train our eyes and ears to see and listen to it."[28] Silence in the aftermath of violence, therefore, beckons us to adopt a mystical approach, one that encourages us to open ourselves up to the unknown and the unheard.

Scholars who investigate the role of silence in collective memory pay attention to distortions in what is perceived as the truth about the past, as well as explore the process through which certain people and events are excluded from collective memory.[29] Like narratives, memory is recalled in certain social frameworks and is "constructed around its own blind spots and silences."[30] As sociologists Vered Vinitzky-Seroussi and Chana Teeger note in their article about collective memory, commemorative activities edit, omit, and ignore certain narratives with the goal of forming a cohesive memory to be accepted by the public. These activities often entail the exclusion, simplification, and amplification of certain parts of memory in order to make some parts of the past "palatable to all tastes—hence, bland and uncontroversial."[31] Those in positions of power determine what can and cannot be discussed about the past, thereby exerting social control over collective memory. Triumphalist, loud, and consumable commemorations are fraught with many political issues and may serve as a way to promote forgetting through excessive talking.[32] We need an approach that allows us to see and listen to what lies behind and beneath the written and spoken words.

When constructing collective memory, therefore, it is important to challenge the privileging of speech over silence. Speech can be used to enhance forgetting, while silence can preserve and reconstruct memory.[33] Speech can also serve as a means to cover up memory, yet silence can be an instrument for reclaiming memory by allowing us to reflect and intentionally build our relationship with the deceased. Silence, furthermore, inserts unexplainable gaps in collective memory and creates room for untold narratives. This "disruptive gap" in discourse resists power by cutting through established communicative norms. It erodes the existing power relations and directs attention to a party that does not or cannot voice their point when the dominant insists on speaking.[34] In a Foucauldian sense, silence can not only be "a hindrance, a stumbling-bock" but also a "starting point for an opposing strategy" and an "instrument and an effect of power."[35] Silence in this respect includes a mystical aspect, serving as a threshold for different insights as well as inviting us to explore new ways of understanding and engaging with traumatic events.

It is, also, when we take heed of this that we begin to recognize that the silence of victims and survivors is not merely an absence of their testimony. Rather, it is a different way of bearing witness that captures the complex and multilayered nature of the event. The mysticism of silence calls for a deeper understanding of the experiences of survivors and the commemoration of those who were lost. Instead of relying solely on the words and testimonies of those directly affected by the tragedy, we must acknowledge the significance of silence that surrounds it. This recognition can lead to a deeper meditation on the impact of the tragedy and a greater sensitivity toward those who are affected by it. It also enhances the opportunity to create a more holistic approach to constructing testimony.

Silence and Testimony

In her book *Trauma, Taboo, and Truth-Telling: Listening to Silence in Postdictatorship Argentina*, Nancy J. Gates-Madsen examines the role of silence in the fictions, films, dramas, and testimonials produced in Argentine literature and artwork in response to the repressive 1976–1983 regime, during which an estimated thirty thousand people were "disappeared."[36] After the regime's fall, postauthoritarian administrations and human rights groups were prompted to expose past crimes and repressed memories. Numerous efforts, including truth commissions and trials, aimed to break the silence and give voice to the voiceless. Gates-Madsen, however, interrogates the tendency to prioritize voice over other modes of testimony in the redress movement. Gates-Madsen's question is based on her challenge to a traditional definition of testimony that is narrowly defined as a formal written or spoken statement given in a court of law or to the public as evidence of state terrorism. The traditional definition of testimony may overlook the unique circumstances and conditions that prevents individuals from confronting and speaking out against repressive powers. I contend that Kimberly Nance's extensive definition of testimony complements the traditional one: testimony is "the body of works in which speaking subjects . . . [represent] a personal experience of injustice, whether directly to the reader or through the offices of a collaborating writer, with the goal of inducing readers to participate in a project of social justice."[37] Nance's definition emphasizes the purpose of testimony to encourage the participation of readers and listeners, rather than solely focusing on a first-person mediated narrative. It creates more space to engage with the silence of the witness, allowing for a more comprehensive understanding of their experience.[38]

Regarding Argentina's postauthoritarian response to military terror, the question about the role of silence is especially pressing due to the physical absence of the disappeared. Gates-Madsen's depiction of the *siluetazo*—an artistic presentation of life-sized silhouettes of human figures in the Plaza de Mayo, Buenos Aires, in September 1983—powerfully illustrates the impact of silence in testimonies, drawing attention to what is hidden or unspoken. The presentation featured thirty thousand disappeared with faceless figures in the plaza, silently confronting passerby and drawing attention to the unheard stories of those absent victims.[39] The visual rendering of the presence of absence reminded the passersby of the disappeared as a part of Argentina's collective trauma and at the same time expressed the impossibility of filling the hole. The use of silence in this testimony reveals a mystical element, allowing the figures to convey the enormity of the tragedy and magnitude of the loss and inviting people to a reflection and remembrance that goes beyond words.

Whether due to physical disappearance, the deprivation of the ability to speak, or the denial of the right to speak, the absence of victims' voices in human rights discourse suggests that testimony is not a "simple battle between speech and silence."[40] When the demand to speak out takes over human rights discourse, the expectation of an "articulate witness" dominates the conversation and places victims and survivors in a passive position.[41] In other words, an excessive emphasis on speech and proof, without considering circumstances and power relationships, could hinder any attempt or desire to express beyond what has already been said or what people expect to hear. Anthropologist Allen Feldman named this challenge "prescriptive expectations," meaning that once testimonies are framed into "legal or therapeutic" needs, the experiences of the victims and survivors are viewed as "episodes scheduled for eventual overcoming through redemptive survival, recovery, and restorative justice."[42] Speech-centered testimony, therefore, often revolves around the traumatic event itself, disregarding the individual humanity and personhood of the victim or survivor. Such an approach can create a narrow and one-dimensional understanding of the person, emphasizing their victimhood and reducing them to a representation of suffering.[43]

Beyond the limitations and demands of verbal testimonies, the lives of the victims and survivors are much richer than the stories of their death or their experience of the traumatic event. When their stories are reduced to political slogans, their personhood is shrunk to a single identity as a victim or a survivor. As feminist scholar Deidre Lashgari argues, "Silence posits the dominant linguistic system when it operates as twisted, unfair, and predirected manners, by disclosing the fact that dominant discourse is already formed and aligned against the subordinate subject."[44] Not only the stories known to us but the stories that remain unsaid and inarticulable await our attention.

To be clear, I do not downplay the critical role of speaking truth and the courageous act of breaking coercive silence. I argue, however, that the hierarchical disposition of speech over silence is inadequate for understanding the complexity of survivors' experiences. The interplay between speech and silence in each traumatic event, therefore, warrants careful examination within its specific context and among the relationships of the multiple players involved in the event. Just as in the case of constructing collective memory, the hierarchy between speech and silence is unhelpful in the context of testimony as well. Speech is not always effective in confronting power; it may at times reinforce violent history by limiting information, presenting only half-truths, and distorting shared memories. Likewise, silence does not always mean a passive submission to power but can be an alternative means to express inarticulable trauma. In his reading of Anne Michaels's Holocaust novel, *Fugitive Pieces*, David F. Ford highlights the importance of taking silence into account in political struggles. Ford argues that speech-dominated testimonies, which generally focus on "what" questions, undercut "how" questions—"how to 'seek by way of silence,' how to cope with the silence of absence and death, how to describe and interpret the forms and codes of silence, how language relates to silence, how silence is part of the 'descent into horror.'"[45] Silence can point to what is unnamed, missing, or misrepresented in contexts of violence, and direct us to ask "how." By considering "how," opportunities for reflection are extended, and we can see fragments of individuals crushed by tragic events as whole and thus connect with them.

Embracing the approach of mystical silence, therefore, encourages a nuanced approach that considers the person's unsaid narrative and undisclosed context, providing a more comprehensive and humanizing portrayal. In a similar fashion to Gates-Madsen's assessment of Argentine testimonial literature and artwork, my exploration of the silence of the numerous victims and survivors under unjust political regimes, coupled with the silence of Jesus's empty tomb, underscores the importance of the role of the mysticism of silence in bringing attention to the unheard stories of the victims and survivors under oppressive regimes. The symbolic significance of Jesus's empty tomb, which reflects the silent cries of the victims and survivors under unjust political realities, links the mysticism of silence with political struggles, ensuring its potential to be a source of remembrance and testimony. The mysticism of silence extends our horizon and allows us to listen to the unspoken while also orienting us toward contemplation through which we can deepen our relationship with others and the divine. When adopted in political actions, mystical and contemplative silence can encourage us to distance ourselves from the impulsive demands of both ourselves and the public and instead engage with uncertainty until it gradually yields to new possibilities—thereby allowing us to reimagine ourselves and the world in new words and images, anchored in our connection with others and with God.

However, what do we actually experience in the silence left after tragedies like Jesus's empty tomb and the gaping open wound of unjust political realities? If we detach the silence of those tragedies from the triumphalist rhetoric and claim that it does not secure any intrinsic constituents for the final victory, how can it be a source of hope or render any significance for our struggle? Simply speaking, what support can we draw from the silence of the empty tomb in order to properly mourn and remember the deceased and let their silent cries be heard? In what way can we still envision a moment of silence that may orient us toward contemplative silence, the deep sense of communion with others and the divine? The following discussion is my attempt to respond to these questions. I will engage particularly with the story of a group of trauma survivors who were involved in the installment of the 4.16 Memory Classroom after South Korea's *Sewol* ferry disaster.

THE 4.16 MEMORY CLASSROOM

April 16, 2014, is a day deeply etched in the memories of those affected by the MV *Sewol* ferry disaster. The MV *Sewol* ferry, carrying 476 passengers and crewmembers, capsized en route from Incheon to Jeju, South Korea.

Initial reports of a successful rescue of all passengers turned out to be false, and what followed was a heart-wrenching display of poor decision-making and inadequate response. For the critical hours in which all could have been saved, the passengers were left without instruction in vain hope of rescue while the captain and fourteen crewmembers made a cowardly escape. The rescue and search operations were slow and ineffective due to the senseless response of the marine salvage system and the government. While private fishing boats were rescuing more passengers than the Coast Guard, the South Korean president at that time, Park Geun-hye, did not even appear in public for about seven long hours after the sinking was reported. As the disaster unfolded, the public watched in horror as the ship slowly sank, taking with it the lives of 304 passengers, including 261 students and teachers from Danwon High School. The families of the victims were forced to bear witness to the tragedy, helpless to do anything but pray for their loved ones.[46]

As the investigation efforts proceeded, the disaster exposed the ugly underside of Korean society—one plagued by government corruption, insufficient safety regulations, and political indiscretion.[47] The disaster was not a mere accident. It was a human-made tragedy resulting from the country's obsessive pursuit of economic success under neoliberal capitalism at the expense of citizens' safety. The disaster also highlighted the widespread incompetence of political leadership, who shirked responsibility for the incident. Three years later, former president Park was impeached on charges of abuse of power, bribery, coercion, and leaking government secrets. Despite this, and ten years after the disaster, the families of the victims are still unsatisfied with the investigation, and many crucial questions about the disaster remain unanswered: Why were the passengers not rescued? Why was no one held accountable for the failed disaster response? What led to the investigation being delayed, and what was Park's involvement and reasoning in the matter?[48] Moreover, the leadership of South Korea has yet to take effective measures to prevent similar tragedies from occurring in the future.

The aftermath of the *Sewol* ferry disaster has been a harrowing experience not only for the families of the victims and survivors but also for the South Korean public at large. The mental health of the survivors and bereaved families has deteriorated significantly, with many suffering from PTSD, chronic insomnia, and physical ailments. The trauma has been so severe that some have passed away from stress-related illnesses or by suicide.[49] The disaster has left a lasting impact on the collective psyche of South Koreans, evoking feelings of anger, frustration, disappointment, and shame. The tragic suicide of Kim Gwan-hong, one of the civilian divers who volunteered to join the rescue operation, highlights the toll this disaster has taken on those who were involved in the rescue effort.[50] The loss of 304 lives and the inadequate response from leaders left a huge wound in Korean society.

The healing process, however, remains distant. Only a few months after the disaster, public opinion began to shift toward moving on from the tragedy in favor of economic recovery. These voices ignored the collective suffering and unresolved grief of the country, framing the ferry disaster as a personal tragedy for the families. However, the families of the victims and their supporters refused to let the memory of the disaster fade away. They organized rallies, sit-ins, hunger strikes, and legislative activism to raise public awareness and demand adequate governmental response. They created yellow ribbons as a symbol for remembrance and distributed them to the public. Groups across various religious traditions stood in solidarity by holding prayer meetings and services. Activists and artists joined the cause by archiving the artifacts of the victims, creating portraits, writing poetry and songs, and performing dances and plays. Their goal was to put a human face to the suffering of each victim and to ensure that the tragedy is properly mourned and remembered.

The remarkable 4.16 Memory Classroom deserves attention for its focus on preserving the ten classrooms of Danwon High School, where the student victims studied before the ferry disaster, as a place of commemoration. The project's primary goal is aligned with the demands of the parents of the student victims, who want to keep their children from being erased from public memory.[51] The parents insisted that the classrooms remain empty and as they were before the disaster. Although government officials suggested erecting a memorial hall as a replacement of the classrooms, the families disagreed, seeing such a move as an artificial gesture that represented political slogans over the individual personality of each student. For the parents, it was crucial to keep the classrooms and reveal their emptiness as a witness to the violent erasure of their children's lives and dreams. Preserving the empty classrooms was essential to remembering each student victim as an individual person. The classrooms contain the vivid life stories of each victim, where they greeted each other every morning, studied, ate, and played together, growing up dreaming of their futures. Friends and visitors of the victims bring paper cranes, photos, school supplies, and letters and cards that tell their stories. Visitors also leave abundant messages on the blackboard, offering condolences for the families of the victims.

The 4.16 Memory Classroom Project encountered opposition from those who believed that removing the classrooms from the current students' view would help them move on. Disagreements and debates have emerged in both civic and governmental spheres regarding how the disaster should be (un)remembered. The public and the government resorted to a disingenuous approach by selectively choosing, simplifying, and amplifying specific memories from the limited records available, in order to craft a politically convenient slogan. Concealment, loss, and distortion of the "official" record of the disaster presented the biggest challenges to honoring the narratives of the victims in the eyes of the public. By ignoring the multifaceted nature of the disaster and the diverse narratives of its victims, this approach served only to obfuscate the truth and perpetuate a distorted narrative for political gain. However, the parents of the student victims were determined to address the issue by safeguarding the empty classrooms that keep the memories of individual victims, elevate their narratives, and direct attention toward them. They fought tirelessly to ensure that their children were not reduced to mere numbers but were recognized as distinct human beings with their own stories and experiences.

Eventually, the classrooms survived, although relocated to the newly constructed 4.16 Education Center for Democratic Citizens. The transfer of all objects from the classrooms was carried out with great care, accompanied by artists and religious leaders and marked with solemn rituals and prayers. Now open to the public, the Memory Classroom serves as both a memorial and an educational space, teaching the value of life over profit and fostering compassion and a sense of shared humanity. The classrooms are preserved exactly as they were, including the desks, chairs, and lockers of the deceased students. The emptiness and absence of the victims in the classroom create an eerie silence that echoes the unforgettable tragedy. The silence that fills the room is a poignant symbol of the grief and mourning that still lingers in the aftermath of the tragedy. It is a tribute to the victims, a reminder of the importance of cherishing every moment of their life, and a call to action to work toward preventing such events from occurring in the future.

The Memory Classroom marks the significance of silence in the formation of a collective memory of the *Sewol* disaster victims. The emptiness and silence of the Memory Classroom facilitated the parents' efforts to preserve and bring to light the life stories and unfulfilled dreams of the deceased youth. The Memory Classroom has the unique ability to revive and renarrate the student victims' life stories, which are conveyed through both the objects left behind and the viewers' capacity for empathy. Even without any personal connection to the victims, viewers can imagine the lives of those who are no longer with us through their interaction with these objects in silence. Silence enables the memory of the victims to be reconstructed in the present, rather than being merely represented as a past event. It strenuously confronts the dominance of words and speech in controlling the process of remembering, while enabling new memories and testimonies to emerge beyond their control.

Regarding the commemoration of the *Sewol* disaster, sociologist Hyeon Jung Lee has noted a role of "relation-generating mourning," which I believe highlights the significance of the Memory Classroom.[52] She argues that political struggles in the aftermath of violence instigate different ways of mourning, namely "discourse-oriented mourning" and "relation-generating mourning." According to Lee, discourse-oriented mourning seeks to establish the factual truth of past events and history, thus becoming an effective political discourse. Conversely, relation-generating mourning values the untold and underrepresented narratives of these events. Extending Lee's theories, I propose that the mystical nature of silence in Memory Classrooms was key to cultivating memories that foster relationships, thereby enhancing and balancing the primarily discourse-driven approach to memory formation.

The aim of discourse-oriented memory is to document and archive facts. It seeks to reconstruct the past in a linear and continuous manner, transforming it into a political discourse. Discourse-oriented memory focuses on uncovering wrongdoings and producing social dialogue regarding the past. It focuses on fact-finding activities and necessitates a political and legal frame and language to fit in public discourse. This type of memory ensures itself to be impersonal because it needs to be objective. Therefore, it cannot preserve the personalities of the individual victims embedded in their narratives. It bases its authenticity on discovered facts and amplifies useful information to make political discourse productive, albeit at the cost of personal narratives of the victims. In contrast, relation-generating memory is often subjective and fragmented, allowing for a diversity of perspectives and interpretations. While discourse-oriented memory aims to be objective and coherent, relation-generating memory can be discontinuous, diverse, and personal. To bring the personalities of the victims to life and forge a meaningful connection with them, relation-generating memory demands a deeper engagement beyond the mere representation of facts. If discourse-oriented memory focuses on investigation, record, and some outcomes brought about for the purpose of making productive discourse, relation-generating memory fosters empathy with the victims. In other words, it always leaves room for more to be remembered and testified in relation to those who engage with the memory.

For the collective memory to be passed down to subsequent generations, discourse-oriented memory and relation-generating memory must go hand in hand. While discourse-oriented memory plays a crucial role in establishing a legitimate historical record and serves to support ongoing investigations and legal proceedings, commemoration should not stop at the mere act of recording information in an archive. Instead, memory should actively connect with the lives of the living through personal participation. Healing from the wounds of the past is not a simple or immediate process. It involves future generations empathizing with the victims of painful history through memory and reconstructing its meaning in their own time. The process is gradual and quiet, necessitating the exertion of each person. For this healing process to occur, relation-generating memory must complement discourse-oriented memory. By creating memories that generate a sense of connection, engaging with one's personal history can animate the personalities of those who were victimized and establish a bond with them. This approach values the unheard and overlooked narratives of the past and contributes to communal understanding and empathy toward historical events.

The role of silent spaces, both physical and interior, is critical in keeping relation-generating memory alive. The silence in the 4.16 Memory Classroom aids visitors in forming an interior space for the deceased, allowing them to recall, connect, and remember them. The profound impact of loss is solemnly revealed through the silence and emptiness of the classrooms, creating an atmosphere that bears witness to the memory of the departed youth. Silence in the classrooms is not equated with oblivion or societal amnesia. Rather, it is the embodiment of the absence of the victims who previously occupied the rooms. It assists individual visitors in forging personal connection with the victims through their attention to the presence of the absence of each victim in the classrooms. Through this active engagement done in silence, the dead are symbolically brought back to life, and their stories are reproduced as different knowledges and messages. The mystical aspect of silence plays a role in reviving each victim to be heard, seen, and felt as well as in anchoring visitors in a space of mourning that transcends political discourse. The following section underscores this silence, drawing from my experience of visiting the 4.16 Memory Classroom and engaging with the parents of the victims.

THE MYSTICISM OF SILENCE AND POLITICAL STRUGGLE

In 2018 I visited the Memory Classroom. As I stepped into the room, guided by a parent of one of the victims, I was met with a haunting and disruptive experience. In that moment, my previous perception of the event was shattered, and I was left with a renewed sense of the ramifications of what had occurred. The once-bustling rooms, now devoid of students, served as a powerful reminder of the lost lives and the impact that the event had on the community. The empty seats and desks represented the unrealized potential of the youth and the impact that their absence continues to have on those who knew and loved them. By leaving the space empty and silent, instead of filling it up or replacing it with another monument, the classrooms enclosed me in the huge hole left behind by the tragedy.

The silence in the 4.16 Memory Classroom was extremely saddening and uncomfortable in that it held visitors in an unsettling experience, recalling the silenced cries of the victims. The objects left behind by the victims exhibited multiple temporalities, merging the memories of the late students' living days in the past, the irrecoverable wound that remained with their families in the present, and the incomplete futures that were tragically cut short. This sense of discomfort and disorientation, however, powerfully challenged the utilitarian approach of seeking a quick fix to alleviate the pain. While the silence did not fit into established models of political discourse, it still posed a significant disruption to the dominant system of meaning that prioritized efficiency. While it did not aim to invoke any immediate meaning in accordance with expectations, it still prompted a pause and a shift in perspective. The tangible absence and ominous silence of the 4.16 Memory Classroom altered my perception, enabling me to reflect on the unseen and unheard aspects of the student victims' lives. This led to a revelation that there was something more to remember, speak about, and act upon. Through the potency of silence in the classrooms, I was able to forge a profound connection with the stories of the victims, engaging with them on a deeper level than I ever thought possible. Unbinding me from manufactured forms of representation of the dead, I learned the various life stories of each victim. What remains unspoken about the stories of the individual victims does not become an absence of meaning. Silence continues to testify to the truth of the disaster without attempting to fix or render any discursive demand for consumable political slogans. In this way, the silence in the classrooms serves as a punctum that is irreducible to any speech or "particular political functionality" and that inhibits any single narrative from dominating the space.[53]

To me, the silence that fills the Memory Classroom was a poignant reminder of the silence of Jesus's empty tomb. Just as the empty tomb preserved the memory of Jesus's life, the silence in the classrooms bears witness to the unspoken stories of the victims and an irreplaceable loss that defies expression through words. Both silences invite us to sit with ambiguity and uncertainty, resisting the urge to hastily impose meaning on the

Figure 3.1. The 4.16 Memory Classroom in Ansan, South Korea. Photos by author.

loss. Through this pause, we can gain a deeper understanding of the impact of tragedy on our lives and find the courage to persevere and continue our journey. Yet, just as the silence of the tomb testified to the death of Jesus, the silence of the classrooms reminds us of the ongoing task of truth-telling. The tasks include that we must honor the stories of each victim as well as the hollowness left by survivors rather than framing the memory into political agenda to find a solution. Amid struggles, the mysticism of silence provides fertile ground for reflection, healing, and transformation, expanding our horizons beyond limited perspectives.

With its reminiscence of the silence of Jesus's empty tomb, the silence in the 4.16 Memory Classroom resonates deeply with the many silences in political struggles to honor those whose voices were lost, removed, and silenced. Examples abound from both the past and present and across cultures: the Silent Protest Parade on July 28, 1917, in which a group of about ten thousand African Americans marched through the streets of New York City to denounce the riot in East Saint Louis; the Day of Silence, which became a US tradition starting in 1996 to spread awareness about the effects of bullying and harassment on LGBTQIA+ youth; a minute of silence on the anniversaries of the Marikana massacre, the killing of thirty-four miners by the South African Police Service in 2012 during the deadliest clash in South Africa since the Apartheid era; and Myanmar's 2021 silent strike, marking the two-year anniversary of the military coup that overthrew a democratically elected government and resulted in thousands of deaths and displacements.[54] The silences in those struggles serve as a reminder of the unheard voices of the marginalized and oppressed, witnessing their unrecognized stories and experiences.

The mysticism revealed by the silence of such political struggles inspires us to see and listen beyond the boundaries set by political agenda and obsession with efficiency, seeking alterity and new possibilities. My exploration of silence within these political struggles aims to highlight its spiritual potential as a resource for persevering through the challenges that arise in the midst of suffering. I illustrate three specific capacities of mystical silence that can be applied to political struggles: the practice of unsaying for the subjugated, openness to the transcendent, and the capacity to build communion with others and the divine.

The Practice of Unsaying

The practice of unsaying is a spiritual discipline rooted in the traditions of apophatic mysticism. Although the cataphatic approach and apophatic approach are not contradictory but complementary, mysticism prioritizes the apophatic approach due to both the ineffable nature of God and the ineffable affairs of experiencing God. The practice of unsaying involves intentionally unsaying or setting aside all concepts and language about the divine in order to create space for an encounter with God beyond language and concepts. In his book *Mystical Languages of Unsaying*, theologian Michael A. Sells argues that mystics of the apophatic traditions do not simply name or deny a name to God; instead, they use language in a way that disrupts and challenges traditional modes of expression by emphasizing the contradiction created by the divine ineffability. Sells suggests that these mystics not only assert the divine ineffability but also "perform" it through language, enacting the unfathomable nature of the transcendent through diverse strategic (un)use of language.[55] The result is to open up fresh avenues for encounter with the transcendent that goes beyond conventional language and thus establishes opportunities for readers to approach the divine in new ways. Thus, mystical language of unsaying serves as a means of challenging the tendency toward reification and dogmatic demarcation within traditional religion.

As mystical unsaying disrupts and transforms power dynamics within the speech traditions of the church, the many examples of silent protests, along with the Memory Classroom, evince that silence in political struggles, too, challenges the preexisting mores of political conduct by unsaying. In this respect, silence holds potency for those who lack the leverage to exert influence on public discourse. It offers them an alternative to the language of politics and law, which often fails to account for the experiences of the marginalized, and it further allows them to express themselves in ways that are authentic and meaningful. Taking inspiration from de Certeau's explorations of quotidian practice, silence in this sense is a deliberate action determined by "the absence of a proper locus."[56] In this context, speech serves as an instance of "strategies" employed by those in power, while silence functions as "tactics" employed by the subjugated. Whereas speech occupies a legitimate place and regulates political discourse, silence appropriates and transforms the products and production of dominant discourses. Thus, silence inserts a space within the discourse outlined by elites, and while its reach is limited, it can challenge those in power.[57] Silence does not define or demand anything but expands the "horizon of political activism and rearranges power relations, by manifesting neglected, unexpected, and previously unexamined forms of political engagement."[58] The practice of unsaying in political struggles like the Memory Classroom therefore sheds light on the unequal forces at play between the dominant and the subjugated.

Mystical insights arise when we detach ourselves from a discourse confined by social norms and consumptive politics produced by those in power. The use of silence in political struggles, manifested through the practice of unsaying, helps us evade total subjugation by dominant power discourses. It opens avenues for envisioning alternative modes of thought, action, and existence.[59] The practice of unsaying, in this respect, is not an inaction but a mystical practice, especially for those who are marginalized. By refraining from entering the realm of speech, silence decenters and destabilizes political relationships.[60] Though it may not constitute power nor suggests a tangible solution, it remains significant and potent since it embodies an alternative way of imagining the future, even when all other means are exhausted.

Openness to the Transcendent

Engaging silence in political struggle also reveals the capacity of silence to urge openness toward the transcendent. By carving out a reflective space, silence invites one to be receptive to the unexpected and to foster a deeper sense of empathy and compassion. In contrast to the frenzied pace of consumptive politics, it encourages us to pause and listen attentively to the voices of those who are silenced. Genuine solidarity with the voiceless can only be achieved when the observer's mind is attuned to listening to the pains and struggles of others. Rather than being driven to action by impulse, a thoughtful response to silent cries must involve first attending to their suffering and then opening oneself up to the possibilities of transformative occasions that emerge organically and unexpectedly, unencumbered by one's own agendas. Such an occasion can be a moment for mysticism, which denotes a manifestation of the pertinent meaning or an opportune circumstance for a significant event to occur, even if it initially remains hidden. The mystical moment can take the form of an idea, realization, or experience that has the potential to release one's thinking and behavior from the trajectory of society, leading toward transcendence—for Christians, the divine. And it can fundamentally challenge one's manner of speaking and thinking about God.

At the outset of his book *The Edge of Words*, based on his 2013 Gifford Lecture, Rowan Williams highlights such liberating potential of silence. He poses a question: "Does the way we talk as human beings tell us anything about God?" In the latter part of the book, Williams argues that silence is indicative of the abundance of the divine and the world that surpasses what can be expressed through words. By "reveal[ing] in the sense of exhibiting depth" and at the same time "conceal[ing] in the sense of marking where supposedly straightforward description and analysis cannot go," mystical and contemplative silence frees both the world and the self from the constraints of the self-centered agenda and the compulsion to dominate others.[61] It is through this liberating aspect of silence we can turn ourselves toward mysticism, the contact to the transcendent.

In our culture of violence that entails immeasurable loss, there is always a demand for effectiveness and productivity that tries forcefully to fill up the holes, cracks, and gaps made by the loss in order to move forward. Such pressing demands trivialize the necessity to take a pause and open ourselves to the unknown, particularly when we face the aftermath of violence. It is important to exercise caution when we feel ethically obligated to "act immediately," as this approach can cause us to overlook important considerations in our haste, potentially leading to unintended consequences. The value of society that cherishes effectiveness and productivity does not align with the mysticism of silence, nor does it give us space to listen to the unknown, unspoken, and unheard. Silence helps us unfold at a pace that prepares us for the deeper and more poignant insights arising in tune with others who suffer together, rather than solely aiming to increase productivity and solve problems. Silence challenges our tendency to quickly articulate the meaning of tragic loss and instead directs our attention toward the voices underneath and the visions beyond. The uncertainty and unknowingness of silence compels us to wait longer and listen deeper. Ultimately, silence leads to contemplative awareness where God initiates, sustains, and renews the foundation of our perception. Here, we can bear witness to the transcendent and pave the way toward a more just and equitable world.

Communion with Others

Silence in political struggle also fosters contemplative space for us to remember others whose lives remain intrinsically interdependent with ours. We enter into silence in political struggle by emptying our impulsive desire to speak and turning our attention to those who reveal their existence through their absence in silence, whether they are deceased or living. The rupture marked by silence reflects the incompleteness of our stories in times of suffering, through which we strive to connect with others. The mysticism of silence inspires us to ponder how our lives depend on our relationships with others, living or dead, and how our future will remain affected by them. It offers us boundless space to connect with the dead as well as the living, forming solidarity with them and remaking ourselves and our communities. If we are willing to uphold our responsibility to remember them, silence can be a condition for renewed speech and action in a world where we experience a sense of disintegration and loss of meaning, hope, and creativity.

Judith Butler's work on the politics of mourning may shed light on the mysticism of silence in political struggle. Butler observes in their book *Precarious Life: The Powers of Mourning and Violence* that numerous forms of loss are often disregarded and unacknowledged, including "the losses of war and genocide, the loss of 'humanness' under slavery; the loss that is undergone with exile; the loss that is effaced through colonization."[62] Butler highlights the act of mourning as an eruption of "unspeakable" losses in public life that obscures the frames by which memory and grief are organized. For instance, the exclusion of the Arabic dead or injured in the public commemoration after the September 11 attacks illustrates a "different allocation of grievability," which "operates to produce and maintain certain exclusionary conceptions of who is normatively human; what counts as a livable life and a grievable death." Butler's politics of mourning underscores solidarity through loss. According to Butler, mourning brings us to realize our susceptibility to suffering and death in a culture of violence and an awareness that our life is fundamentally dependent upon anonymous others, both human and nonhuman. Mourning puts us in a mode of "unknowingness," in which we realize we are intrinsically connected to the dead through their absence.[63] In this light, mourning does not end with overcoming sorrow over the loss of loved ones. It involves a long process for the living to ponder the implications of the loss and to form a new relationship with what we have lost. Mourning never cuts off life and death but crosses between this chasm to envision a future that remembers the loss.

I extend Butler's perspective on collective mourning to emphasize the impact of mystical silence leading to contemplation in the aftermath of traumatic events. As shown in the case of the Memory Classroom, silence forges a relationship between the living and the dead. It helps us listen to the dead and suspends us in a space between the unresolved past and the present, where we are connected with their forgotten stories. The memories of the dead then convey meaning and interrelatedness to the living, reminding us of our indebtedness to them and our responsibility to future generations. Drawing inspiration from the Christian belief in the Communion of Saints, the dead become "a cloud of witnesses" (Heb. 12:1) to the lives of the living. They "bespeak an unfinished agenda that is now in our hands.... Their companionship points the way," as theologian Elizabeth Johnson says in her reflection on the Communion of Saints.[64] In the deepening silence of contemplation, we encounter the silent God who is present with us across life and death.

As such, silence in political struggle can transform our vision. It invites us to recognize our dependence upon the lives that have gone before us. Refusing to be filled or fixed, silence urges us to pause, reflect, and mourn the unfathomable. The memories of those who have been isolated from the future join the living, and silence becomes an abundant and limitless reservoir containing the stories of the unsaid and unheard, just like Jesus's empty tomb did for his followers. The role of silence in this light is its ability to preserve and reproduce memories of the dead and embrace them as a part of the lives of the living. Paradoxically, silence turns the voices of those who are lost and unheard into a perpetual accompaniment to our obligation to bear witness to the truth.

THE EMPTY TOMB, POLITICAL STRUGGLE, AND SPIRITUAL PRACTICE

The silence of Jesus's empty tomb and its echo in countless silent gravesites in our strife-filled world of violence and suffering will always haunt and remain with us, containing all the unaddressed and unfathomable pains and sorrows of human history. Their silence is a part of our lives, just as there is always silence before, after, between, under, and above our speaking and thinking. We must learn to attend to silence and listen to the unheard aspects of our lives because there is God in silence—the God who emptied the divine privilege into silence on Holy Saturday and descended into the lower places to be present with the silenced. When we relinquish our own words and open our ears to the unheard stories of those who are silenced, the shared silence between God and the abandoned is remembered and revived in our lives, inviting us to envision a better world.

The mysticism of silence in political struggles does not lie in its usefulness. It lies in its ability to draw our attention to the unheard and unrecognized and open a new horizon. Silence does not always produce the possibility of declaring an injustice, but it enriches the possibility. Rather than exerting power, silence allows inarticulable expectations to manifest and intervene in ways we never imagined. It leads us to acknowledge our own limitations and humbly pause before the unfathomable depth of the mystery of suffering. It makes us aware that the need for healing should not be reduced to political slogans and shallow forms of communication. It transforms the way we speak and act and aids us in recovering our spiritual and political needs to listen and practice humility. Then, it urges us to a radical trust in unprecedented experiences and the goodness of others who will join in remembering the loss. It shapes us to view ourselves in relation to the God who chooses to be silent in order to reveal the presence of the people who are silenced. In this prayerful vulnerability, we listen to the silent God, who listens to the ineffable suffering of the world, and strive to form a community with others who are willing to listen.

NOTES

1. The Indonesian mass killings of 1965–1966, also referred to as the Indonesian Communist Purge or Indonesian Politicide, were a genocide that occurred in Indonesia over several months, resulting in the estimated murder of two to three million people who were involved with the Communist Party of Indonesia or who were Communist sympathizers, Gerwani women, ethnic Javanese Abangan, ethnic Chinese, and alleged leftists.
2. *The Look of Silence* is a companion piece to *The Act of Killing*, Oppenheimer's 2012 documentary film in which the director invited the perpetrators to recount their murderous experiences for the cameras and to make scenes describing their memories and emotions about the murders. The Indonesian government responded negatively to both films.
3. Oppenheimer, "Director's Notes."
4. Dana Stevens, "'It's as Though I'm in Germany 40 Years after the Holocaust, but the Nazis Are Still in Power': A Conversation with Joshua Oppenheimer about How to Make an Effective Documentary about Genocide," *Slate*, July 17, 2015, https://slate.com/culture/2015/07/joshua-oppenheimer-interview-the-director-of-the-look-of-silence-and-the-act-of-killing-on-his-extraordinary-documentaries-about-the-indonesian-genocide.html.
5. Stevens, "A Conversation with Joshua Oppenheimer."
6. McLauchlan, *Saturday's Silence*, 1.
7. Mark 16:1–4; Matthew 28:1–10; Luke 24:1–12; John 20:1–18.
8. Barth, *Church Dogmatics*, 382–83.
9. Kasper, *Jesus the Christ*, 127.
10. Rambo, *Spirit and Trauma*, 143.
11. Balthasar, *Mysterium Paschale*, 50–51.
12. In discussing classical Western theism, I am referring to those theologians who advocate for a conception of God as the "supreme self" or person, characterized by omniscience, omnipotence, and omnibenevolence. God is an absolutely perfect being who governs Creation, ensuring all things work toward good. Being omniscient, God knows all truths and falsehoods across time, with this knowledge being unchanging, eternal, and infallible. As omnipotent, God can do anything that is logically possible. Finally, God's perfect goodness means God always acts for the best, intending the most favorable outcomes in all situations. In this view, God is the creator, sustainer, and governor of the world, remaining unaffected by it. While the world is subject to God's influence, God himself is not causally impacted by worldly events or actions. William Wainwright, "Concepts of God," *Stanford Encyclopedia of Philosophy*, accessed November 27, 2023, https://plato.stanford.edu/Archives/Win2017/entries/concepts-god/. For further reading, see Davis, *Logic and the Nature of God*; Morris, *Our Idea of God*; Johnson, "Calvinism and the Problem of Evil"; and Hart, "Calvinism and the Problem of Hell."

13. For further information, see Rogers, *Christianity and Western Theism*.
14. von Sass and Hall, *Groundless Gods*, 9; and Rubenstein, "Dionysius, Derrida, and the Critique of 'Ontotheology.'"
15. Crosby, "The Spirit of a Weak God."
16. Notable works in the vein of contemporary apophatic theology that have also influenced my book include Boesel and Keller, *Apophatic Bodies*; Caputo, *Specters of God*; Hart, *Trespass of the Sign*; Knepper, *Negating Negation*; Sells, *Mystical Languages of Unsaying*; Stang, *Apophasis and Pseudonymity*; Turner, *Darkness of God*; Williams, *Seeking the God Beyond*.
17. R. S. Thomas, "The Absence" and "The Gap," in Thomas, *Collected Poems*, 361 and 324.
18. R. S. Thomas, "Shadows," in Thomas, *Collected Poems*, 343.
19. Balthasar, *Man in History*, 95.
20. McLauchlan, *Saturday's Silence*, 1.
21. Martin F. Connell, "Descensus Christi ad Infernos: Christ's Descent to the Dead," *Theological Studies* 62 (2001): 266, quoted in Sanders, *Tenebrae*, 149.
22. Balthasar, *Mysterium Paschale*, 168, 172, 175.
23. Balthasar, 165, 181.
24. Lewis, *Between Cross and Resurrection*, 29–30.
25. McLauchlan, *Saturday's Silence*, 129.
26. Winter, *Sites of Memory*, 104, 105–6.
27. Vinitzky-Seroussi and Teeger, "Silence and Collective Memory," 664.
28. Winchakul, *Moments of Silence*, 9, 18.
29. For the research related to this argument, see Choi, "Politics of War Memories," 395–409; Stora, "Algerian War in French Memory," 151–74; Aguilar, "Agents of Memory," 84–103.
30. Brink, "Stories of History," i37.
31. Schudson, "Dynamic of Distortion in Collective Memory," 354.
32. Vinitzky-Seroussi and Teeger, "Silence and Collective Memory," 665, 669.
33. Vinitzky-Seroussi and Teeger, 669.
34. Glenn, *Unspoken*, 6.
35. Foucault, *The History of Sexuality: An Introduction*, 101.
36. The Dirty War (Spanish: *Guerra sucia*) refers to the state terrorism done by the military junta in Argentina during 1976 to 1983 as part of Operation Condor. Military and security forces and right-wing armed groups, in the name of the Argentine Anticommunist Alliance, hunted down anyone who was believed to be associated with socialism, left-wing Peronism, or the Montoneros movement. Between nine thousand and thirty thousand people were murdered or disappeared, and state terrorism made it impossible to report many of the victims. For more studies, see Esparza, Huttenbach, and Feierstein, *State Violence and Genocide*.
37. Nance, *Can Literature Promote Justice*, 7.
38. Gates-Madsen, *Trauma, Taboo, and Truth-Telling*, 18.
39. Gates-Madsen, 51.
40. Gates-Madsen, 70.
41. Gandsman, "The Limits of Kinship Mobilizations," 197–98.
42. Allen Feldman, "Memory Theaters, Visual Witnessing, and the Trauma-Aesthetic," *Biography: An Interdisciplinary Quarterly* 27, no. 1 (2004): 163–202, quoted in Gates-Madsen, *Trauma, Taboo, and Truth-Telling*, 66.
43. Carlson, *I Remember Julia*, xvii, xiii, xv.
44. Lashgari, "Introduction," 8.

45. Ford, "Apophasis and the Shoah"; Michaels, *Fugitive Pieces*.
46. Mitch Shin, "7 Years after Sewol Ferry Disaster, Bereaved Families Still Urge Government to Reveal the Truth," *The Diplomat*, April 16, 2021, https://thediplomat.com/2021/04/7-years-after-sewol-ferry-disaster-bereaved-families-still-urge-government-to-reveal-the-truth/.
47. The disaster resulted in broad social and political reactions within and beyond South Korea. Criticisms include 1) the actions of the captain and most of the crew who escaped from the ferry while hundreds of passengers remained trapped inside; 2) the ferry operator and the regulators who oversaw its operations; 3) the South Korean government's failure to rescue the victims and to take responsibility for the failed safety systems; and 4) South Korean media for its disaster response and attempts to downplay government culpability. The families of the victims continue to protest, demanding the government investigate the disaster to the fullest extent and establish laws and systems to prevent the reoccurrence of such a disaster. Korean citizens have supported the families by holding nationwide and international protests.
48. "Life and Safety Park," 4.16 Foundation, https://416foundation.org/en/4-16-ferry-sewol-tragedy/life-and-safety-park/.
49. Lee et al., "Factors Associated with Post-traumatic Stress Disorder"; Jin Shin, "The Trauma of Sewol Families after Two and a Half Years," *JTBC News Report*, July 20, 2016, https://news.jtbc.joins.com/article/article.aspx?news_id=NB11276162.
50. Steven Borowiec, "A Diver's Pain: Living with the Ghost of Sewol Tragedy," *Al Jazeera*, July 27, 2016, https://www.aljazeera.com/features/2016/7/27/a-divers-pain-living-with-the-ghost-of-sewol-tragedy.
51. Lee, "The Struggle Surrounding the 4.16 Classrooms," 145–88.
52. Lee, "The Struggle Surrounding the 4.16 Classrooms," 152.
53. Glenn, *Unspoken*, xi, 512.
54. The riot in East Saint Louis in 1917 included a series of outbreaks of labor and race-related violence by White Americans. They murdered between 39 and 150 African Americans in late May and early July 1917. In addition to the murders, about 6,000 Black people were left without homes because of the riot, and the burning and vandalism cost approximately $400,000 in property damage. "Marikana Massacre 16 August 2012," South Africa History Online, https://www.sahistory.org.za/article/marikana-massacre-16-august-2012; The Nelson Mandela Foundation, "Remember the Slain of Marikana," Google Arts & Culture, https://artsandculture.google.com/story/the-phenomenon-of-protests-in-south-africa-nelson-mandela-centre-of-memory/1QVRk_LBbfFJLw; Jonathan Head and Oliver Slow, "Myanmar Coup Anniversary: 'Silent Strike' Marks Two Years of Military Rule," *BBC*, February 1, 2023, https://www.bbc.com/news/world-asia-64481138; U.S. Department of State, "Marking Two Years Since the Military Coup in Burma," press statement, January 31, 2023, https://www.state.gov/marking-two-years-since-the-military-coup-in-burma/.
55. Sells, *Mystical Languages of Unsaying*, 3; Hollywood, Review of *Mystical Languages of Unsaying* by Michael A. Sells, 564–65.
56. de Certeau, *Practice of Everyday Life*, 36–37; My discussion is inspired by political scientist Sophia Hatzisavvidou's article "Disturbing Binaries in Political Thought," 509–22. Hatzisavvidou explores the significance of the silent protest at UC Davis following an event on November 18, 2011, during which campus police pepper sprayed a group of students who were protesting against budget cuts and tuition hikes. When UC Davis

chancellor Linda Katehi did not respond to the students' chants for justice, the students sat down, locked their hands, and formed a silent "walk of shame" as Katehi walked three blocks to her car surrounded by crowds of silent students.

57. de Certeau, *Practice of Everyday Life*, xix.
58. Hatzisavvidou, "Disturbing Binaries," 517.
59. I was inspired by Claire E. Wolfteich's article "Practices of 'Unsaying.'"
60. Guillaume, "How to Do Things with Silence," 488.
61. Williams, *The Edge of Words*, ix, 162, 165.
62. Butler, "Afterword," 467.
63. Butler, *Precarious Life*, xiv–xv, 13; McIvor, "Bringing Ourselves to Grief," 411.
64. Johnson, *Friends of God and Prophets*, 182.

4

THE SILENT WOMEN AND THE EMPTY TOMB

Listening to Unheard Stories

"Remember how he told you, while he was still in Galilee, that the Son of Man must be handed over into the sinners and be crucified, and on the third day rise again." Then they remembered his words, and returning from the tomb they told all this to the eleven and to all the rest. Now it was Mary Magdalene, Joanna, Mary the mother of James, and the other women with them who told this to the apostles. But these words seemed to them an idle tale, and they did not believe them.

—Luke 24:6–11 (NRSV)

You and I are close, we intertwine; you may stand on the other side of the hill once in a while, but you may also be me while remaining what you are and what I am not.

—Trinh Minh-ha, *Woman, Native, Other*

I said to my soul, be still, and wait without hope.

—T. S. Eliot, "East Coker"

Living in a land where my native tongue is considered foreign, speaking has never been a natural activity for me. Whenever I utter a word, a fear of looking and sounding different lingers on the tip of my tongue. Decades-old doubt, frustration, and impostor syndrome arise. Speaking is a perpetually unfinished task, one that often fades away before I can even utter a word in the first place. As Vietnamese writer and filmmaker Trinh T. Minh-ha says, "If I tell you now what I would like to hear myself tell you, I will miss it. . . . Whenever I try my best to say, I never fail to utter the wrong words."[1] The unuttered words of mine, like an endless sea, are never given a chance to make it ashore.

They are stored in silence, hoping for rest and yearning for another opportunity to spill out of me.

Silence, however, does not always provide solace or a safe haven for me. Facing the external and internal urge to communicate, silence aligns with many different and even contradictory emotions: relief and anxiety, resilience and vulnerability, contentment and frustration, freedom and fear. Furthermore, the culture of the United States, where I currently reside, often exhibits a discomfort toward silence. The culture demands binary answers in yes or no, views in either this or that, and feelings in either pleasure or detestation. The idea of deviating from one's own expectations and embracing uncertainty can be daunting for a majority of this culture. The culture interprets silence as an inability to communicate, a lack of understanding, or a lack of desire and will to interact with anybody or anything. In the dichotomous context of speech and silence, power dynamics can disrupt authentic communication, leading to instances where silence is misconstrued as conveying a particular message or stance. Sometimes, it expresses more than words—more accurately, eloquently, and defiantly—yet other times its impact has the opposite effect. From my personal experience and as a cultural phenomenon, I have observed that silence can be just as ambiguous and difficult to navigate as speaking. Silence is a complex and compound matter, particularly for minorities in American society.

The ambiguity of silence presents ethical challenges as well. When facing forces of subjugation, the urge to speak out is necessary and often compelling. Although silence is often considered a passive agreement to certain things, one may choose to avoid speaking because responding with words can reinforce oppressive power dynamics. When hate, bigotry, and divisive rhetoric are weaponized against one, responding to them with words may only perpetuate the harm. Hence, the challenge lies in finding alternative ways to voice oneself, to resist subjugation, and to reclaim agency. This demands creativity, courage, and a willingness to explore new avenues of expression. However, can silence serve as a viable alternative to confront the violence of speech, instead of surrendering itself to the force of violence?

The prevailing culture, which finds silence uneasy, is equally unnerved by the profound mystery that shrouds the divine silence of God. However, Christian mystical and contemplative traditions suggest a path otherwise. The traditions describe and pursue silence as a source of mystery and the pinnacle of union with God. Silence orients the mystic to the ultimacy of their experience in which they dwell with God. Silence also sustains the exterior and interior ground that enables mystics to renew their desire to express God. As an individual who understands both the intricacies of silence in daily struggle and the value of silence drawn from spiritual traditions, I am compelled to consider the following questions in hopes of finding a balance between the two different paths of silence: How can we engage with and listen to silence that contains rich and complicated emotions and thoughts, and at the same time differentiate it from possible harmful effects of silence? Although for the vulnerable the daily experience of silence is often complex and even oppressive, is it possible to find mystical and contemplative opportunities within it? Above all, how might we cultivate our daily experience of silence as a spiritual resource, a space to wait for and embrace others and the divine, without perpetuating coercive and complicit silence?

These guiding questions are not only born out of my own personal experiences but also fueled by my longing to connect with other linguistic minorities who face similar challenges in navigating the complexities of both speech and silence. It can be a constant struggle to find the right balance between expressing oneself and honoring the value of silence, especially when the nuances of one's speech and silence may go unrecognized or be misunderstood by others. In the daily lives of individuals who face many societal challenges, the various roles that silence plays require attentive ears to engage. It is not enough to listen to others' speech; one must also learn to listen to others' silence, which captures the ineffable and unspeakable depth of their experiences and may become manifest in a disguise of cries and screams.

This chapter aims to offer a theological reflection on the political dynamics that surround the silence experienced by linguistic minorities and to engage in a dialogue with the Christian mystical and contemplative traditions through the lens of the experiences of women of color in particular. To begin my discussion, I revisit the biblical scene of Jesus's empty tomb with a focus on the silence of women disciples. I believe this silence echoes the entangled and layered ways that silence affects women of color in the United States, drawing on both my personal experience and observation. Despite feeling overwhelmed and fearful upon encountering the absence of Jesus's body, the first witnesses knew he had been resurrected. Their testimony, however, was unheard, misinterpreted, and ignored. The women disciples' experience of being silenced in the Gospel stories serves as a poignant reminder of the silence often imposed upon women of color in the United States. By differentiating the coercive and complicit silences that weigh down the lives of women of color, I explore three types of their silence—"loud" silence, melancholic silence, and defiant silence—and how these manifestations of silence generate mystical and contemplative opportunities that can be used to build a community among different groups of women of color and create a space to struggle together.

To fully engage with the spiritual potential of silence for women of color in their daily struggles, it is crucial to incorporate attentive listening as a fundamental component of the practice. The important task of forming relationship among women of color entails not only amplifying their voices to challenge the dominant but also listening to each other's silence that contains the ineffable and unspeakable experiences of pain. Therefore, this chapter provides theological insights into the significance of listening and emphasizes the necessity of intentional silence as a space in which the listener and the silent participant can be present for each other while maintaining a respectful distance. This intentional silence enables mutual recognition and appreciation of differences, a willingness to embrace ambiguity, and a sustained curiosity toward each other. In this regard, mystical and contemplative silence can serve as a catalyst for different groups of women of color to practice listening and building community together. Within the scope of this exploration, I specifically observe potential for partnership between Black and Asian American women. However, I believe that the practice of mystical and contemplative silence is relevant to all who experience racial and gender subjection within the dominant White heteropatriarchal culture, including Latina, Indigenous and Native women, LGBTQIA+ individuals, and all those who identify as marginalized.

As I conclude this chapter, I turn to the works of the late Korean American poet and artist Theresa Hak Kyung Cha to illustrate the practice of listening to silence. Cha's personal experience of exile and migration informs her use of silence as an indispensable motif in her works, which expresses her yearning to connect with others and transcend toward the unknown. By doing so, she transforms silence into a resource that bridges the inner needs of introspection and the outward expression of truth. Cha's artworks inspire me to affirm that mystical and contemplative silence provides the necessary foundation for spiritual practices that are attuned to transformative social action.

"THESE WORDS SEEMED TO THEM AN IDLE TALE"

In the empty tomb from which the Incarnate Word of God had vanished, the first witnesses were left with fear, confusion, amazement, and a struggle to find a word. Their initial response to the event of the empty tomb was silence. The first witnesses' silence at encountering the absence of

Jesus's body is portrayed differently in each Gospel account, providing a unique perspective from each evangelist. Mark ends the story by stating, "So they went out and fled from the tomb, for terror and amazement had seized them; and they said nothing to anyone, for they were afraid" (16:8). Matthew elaborates the story adding the dramatic appearance of an angel amid an earthquake. He also describes how Jesus met the women as they were returning to the men disciples, and how the women took hold of his feet and worshipped him, while still remaining silent. The news of the Resurrection was not broken by the women disciples but by the guards of Jesus's tomb, who did not understand the implications of the empty tomb (28:1–11). In John's account, the women disciples are briefly depicted, and more weight is given to the scene in which two men disciples visit the tomb. However, John then shifts his focus to spotlight Mary Magdalene's encounter with the risen Jesus (20:1–10). Meanwhile, Luke includes a disturbing detail that illustrates the challenges faced by the women as they testified about the Resurrection. According to Luke, the women disciples were told by two strangers that Jesus was risen. They understood what was happening. Though terrified, they plunged themselves to the ground in an act of veneration.[2] Then they "remembered" the words of Jesus—reminded by the strangers, returned from the tomb—and "told all this to the eleven and to all the rest" (24:5–9). However, the men disciples dismissed their words as "an idle tale" and refused to trust them (24:10–11). The women's claim became a reliable confirmation only after it was affirmed by two men disciples who encountered Jesus on their road to Emmaus (24:12–35). In each of these Gospel accounts, the silence or silencing of women's voices has different implications for Christ's legacy.

The subject of the silence or silencing of the women disciples in the Gospel stories has been met with mixed interpretations from biblical scholars. A widely accepted explanation is that the men disciples failed to understand the women's testimony because the message of the Resurrection was too strange and shocking for them to accept. Another traditional interpretation puts a blame on the women disciples, arguing that their timidity prevented them from delivering the truth in a comprehensible manner. However, feminist scholars such as Elisabeth Schüssler Fiorenza and Mary Rose D'Angelo observe the patriarchal context of the Gospels that distanced women from prophesy and ministry.[3] They argue that the Gospel writers intended to downplay the significance of women's testimony in establishing the account of the Resurrection. Instead, they emphasized the preeminence of men disciples who not only confirmed the women's words but also had their own encounters with the risen Jesus.[4] The feminist perspective invites a closer examination of the wider social context of first-century Palestine, which was characterized by hostility toward the legitimacy of women's voices.[5]

In the first century, the Roman empire aimed to forge a trans-imperial identity in Palestine, establishing power in its colonies by promoting a cultural ideology based on the ideals of the Greek and Roman elites. Language was a crucial element in the construction of a unified identity. The elites in the Greek colonies were taught in Attic Greek and schooled in rhetorical and literary styles, as well as other classical skills.[6] Unsurprisingly, such education was available solely for men. The Greek ideal of masculinity prescribed that physical strength was necessary to keep the voice from decreasing to a faint shrill; masculine ideals excluded "eunuchs, women, and invalids" from education.[7] Consequently, the empire's colonial culture understood the male subject as the normative human being, which led to the belief that women and minorities were inferior and unintelligible. Jewish law was no different from Greek and Roman norms with regard to the rights of women.[8] The culture of first-century Palestine did not allow women to access "legible, educated, and logical" language, nor did it afford them the authority to communicate what they saw or remembered. This cultural belief bleeds into the social interactions of even the men disciples, who, despite being perhaps the most sympathetic group of men present, still judged women as unreliable and failed to listen to the news of the Resurrection due to conventional cultural bias. The cultural disrespect of women and the consequent silence of the women in the empty tomb narratives uncomfortably mirror the experience of women across time and culture. The dominant heteropatriarchal logic and masculine narratives associated with language that pervaded the first century remain as a force to silence women, children, and other marginalized individuals in modernity.[9]

Upon examining the silence of women in the biblical narrative, however, I have observed a complex dynamic at play that goes beyond a simple binary of speech and silence. Despite not speaking out, the women disciples preserved the truth, adding another layer to their silence. Recent scholarship on the multifaced nature of silence offers an alternative angle to view the silence of linguistic minorities, including that of the women disciples, by challenging the dichotomy between speech and silence. When a marginalized person experiences something that separates them from the dominant system, as the women disciples did, language can no longer serve as a reliable medium to express their feelings, ideas, experiences, needs, and desires, since language itself is a product of the social order. In such situations, language becomes the source of their suffering as it fails to accurately describe what their experiences. The binary between speech and silence is not helpful in such a context because it does not account for the limitation of language, the cultural differences regarding silence, and the complex power dynamics operating in both discursive and nondiscursive actions. As the political scientist Jenny Edkins aptly describes in her book about the survivors of state and political violence, the subordinate individuals face a dilemma: "What [they] *can* say no longer makes sense; what [they] *want* to say, [they] can't. There are no words for it.... The only words they have are the words of the very political community that is the source of their suffering."[10] The demand to speak places the linguistic minority in an untenable position. On the one hand, if they adopt the dominant language and speak in the ways of the oppressor, their speech and resistance against normative treatment may lack credibility. On the other hand, if they reject the dominant language and speak in their own tongue, they risk being forced into a conceptual and linguistic framework that marginalizes their culture, language, and existence, causing their narrative to be seen as lacking legitimacy. Communication is never free from existing power relationships. As Gayatri Spivak and many other postcolonial scholars argue, knowledge production is inherently colonial in that it defines the Other as a distant and politically unequal object of study.[11]

When the linguistic minority find language inadequate to communicate for many reasons beyond fear, shock, or confusion, they choose to remain silent or find alternative means other than verbal communication. Then their repressed expressions morph into "illegible" communication, such as body language, paralanguage, and spatial communications, all of which can have various meanings depending on the culture in which they are being used.[12] In such a context, silence then cannot be described as a simple absence of speech but as a mark of disclosing a strong presence of subjugation. The "illegible" nonverbal expressions, which can manifest in various forms, serve to eloquently testify the ineffability of their experience. Silence has the potential to perpetuate oppression and marginalization, but it can also have the profound ability to express the critical needs of marginalized individuals, including protection, refusal, resistance, and defiance. The prevailing understanding of language hierarchy fails to recognize the complex nature of silence and thus fosters negative perceptions of women and the marginalized as inadequate communicators, just as we see in the case of the women disciples in first-century Palestine.

Based on the careful study of the limitations of language, recent feminist and postcolonial biblical hermeneutics scholarship highlights the complex dynamic underlying the silence of the women in the empty tomb narratives and proposes refreshing perspectives.[13] For example, New Testament scholar Jin Young Choi argues that the silence of the women disciples is an alternative form of resistance and a way to claim voice, echoing the experience of women and the colonized across time and culture whose voices go unheard in public.[14] By challenging the premise that speech equals power and silence equals weakness, these scholars suggest that the silence of the women disciples should not be judged as a frightened reaction or simple failure. Though terrified and confused, the women "remembered [ἐμνήσθησαν]" the words of Jesus (Luke 24:8). The Greek word ἐμνήσθησαν as used by Luke implies an active, purposeful act of retaining something significant. In contrast to the men disciples, who did not take women's words seriously due to conventional prejudice, the women disciples were fully receptive of the words of two strangers who reminded of what Jesus had spoken. The women's silence is not a sign of timidity or evidence that they lacked confidence. Their silence exposes a subversive potential that hoards the liberating news of the Resurrection. In their silence, the women exemplified bravery in listening to the words of complete strangers and modeled tenacity in defending the truth they held dear, even when they were ignored. Their silence ultimately highlights their receptiveness to unfamiliar truths and their openness to ineffable possibilities, qualities the men disciples lacked.

Examining the Gospel narratives through the lens of contemporary experiences of women and marginalized individuals leads us to the intersection where linguistic hierarchy impinges on their speech and their silence, thereby inviting us to a deeper understanding of their struggles. As linguistic minorities are often relegated to the margins of society, we are compelled to examine the subtle nuances of silence and illuminate its potential to challenge the linguistic hierarchy. The silence of marginalized individuals, particularly women of color in the United States, can offer resistive and transformative potential. The story of the women disciples encourages us to explore the mystical and contemplative opportunities of silence in our daily experience as we learn to listen to the subjugated and the marginalized and to connect with others in our struggles.

WOMEN OF COLOR IN THE UNITED STATES

Within the lives of women of color in the United States, silence has various negative connotations. The silences coerced by the dominant White heteropatriarchal culture are the most obvious and tangible. The dominant culture weaponizes silence to control and oppress minority groups, as evident in the history of women of color in the United States. In the case of Asian American women in particular, there is also the silence of complicity coupled with the Asian American model minority myth. Asian American groups and individuals have faced pressure from within the United States and beyond to break their customary culture of silence, which perpetuates racism against them and justifies racism against other racial and ethnic minority groups. The events of the past few years, including the COVID-19 pandemic and the Black Lives Matter movement, have brought this intricate nature of silence to the forefront.[15]

First, the spike of racially motivated violence and hate crimes against racial and ethnic minority groups during the pandemic unearthed the injustice that has made people of color use their voices. Through discriminatory speech and exclusionary policies, the state has implicitly and often even explicitly reinforced and perpetuated racial violence at the institutional level. State-supported racism and xenophobia against people of color are linked to centuries of racism in the United States, which oppresses diverse communities of color in various ways.[16] And silencing is one of the notable instruments of suppression that affects all groups. Such forced silence manifests in different ways, including overt forms of physical violence, which we often witness in racism against Black communities, as well as more covert forms such as stigmatization, othering, isolation, deportation, and bullying, which we see in the cases of Latine Americans, Indigenous peoples, and Asian Americans.

The current surge in anti-Asian crimes has called for urgency in people of color to address race-related political and social issues. However, the discussions of race in North America have frequently been reduced to the Black–White binary, neglecting the perspectives and experiences of non-Black communities and obscuring the complex nature of race in America.[17] Distinct from conspicuous forms of racism such as the suffering of enslavement and campaigns of lynching that Black Americans have experienced, Latine Americans, Indigenous peoples, and Asian Americans have suffered civic ostracism, being regarded as "probationary citizens" or "perpetual foreigners." Especially for Asian American communities, the dominant culture has adopted the strategy of silencing as a means of oppression, which manifests in many forms, such as "namelessness, denial, secrets, taboo subjects, erasure, false-naming, non-naming, encoding, omission, veiling, fragmentation, and lying," by making Asian American experiences invisible, ridiculing their culture and language, and censoring their political appeals.[18] Yet the Black–White binary often excludes the experience of other ethnic minority groups from conversations about race and racism by portraying their discriminatory experience as irrelevant and denigrating them as sharing responsibility in anti-Black racism.[19]

While it is necessary to recognize the various and distinct forms of coercive silence that people of color experience at all levels of society, it is also true that ethnic and racial minority individuals sometimes choose to practice a type of silence that perpetuates the coercive silence against other communities. In particular, the Asian American community must be held accountable for its complicit silence, notably in relation to the racism against Black Americans. Asian Americans occupy a unique location from which to understand the coalitional imperative of movements against racial violence, since they have been posited as the antipode to a "pathologized defiant Blackness" on the basis of two key characteristics: silence and submission to authority.[20] The death of George Floyd on May 25, 2020, at the hands of a Minneapolis police officer is only the tip of the iceberg demonstrating how dangerously entrenched anti-Black racism is in the United States. White supremacy and structural racism rely on the majority's silence and complicity to sustain the structures and practices that keep the status quo in place, and Asian Americans have been reprimanded for their complicit silence, through which they may benefit from the system that maintains Black subordination. Given the relative newness of migration and better level of socioeconomic resources for certain members of the population, Asian Americans as a whole have been labeled as a "model minority" and utilized as a benchmark for minority achievement.[21] As Claire Jean Kim accurately describes, despite their own experience of exclusion, discrimination, and dehumanization, Asian Americans have also been "protected by institutionalized anti-Blackness, where 'white supremacy has pushed them down, and anti-Blackness has provided the floor beneath which they cannot fall.'" The model minority myth has been vigorously disputed by academics and activists because it is based on a fallacy that flattens diverse experiences of Asian Americans into a single restricted narrative and thus provides a deceptive picture of the community that does not correspond with current statistics. However, Asian Americans often adopt and internalize the myth, reinforcing the ideology of anti-Black racism and sustaining the racialized subjugation imposed upon them by White supremacy.[22]

While complicit silence is certainly an individual choice, it must still be carefully investigated in relation to structural racism. Within a racialized society, a person of color is confined to what Frantz Fanon calls "the historico-racial schema," which through the imaginary of Whiteness scripts, reads, and imposes assumptions on bodies of color. The concept of Whiteness has been constructed as a normative standard within Western societies, setting up a system where those who do not fit into this category are considered Other. Asian American individuals are often expected to assimilate to white norms and values, which can lead to the erasure of their own cultural identities. As a result, they find themselves in a difficult position of navigating a society that does not fully embrace them. On one hand, embracing their cultural heritage can be challenging within this ambivalent position, as it can be seen as deviating from the expected assimilation. Denying their heritage, on the other hand, can result in a loss of personal identity and the lack of a solid foundation for relationships with others. According to Fanon, to survive in society the racially oppressed must choose either "amputating" the self from their skin or continuing to bleed, which will spatter their blood across the entire body.[23] By choosing complicity, members of the Asian American community cut the self from their skin and accept subordinate positions. They become subject to pejorative modes of labeling and in turn view themselves as inferior members of society. While they are able to participate to some extent in the social order, that participation comes at the cost of not only their own dignity and autonomy but also the dignity and autonomy of other minority groups and individuals. The systematic issues behind the complicit silences of Asian American community members reveal the difficult but important task of challenging the nature of the Asian American silence in upholding an anti-Black racial social order.

Considering the coercive silence against the Asian American community and the complicit silence of Asian Americans toward Black communities, I would like to pose a question: Can the silence drawn from the mystical and contemplative traditions work positively to foster dialogue among racially subjugated groups, particularly between Black women and Asian American women? Challenging both coercive silence and complicit silence, women of color scholars and activists have prioritized the necessity of breaking silence, considering it the most successful act of emancipation by which one unshackles the control and censorship of the dominant. While the urgency of breaking the coercive and complicit silences must remain at the forefront of confrontation against racism, one may also acknowledge that ways of addressing and being accountable for the racism that affects the ethnic groups and individuals other than their own may be limited, because we are not able to fully fathom others' pain. Furthermore, the allegiance of the dominant society to White heteropatriarchal supremacist and neoliberal logic makes it nearly impossible to truly recognize the struggle of communities other than our own, thus often resulting in oppression Olympics.[24]

Just as the men disciples failed to grasp the significance of the silence in Jesus's empty tomb and dismissed the "illegible" words of testimony from the women disciples, I have observed moments in the United States when both Black and Asian American communities have misunderstood and ignored the diverse forms of silence that individuals experience in their respective life contexts. The challenge of communication lies in the lack of training to listen not only to each other's demands but also to each other's silence—the unspeakable and ineffable cries that remain repressed under coercive and complicit silences, causing perpetual pain or erupting as a loud scream. A more nuanced perspective that draws on the mystical and contemplative perspective allows us to view silence as a bridge rather than a barrier. Silence can be used as a means of fostering compassionate dialogue by encouraging a deeper introspection. While forced silence prolongs subjugation and complicit silence contributes to only partial survival in a racist society, a mystical and contemplative approach to silence can invite us to work toward a new vision and imagination. This approach recognizes the potency of silence in daily struggle as an avenue for alterity and utilizes it as a means to promote dialogue.

The task of seeking mystical and contemplative approaches to the silence of women of color must begin with acknowledging the shortcomings of the guiding political imperative of breaking silence and coming to voice, as well as the narrow understanding of silence simply as the absence of sound, both of which stem from the speech and silence binary created by dominant culture. Although much needed for confronting injustice, speech does not always facilitate an emancipatory dialogue for the vulnerable. The speech–silence binary can instead perpetuate the stereotype of women of color lacking agency and being inadequate communicators. When addressing the power relations that define society's margins, one must first interrogate who can and cannot speak.[25] Furthermore, one must acknowledge that silence can express more eloquently than speech in contexts where the freedom to speak is limited. As Deidre Lashgari says, where there is a dominant voice, "there are always numerous other voices, subverting, transgressing boundaries, working to disrupt its centripetal certainties," whether those manifest through speech or not.[26] The hierarchy of speech over silence hinders us from recognizing the creative potential of silence as a means to resist and build new relationships among women of color. Taken with mystical and contemplative approaches, silence can be a powerful space for dialogue that allows "the freedom of not having to exist constantly in reaction to what is said" and instead brings to the forefront the significance of listening to one another.[27]

By ruminating on various manifestations of the silences of the women of color and recognizing the mystical and contemplative opportunities stemming from them, the following section challenges the racialized and patriarchal attire of silence in daily struggles. I hope to release those silences from the gaze of the dominant and privileged and describe them instead as a shared space for women of color to build community. By mystical opportunities, I refer to situations or moments in which individuals take inspiration from silence in order to subvert the narrow confines of society's definition of the self. By contemplative opportunities, I refer to the disposition through which one can engage in deep, reflective meditation, reorienting oneself toward a deeper relationship with others and developing mental patterns that facilitate a constant inclination and connection to the divine at the core of all beings. The spatial metaphor for the spirituality of silence is useful in this regard because it helps us understand silence as an experience instead of as the opposite of sound or speech, recognizing the relationality of silence and presenting it as a workable space performed by participants. I explore the ways in which we can take the silence of women of color for consideration of mysticism and contemplation through three manifestations of their silence distinct from forced or complicit silence: "loud" silence, melancholic silence, and defiant silence.

MYSTICAL AND CONTEMPLATIVE OPPORTUNITIES OF SILENCE

"Loud" Silence

People who experience extreme anguish and grief typically rely on nonverbal modes of communication to express their ineffable pain or to get their message through to others.[28] Varied in meaning across cultures and individual contexts, the wide spectrum of nonverbal communication includes gestures, facial expressions, interpersonal distances, posture, touching, eye contact, or nonverbal sounds such as moaning, yelling, and crying.[29] Paradoxically yet unsurprisingly, the unspeakable depth of suffering can externalize by a cacophonous sound and excessive body language, which I name "loud" silence. In this context, silence can be a complex phenomenon that encompasses a range of experiences, making it difficult for individuals to understand and express themselves legibly. Experts agree that nonverbal mediums depict one's physical and emotional state in crisis even more accurately than words, so research and practice have emphasized how to interpret them and translate them into verbal cues.[30] Although interpreting the message properly and responding to the crisis situation immediately are crucial, it is equally necessary to recognize that not all messages can be translated into words, no matter how loud and vocal. This recognition represents the first manifestation of the mystical and contemplative approach to silence.

In her book *Joy Unspeakable*, Barbara A. Holmes illuminates the contemplative dimension of African American experiences, focusing on nonverbal expressions of suffering manifested in the history of enslavement.[31] Holmes proposes a nuanced understanding of contemplation outside the confines of religious expectations and encourages the recovery of Indigenous African contemplative practices because both enable healing for communities harmed and scarred by racism. Holmes's exploration of the contemplative opportunities, particularly through the narratives of captured Africans during the Middle Passage, in the holds of slave ships, on auction blocks, and within hush harbors, reveals how members of the Black diaspora conveyed their unfathomable sufferings through nonverbal means. In the face of the horrendous transition from personhood to property, and ultimately nonidentity, they could not speak. Their anguish was "too profound for words."[32] Bearing and witnessing the beating, torturing, raping, and murdering upon themselves and their people, their excruciating fears erupted into moans and screams.[33] They sang because words were too small to contain their pain. They drummed and danced because they needed instruments more than their voices to express the suffering that lacerated their bodies and souls. Their secret silence to gather for a meeting in the hush harbor burst into tears and shouts. The silence that kept their thoughts, sorrows, and joys from the ears of perpetrators was often transformed into charismatic experiences or, in the words of Dwight Hopkins, "a total yielding of the self to spiritual possession."[34] In the experience of Africans in America, the distance between silence and shout is not as vast as it appears because both have roots in unfathomable pain that only God can truly understand.

The inner and outer lives of enslaved Africans illuminate the profound intersection between silence and shout as ways to respond to extreme suffering. Whether "introspective or charismatic," silence in the midst of extreme suffering can only be approached by a mystical and contemplative outlook because it is rooted in a desire to imagine a different world as well as a complete trust in and dependence on God. The experiences of enslaved African people in America resonate with those of different groups of people of color, including Indigenous peoples on the Trail of Tears, Japanese Americans in internment camps, Latine migrants in US detention centers, and numerous other cases. When dire circumstances prevent bereaved people from speaking their hearts, "loud" silence serves as a vehicle for mysticism and contemplation.[35] Words are substituted with cries and screams, pointing to the furnace where they utter their supplication to God. Moaning, murmuring, sighing, shouting, weeping, drumming, and dancing are the "spiritual vocabularies" of the minority in the crucible of crisis.[36] Just like silence, these vocabularies too are prayers, critiques, hymns, and sermons that transform terrified souls into a state of mystical attenuation, allowing a mental and spiritual space distanced from horrid circumstances.[37] To honor the depth of loud silence, one must listen to the unknowable and patiently remain by the side of the suffering person rather than attempting to construe or translate their pain into legible speech.

Melancholic Silence

In her short story "The Loom," Japanese American novelist Ruth A. Sasaki portrays a quiet student in a school classroom. Being the only Japanese girl in her class, she seldom speaks out because she is at a loss for words in a language that is not her mother tongue and she feels unfamiliar with the Anglo-American norms and mores.[38] "She muted her colors and blended in" because she feels uncomfortable with her uniqueness and aloneness.[39] These kinds of feelings are prevalent in the experience of immigrants, and even those who were born into and grew up in the dominant culture share a similar feeling if they come from a marginalized background, whether by their race, gender, class, sexual orientation, physical and mental disability, religion, age, or other such factors. As the author Joanna Kadi says, "If you feel comfortable and speak easily, it's because those spaces have been set up for and by your own particular group of people."[40] Marginalized individuals often feel that the culture was built for others and that they do not have the vocabulary to express themselves adequately.[41]

However, lack of proficiency with the dominant language and culture is not the only reason the marginalized choose silence. For those who have been uprooted from their homes and have come to rely on a foreign language as their primary means of communication, silence can reflect complex internal and external struggles. For example, when one experiences abrupt separation, especially coupled with an asymmetrical power balance between the dominant culture and their own, the marginalized may feel that it is impossible to communicate. To distinguish this experience from ignorance or inability, postcolonial scholars adopt the clinical term "colonial aphasia," which describes the difficulty to speak up or to come up with a vocabulary that can link words with the appropriate concepts.[42] While I am cautious of using such impairment rhetoric because it is steeped in ableism and "reinforces a belief in a true, right, strong, free perceptual awareness and its diseased or impaired other,"[43] the experience of the marginalized resonates with the symptoms of aphasia. In this situation, their silence exposes dislocation, dissociation, and the loss of access to the source beyond the lack of proficiency to speak.

Hongkongese American scholar Rey Chow further adopts the Freudian melancholy to expand the significance of the "colonial aphasia," describing it as the limit of having voice caused by lingering cultural orientations and political power relations.[44] Freudian melancholy refers to a state of deep and persistent sadness or depression that arises from the loss of a loved object, which can be a person, an ideal, or even an aspect of oneself. Melancholy involves a process of internalization in which the lost object is incorporated into the ego, resulting in a sense of self-devaluation and guilt, then feelings of hopelessness and a diminished sense of self-worth. According to Freud, melancholy is a peculiar kind of mourning for a broken or destroyed relationship in which the mourner connects with the object of their affection rather than letting it go and, as a result, develops intense self-criticism. While Freud viewed melancholy as a pathological condition, Judith Butler emphasizes the ways in which social norms and power structures can shape our mourning and grief and view it as a form of melancholy. They argue that societal expectations can limit our ability to fully process loss and can even result in the internalization of oppressive systems.[45]

Chow employs both Freudian and Butlerian concepts of melancholy and says the formerly colonized—and I would add the immigrant and marginalized who are pushed aside from the dominant society—find themselves "condemned to a vicious circle of melancholic longing: displaced from [their] own indigenous language and accustomed to seeing [themselves] and [their] culture from the outside, [they are] afflicted with grief, yearn for a return to a lost harmony, yet must continue to survive in a world in which such a return is impossible."[46] Their silence, which I name "melancholic" silence, thus manifests an undone grief over the experience of loss, embodying their concomitant struggle that intersect with many other discriminatory categories.

While melancholic silence is a manifestation of being a linguistic minority and reflects one's cultural location, it must be approached with caution.[47] If left unaddressed, it can lead to individuals being trapped in their own bubbles, unable to disclose the root causes of their feelings of inequity and isolation or to suggest any transformative potential to challenge dominant forces. Indebted with postcolonial theory, Chow is wary of the risk and even the impossibility of attempting to fill silence with words and translating them into the dominant language.[48] Instead, she finds creative potential in their experience of loss, dislocation, liminality, and mimicry. The postcolonial and immigrant experience involves conflicting language politics, including both the subjugation of the dominant language and subversive acts of reconstructing language from the bottom up. Although it may be unsettling and uncomfortable, the precarious status of the postcolonial and immigrant experience can serve as a catalyst for creative, anarchical, and insubordinate linguistic activity. In order to transform melancholy into something inventive and fruitful, Chow proposes the concept of "xenophone," which refers to the sound or tone of foreign language that disturbs the alleged unity of dominant languages and embraces linguistic multiplicities. Xenophones share a commonality with loud silence in that both are a form of expression that remains impossible to fully express; however, unlike loud silence, xenophones demonstrate one's attempt to anchor oneself in a certain linguistic practice while constantly slipping away from a supposed sense of security. Navigating in the realm between legible and illegible language, xenophones constantly evolve a blend of various accents and tones and perplexes with their dissonant melody of diverse sounds, thereby creating space for small noises that were once silenced.[49] The xenophone bears the marks of individual and communal subjugation, lived inequality, and failed expectations of the life at the margin, yet it burgeons into cultural conviviality, diversity, and inclusion.

Nevertheless, the opportunity for the xenophone cannot be realized without first intentionally embracing a period of silence during which both the speaker and listener are present with each other. Without a trained ear to discern the nuances of the xenophone, its differences may be perceived as mere noise or, worse yet, ridiculed, fetishized, and exoticized in an Orientalist fashion that detaches it from its cultural context. The utterance of a xenophone always includes the clandestine aspects of language that remain fundamentally untranslatable and incomprehensible but which silence can contain, remember, and remind us of. The mystical and contemplative opportunities of melancholic silence can support the creative potential for the xenophone and the possibility of transforming it into a space for new inspiration. One can cultivate a positive attitude toward this new interlingual possibility by paying close attention to the inaudible within words and patiently waiting for a new meaning to arrive. By keeping xenophones open in character and promising their newness in the unexpected, mystical and contemplative engagement enable xenophones to emerge and connect with listeners. For such engagement creates space in our mind and heart where we unlearn our knowledge so that we become receptive to new insights. It enables and encourages the poetic fervor in our communication and guides us on our never-ending search to broaden our horizons toward a more profound communication.

Defiant Silence

Subordinate individuals often deliberately use silence as a means to resist the system of dominance and disrupt the linguistic order when they feel precarious in their use of language. In situations where power relations lead to subjugation, speech often requires conformity to dominant norms, which in turn marginalizes linguistic minorities and undermines their ability to communicate authentically and to exist fully. In such a milieu, an individual may choose "defiant" silence as a pathway to challenge the hegemonic language and to protect their agency.[50] Unlike complicit silence, the subversive act of defiant silence creates mystical and contemplative opportunities. Adrienne Rich once said that when one's words cannot withstand the noise and chaos of the world, silence can serve as a "pond where drowned things live."[51] In this way, silence becomes a space in which the unspeakable can persist and await new opportunities for confrontation.

The narrative of Harriet Jacobs (1813–1897), an African American author and a survivor of sexual violence, reveals this defiant modality of silence. In her autobiography *Incidents in the Life of a Slave Girl*, Jacobs indicates the dilemma of language and the appropriateness of silence to cope with the dilemma: "I have not written my experience in order to attract attention to myself; on the contrary, it would have been more pleasant to me to have been silent about my own history."[52] Grappling with the constraints of the literary standards of her time, Jacobs discovered that language was not always useful when responding to repeated requests to describe her experience of systematic violence. She was well aware that her testimony could be used to expose the ongoing brutality against Black women and maintain her audience's sympathy, which would benefit abolitionist campaign rallies. Yet she also knew that the audience "might read about her suffering voyeuristically." In her reading of Jacobs's narrative, Anne B. Dalton describes that Jacobs, as a woman who had been sexually abused by White men and betrayed by her White mistress, might have felt conflicted to speak truth to White women audiences because the audience could take her experience as evidence of the stereotype of the hypersexualized Black woman.[53] Jacobs's careful consideration of silence demonstrates her strong agency against the restriction and limitation of verbal expression in discourse for women of color and simultaneously discloses a tactical use of silence to shield a minority person from systematic humiliation, violence, and degradation of dignity. In her situation, silence can be seen as resolutely defiant, if not outright belligerent.

American literary critic King-Kok Cheung's book *Articulate Silence* eloquently discloses such defiant silence in the context of Asian American women while challenging both Anglo-American feminists' exaltation of speech and revisionist Asian American men critics' disavowal of silence in their confrontation of Orientalist stereotypes.[54] Drawing on the novels of Asian American women writers such as Hisaye Yamamoto, Maxine Hong Kingston, and Joy Kogawa, Cheung demonstrates how silence, coupled with nonverbal gestures and authorial hesitations, can be expressive and articulate. According to Cheung, the women writers' use of silence displays several common characteristics that expose the distinctive potential of defiant silence: first, the writers reveal the many barriers to women's expression while at the same time uncovering various "strategies of reticence" such as "irony, hedging, coded language, and muted plots"; second, despite their skepticism about inherited language, they are unwilling to proclaim themselves as "*the* voice of truth" and instead leave room for other voices; third, as a result of their reservation for language and textual authority, they embrace "open-endedness and multiplicity" in their writing.[55] In other words, Cheung shows that the silence of women of color not only reveals the difficulties of speaking out and the unreliability of official records but also sheds light on the stories of others who have been marginalized and silenced. This requires an acknowledgment of the fragility of speech and the complexity of silence, along with a deliberate attention to the presence of silent others in the discourse and a willingness to make space for their perspectives to be heard.

Jacobs's narrative and Cheung's analysis of these three Asian American women writers demonstrate that the silence of women of color has a defiant character against oppressive power structures. While their defiant silence echoes the struggles manifested in loud and melancholic silence, it also adds another layer to the silence of women of color, revealing that silence can be an intentional and purposeful act of challenging dominant forces. However, just like "loud" silence and melancholic silence, defiant silence also presents mystical and contemplative opportunities. On one hand, defiant silence disrupts the accepted operation of discourse, thus loosening the grip of power held by dominant forces. This creates a discreet space for women of color in vulnerable circumstances to protect each other without the need for verbal articulation.[56] Yet on the other hand, it becomes a mystical and contemplative space that allows the recognition of many unnamed, missing, and misrepresented voices in their respective cultural, societal, and personal contexts. Instead of attempting to claim the voice of the self as the only alternative, this space acknowledges and opens the scene to others. As such, silence for women of color endures the lack of control over one's speech yet strives toward better relations, particularly with others in struggle, at the junction of the impossibility of speech. It never settles into a single meaning and always anticipates the emergence of another meaning.

These three forms of silence experienced by women of color in their daily struggles—"loud" silence, melancholic silence, and defiant silence—suggest that when language fails, silence can be potent in expressing what cannot be articulated. However, these silences also offer mystical and contemplative opportunities because they ultimately point toward a longing for connection with others that involves relinquishing self-centered desires. The mystical and contemplative opportunities drawn from these silences invite us to pay attention to the unsaid and unspeakable experiences of suffering and listen to them without hastily attempting to react, translate, speak for, or instruct.

Silence can also be a transformative tool to build community among women of color. Through engaging mystical and contemplative silence in their daily experiences, women of color can find a shared space for prayer and protest, both of which serve as permeable points of reference for reducing the likelihood of perpetuating harmful systems and for starting the healing process from within.[57] Such silence is a fluid space where participants are not constrained by rules or an attempt to dismiss others but can allow each other freedom to be present and accepted as they are. Through this freedom, women of color can work toward developing an alternative political imagination that recognizes each other's unrelieved pain and fosters a struggle together.[58]

Realizing the mystical and contemplative potential of the silence of women of color, however, requires a practice of listening. Valorizing silence can be a precarious undertaking, as it can be challenging to distinguish mystical and contemplative silence from coerced or complicit silence.[59] The capacity of listeners to distinguish between mystical, contemplative silence and coercive silence is crucial. Through listening to each other, women of color can cultivate confidence in the possibilities of relationship building and eventually propel sacred opportunities. Without attentive listening mystical and contemplative silence cannot be entangled from repression; listening is an intrinsic part of mystical and contemplative silence.

THE PRACTICE OF LISTENING TO SILENCE

For linguistic minorities who are suffering or have experienced trauma, it is necessary to have their experiences recognized in a safe environment, whether through verbal or nonverbal means, in order to resist oppression and heal. When it comes to listening during such occasions, I suggest adopting a contemplative disposition. This can aid in directing one's attention away from external and internal distractions and misleading thoughts and instead toward a profound connection with the sacred nature that resides within oneself and others. Contemplative silence is different from merely not having a word in the face of suffering. Contemplative silence is to listen to the other and give one's presence to the other without trying to control the other's presence. As Thomas Merton says, "the true contemplative is not the one who prepares his mind for a particular message that he wants or expects to hear, but who remains empty because he knows that he can never expect or anticipate the word that will transform his darkness into light. He does not demand light instead of darkness."[60] Ultimately, contemplation seeks truth through listening to the divine, and truth for the contemplative is always relational in that it is about and for one's communion with the divine. Discovering contemplative opportunities within the silence of daily struggles, therefore, entails opening ourselves up to the presence of others who are silent, even though we may not fully comprehend them, just as we open ourselves up to the divine despite our inability to comprehend the divine mystery.

Without witnesses to our suffering, our pain increases. Unrecognized memories of suffering can turn into anger and resentment and entangle relationships with violence and hate. As Robin P. Clair discusses in her book *Organizing Silence*, when marginalized members are forced into silence, they silence each other by hurting themselves and others, respectively.[61] In the case of structural violence, everyone in society becomes a victim, perpetrator, or both, as the violence is directed toward the most vulnerable members of society. Within this context, oppression and resistance exist in a constant tension whose noisy clash can drown out authentic relationship. Contemplative silence seeks to resist the dilution of healing by rejecting the patterns of coercive silence and reactive vocal response. It creates a space for listening to one another, where authenticity and connection can thrive. In this new way of being present with others, listening becomes essential.

However, what does it mean to listen to the silent other? What does one do in the presence of the other whose loud, melancholic, or defiant silence fills the room? How can one respond to the cause of their pain by refraining from speaking? In what ways can one take mystical and contemplative opportunities from the silences of daily struggle and transform them into spiritual resources? The aim of this section is not to prescribe specific actions or solutions to the issues at hand but to offer a theological reflection on the role of listening in silence. By examining how listening can create a space for contemplative silence, we can discern ways to be fully present with the silent other, which I believe is the beginning of the practice of listening. I want to emphasize that the practice of listening is integral in promoting openness and curiosity toward others, allowing uncertainty and wonder to flourish.

The Practice of Listening at a Silent Distance

The practice of attentive listening involves creating a sense of distance between the listener and the silent other, particularly during moments of silence, in order to guard each other's silence and respect each other's boundaries. The sense of distance between the listener and the silent other highlights the fact that both parties are distinct from one another and are not reducible to one another. Distance, therefore, is the primary condition for trustful relationship during contemplative silence. According to Jewish philosopher Martin Buber, relation (*Beziehung*) presupposes distance (*Urdistanz*). In the act of listening, distance and relation must correspond. For two parties to recognize each other as whole people, they must maintain a sense of independence and distance from each other. Distance withstands and simultaneously confirms the presence of both the self and the other, recalling their instinct for relation.[62]

Even when two parties share a common goal and seek to build solidarity, maintaining a sense of distance between them remains crucial. This distance allows each party to fully express their perspective and experiences while also promoting active listening and understanding. By recognizing and respecting each other's unique perspectives, the parties can come together to achieve their shared objective with greater empathy and collaboration. In their discussion on the ethics of listening for racial justice, feminist scholars Michelle Ballif, D. Diane Davis, and Roxanne Mountford emphasize the significance of maintaining a sense of distance. They argue that the distance between the I and the other is "originary and uncloseable" and that "listening itself does not and cannot close this distance; it can only attend to it." Furthermore, they claim listening is not so much "hearing what the other says" as "hearing that the Other speaks as Other."[63] To put it another way, even as one offers their presence to be shared, one must acknowledge the difference of the other and the fundamental inability to fully share the other's suffering. Everyone's pain is unique in its depth, and no one can fully comprehend another's pain.

My aim in exploring the significance of distance in silence as a prerequisite for listening is to forge a connection between the practice of listening to the silent other and the practice of listening to the silent God in the Christian mystical tradition. While listening, it is critical to acknowledge that there is risk involved in the attempt to comprehend the other's silence. Vulnerability can create a window of opportunity for anyone, whether with good or malicious intentions, to interfere with or exert their power over another. This risk is more likely to occur where the listener does not acknowledge the incomprehensibility of the other. The emphasis on the incomprehensibility of the divine and radical openness to the unknown in mystical and contemplative traditions may serve as a reminder of the necessity of maintaining a respectful distance when building a community of listening.

Unlike speaking, silence creates an in-between space that must remain empty and distant, inviting both parties to engage in a moment of reflection. When speaking, individuals may have presuppositions and fantasies about the other person that can reduce them to an object, serving the speaker's own needs. However, in moments of intentional silence, the unknown aspects of each other are preserved and a sense of openness to connect is maintained. The distance between the speaker and listener during such moments is not a wasteland devoid of feeling and meaning, nor does it force the vulnerable into a coercive silence. Instead, it allows individuals to relinquish their attempt to interpret and analyze and to choose not to impose underlying meanings or predetermined purposes onto the relationship. In this way, contemplative silence "lets the other be."[64] Listening to the silence of the other is listening to the other as fully other. To make room for silence is to wait for recognition of what is ineffable and unspoken in the sacred distance; it allows the two parties to build the trust necessary to engage authentically with each other.

The fundamental distance between listener and silent other inevitably entails uncertainty. To listen to silence is to turn toward the unfathomable, which does not allow "immediacy [to be] available to 'us.'"[65] When one engages the silence of the other, the two parties will never satisfy the assumed expectation of the reception of accurate information. The purpose of silence in this space is not to deliver or produce an objective truth. Rather, it is to "break a mold of discourse," as Adrienne Rich exclaims in her poem. Silence, Rich continues, is the space of the "unnamable by choice ... beyond all places, beyond boundaries, green lines, wire-netted walls / the place beyond documents."[66] Silence exists as a consistent companion for both the listener and the silent other, making them equal in the empty space of distance, beckoning them away from the routine of banal and hectic reactionary noise. Before working on a practical solution or even considering solution-oriented politics, contemplative silence allows the other, no matter how fragile or finite they are, to hold space for being together without being overcome by anger, resentment, guilt, or even good intention.

To hold uncertainty in contemplative silence, nonetheless, does not invite both parties to succumbing to nihilism or to be left without any possibility to create together. When two parties desire to build a relationship, embracing uncertainty can offer new possibilities and experiences, bridging the threshold from indifference to curiosity. Unlike voyeuristic desire, which involves watching or observing others without their knowledge or consent, practicing silent listening ensures that both parties remain curious about each other. It fosters a sense of responsiveness and connection that affirms both parties' willingness to visit and revisit each other's perspectives based on consent. Curiosity maintains support for the other by allowing the multitude of different priorities and preferences to coexist, providing space for them to linger and potentially invite second thoughts. The gesture to protect and fortify the silent other by praising them as beacons for the like-minded may appear generous, charitable, and even compassionate, yet it is frequently motivated by a desire to assimilate the truth of the other into a cohesive, understandable narrative for one's own self-interest. On the contrary, when one engages in silent listening, accompanied by embracing uncertainty and maintaining curiosity, both parties are given the freedom to be themselves while trusting each other's perspectives and confidently exploring the self and the other—until, as Rich puts it, "little by little minds change / but . . . they do change."[67]

The ability to stay curious and be amazed is integral to mystical silence, and we achieve it by dispossessing our language and unlearning ourselves to remain in a loving relationship with the divine. While mystical silence keeps us from fixating on self and society and their trivialities, it also guides us in the search for God. Mysticism is founded and sustained by its orientation toward union with God, where God remains unfathomable and ineffable. The divine unknowability does not create fear; instead, it generates joy in the state of mind that is enthralled by love and that trusts in the divine mystery, leading us toward greater love. Drawing from mystical and contemplative traditions, we can learn to honor the incomprehensibility of others. Just as the divine is unfathomable, each person's experiences and perspectives are unique and incomprehensible. Silence inspires us to let go of the compulsion to control uncertainty and instead embrace it as a fundamental aspect of life. We can still desire connection with others based on wonder and amazement while recognizing and respecting their incomprehensibility. Mystical and contemplative silence can help us build mutual support and the trust necessary for this engagement. Listening may be practiced at a distance in a way that fosters wonder and trust toward others.[68] I am inspired by the artistic expressions of the late Korean American artist Theresa Hak Kyung Cha, which exemplify the embodiment, enactment, and practice of listening from a silent distance within the context of linguistic minorities.

The Silent Other and the Dream of the Listener

Looking for mystical and contemplative opportunities through art is not an unusual pursuit. Susan Sontag notes that an artist's goal is not only to present an image but also to create a silence that encourages the observer to engage with what has not yet been articulated and to capture what precedes and follows the act of utterance. Sontag believes that art and mysticism are intrinsically connected: "the antecedents of art's dilemmas and strategies are also found in the radical wing of the mystical tradition."[69] Art embodies key characteristics of mysticism, including inward awareness and a willingness to engage with what cannot be fully expressed. Through its embrace of ambiguity, indeterminacy, and uncertainty, art opens up space for the pursuit of the transcendental, inviting viewers to adopt an entirely new way of seeing. Theresa Hak Kyung Cha's works demonstrate such mystical and contemplative characteristics of silence within the life context of the subjugated. Via the experiences of women of color, Cha presents the unbridgeable distance between the silent other and listener as a space of longing, where both parties together strive for transcendence and form community.

Theresa Hak Kyung Cha was a Korean American poet, producer, and artist. She was born in Busan, South Korea, in 1951, during the Korean War, and immigrated to the United States in 1962. She studied literature and art at the University of California, Berkeley, and film theory at the Centre d'Études Américain du Cinéma in Paris. Cha began her career as a performance artist, writer, director, and producer in California after returning from Paris in 1974. She relocated to New York in 1980, where she began teaching video art and worked in the Metropolitan Museum of Art's design department. On November 5, 1982, when Cha was thirty-one years old, a serial killer raped and murdered her in lower Manhattan.

Cha's best-known work, *Dictee*, is a genre-defying poetry collection published only one week before her death. Interspersed throughout the nine chapters of the book are letters, calligraphy, photographs, and diagrams, depicting the lives of historical and mythical women who endured perilous conditions and the cruelty of patriarchy. They were martyrs (Joan of Arc and Yu Guan Soon), mystics (Saint Thérèse of Lisieux), separated mother and daughter (Demeter and Persephone), and Cha's own mother (Hyung Soon Huo). Despite their distinct contexts, they share a journey as women who were silenced, misrepresented, and appropriated. Although Cha weaves together the narratives of these women, her collection disrupts the reader's expectation of reading them as a complete, linear story. Instead, she leaves space between the narratives for others, as if making a spiral connection. Cha names her distinct approach to presenting the narratives of women as a "concentric circle," as if "one woman's life is a 'circle within a circle' and all the women's lives are a series of concentric circles," as the Korean American scholar Kun Jong Lee describes.[70] Cha moves back and forth between the layers of the "concentric circle," placing each woman in *Dictee* within other women's narratives so that they listen to one another.

Within and beyond *Dictee*, the consistent themes of Cha's works are time, language, and memory. Cha lived in diaspora experiencing displacement and adapting to the language and culture of dominance. Although she was fluent in Korean, English, and French, she never felt at ease in any of them. Her works frequently address the anxiety of being silenced, misunderstood, or forgotten and the difficulty of learning a new language to replace another.[71] By experimenting with multiple languages, she mirrors her experience of loss, isolation, and confusion. Yet she does not represent the experiences of those women and herself as stories of victimhood or subjugation but challenges "the dichotomous understandings of displacement and belonging, repression and freedom, detachment and connection, testimony and silence" and finds creative potential in the clash.[72]

Silence takes a prominent place in Cha's works. She frequently uses silence to express displacement and loss entangled with a convoluted sense of time, language, and memory, reflecting her life as a woman of color and immigrant. In *Dictee*, Cha visualizes silence to be seen as blank pages, ellipses, deliberate punctuation errors, and a nonsensical arrangement of words that cuts and redirects the flow of meaning. In her visual artworks, she leaves images uncaptioned and intentionally blurs them. In her performance artworks, she spatializes silence to communicate with viewers beyond conceptual frames. As a whole, her works give flesh to the silence of women of color and linguistic minorities. Her work demonstrates that the many presences of women of color can be seen and resonate with each other through silence's various manifestations, without being arranged a linearly or hierarchically.

In Cha's works, the three forms of silence I discussed as opportunities for mysticism and contemplation experienced by women of color are quite noticeable. Her intentional disarrangement of words and speeches in her written, visual, and performance art creates a disturbing and cacophonous sound that echoes the "loud" silence of women of color. Her insatiable desire for her mother tongue poignantly reflects the melancholic silence of women of color. Finally, her refusal to speak and be dictated by dominant language correlates with the defiant silence of women of color. Cha's works attest to the experience of women of color in which speech is fractured through dislocation and trauma, making silence a potent tool of expression.

In her performances, Cha often incorporates sound, including her own live or recorded voice, to paradoxically emphasize the significance of silence. In other words, while sound has a role to play in Cha's performance, it does not convey one comprehensible meaning. Her "almost incantational way of speaking" and use of sound rather scatter meaning, persistently resisting conceptualization.[73] By sliding, dimming, and oddly lapsing her voice, Cha disrupts the audience's habit of seeking a singular meaning and brings awareness to the dominant need to focus on concepts, storylines, and decipherability, as well as fear that art may go off "the rails of access and communication."[74] Through her art, Cha challenges the audience to confront their preconceived notions of how an artist should communicate, inviting them to let go of their own agenda and instead enter a shared temporal space. The artist and the audience remain attentively present with each other and form a new relationship by silently engaging with the space. The space allows the artist and audience to traverse together with curiosity and uncertainty by recalling their experiences and anticipating a shared imagination for the future.

Cha's handmade artist book *Audience Distant Relative*, created in 1978 and displayed at Galerie Lóa in Haarlem, the Netherlands, the same year, provides a glimpse into the interaction between the artist and the audience in silence. The artist book consists of seven sheets of paper folded in half, forming seven cards. On the front of six of the folded papers are the titles or subjects printed in black ink: "audience distant relative," "letter senderceiver," "object/subject," "messenger," "between delivery," and "echo." The text inside each card explores the title or subject. As seen in figure 4.1, for example, "audience distant relative" is expanded.

Along with the printed texts, Cha's artist book draws the viewer's attention to the intentional empty space surrounding the texts. Whether placed between words or in the margins of a card, the space is where the unspoken "between delivery" discloses its invisible but tangible presence. In other words, the space between words or in images is not empty but carries unspoken yet tangible messages and emotions that are integral to communication.[75] In this context, silence takes form as a visible absence of words, creating a distance between the artist and viewer. This presence of absence

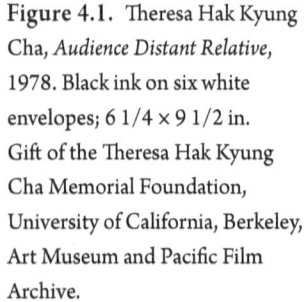

Figure 4.1. Theresa Hak Kyung Cha, *Audience Distant Relative*, 1978. Black ink on six white envelopes; 6 1/4 × 9 1/2 in. Gift of the Theresa Hak Kyung Cha Memorial Foundation, University of California, Berkeley, Art Museum and Pacific Film Archive.

is both unsettling and intriguing for the viewer, as it underscores both the artist's desire to connect and her failure to do so. In other words, Cha's embodiment of silence on each card has an effect on the viewer's perceptions and emotions that is just as significant as that of a presence. This tangible enactment of silent distance exemplifies that relations are formed and performed "not only around the presence, what is there, but also around the absence, what is not there."[76] For Cha, silence refers not to a hidden meaning to be dug out to light but to the "unsayability" at the moment and the "sayability" that has not arrived, both awaiting the viewer's engagement.

I want to draw attention to the phrase "distant relative," which is the title of the artist book and refers to Cha's audience. The connection between the artist and the audience exists only in distance. Whether pushing or pulling, that connection has no significant effect unless both parties recognize and bring about each other's presence. Yet the presence of the artist and the audience can be uneasy and disturbing to the other, similar to the Freudian

THE SILENT WOMEN AND THE EMPTY TOMB   129

> you are the audience
> you are my distant audience
> i address you
> as i would a distant relative
> as if a distant relative
> seen only heard only through someone else's description.
>
> neither you nor i
> are visible to each other
> i can only assume that you can hear me
> i can only hope that you hear me

uncanny, because they exist in a strangely familiar way, recalling suppressed memories of each other. The repressed memories of each other may or may not share the same root, but they serve as a reminder of the losses and pains embedded in their skin. The presence of the artist to the audience, and vice versa, is "nothing new or alien" but "something which is familiar and old-established" in the mind of each other, like a distant relative who "has become alienated from [them] through the process of repression."[77] Lingering around remembrance and prefiguration, the distant relative reveals their presence most often in the forms of silence and absence.[78]

Cha does not require the audience to attend to a prescribed truth or to decipher the silence in order to identify who the distant relatives are. Rather, she "want[s] to be the dream of the audience," as she once wrote in a note.[79] In someone else's dream, one neither has control nor follows a lineal trace but navigates space where they are "suspended between consciousness and unconsciousness."[80] In the dream-like space into which she invites her audience, Cha assumes the role of a *diseuse*, through which her book *Dictee* thematically tracks her emergence. A *diseuse* is a woman performer who presents or recites a monologue, her own story or the story of others. Yet the diseuse in Cha's works cannot speak for herself. While she desires to speak, she struggles to express her trauma due to the precariousness of speech. The experience of the other can never be fully conveyed. "To the others, these accounts are about (one more) distant land, like (any other) distant land, without any discernable features in the narrative, (all the same) distant like any other," she writes. Thus, the diseuse cannot speak, and she refuses to speak: "Greater than is the pain not to say. To not say. Says nothing against the pain to speak. It festers inside."[81] Although she stays silent in the distance, she does not want members of her audience to speak for her or interpret her unspeakable cries and murmurs for their own sake. Instead, she waits for the audience to cultivate receptivity and grapple with strangely familiar memories.

What Cha presents through her artworks is a new mode of listening rather than a new mode of speaking. In this mode of listening, the predetermined schema is lost; instead, the bodily presence of the diseuse—the silent other—becomes a parenthesis that opens a nascent context for engaging. What she bears inside remains unfathomable to her audience. However, by elevating the precise moment when her desire for connection reaches out to her audience members, Cha invokes in them a heightened attention that causes a silent pause within themselves, a state of uncertainty. The silent pause keeps both the artist and the audience awake, inspiring them to strive for connection and emboldening them with new imagination and possibilities. It transforms the distance between them into an open space that welcomes the suppressed narratives of both individuals, as well as of those who have yet to arrive.

Cha repeats over and over throughout her works the lingering urge to *wait*. The artist waits for her audience in distance and in turn desires her audience to wait for her in distance until both parties open themselves, see, and listen to each other. The silence that fills the distance can be confusing and perplexing, but Cha desires her audience to stay in silence with her. For it is only by pausing and embracing uncertainty that one can fully recognize the other's presence. Only when we refrain from imposing our own assumptions and judgments on other's stories can we become curious about others and dream together, creating a new and shared experience. A "concentric circle" of women of color is at work here, standing together and forming a spiral of enticement and curiosity toward one another. Although the goal is not to merge with each other, we remain in a state of silent vigilance, continually waiting for each other's stories to depart and return, to receive and give, both for ourselves and for others in the circle of women of color.

CONTEMPLATIVE LISTENING

"Wait" is a mystical and contemplative call. When one waits with patience and openness, they create a space for the divine to reveal its presence. Waiting allows the divine incomprehensible to unfold in its own time and reveals insights that may have been previously obscured by the noise of everyday life. The women disciples in the tomb waited for the news of the Resurrection, and it finally revealed itself. They witnessed the empty tomb of Jesus and continued to honor the truth of his Resurrection through trusting in God as well as each other's presence. The mystics in the Christian traditions, too, taught us to wait because it may not yet be time for mystery to arrive in language. In this call to wait in silent listening, the mystical longing for the divine echoes the desires of women of color to connect with one another.

Just as contemplative silence for the mystic is not about subjecting oneself to the force of suppression, the silence of women of color in mystical and contemplative waiting is not self-effacement nor self-degradation. Silence for the mystic, as the writer Jean N. Evans says, is "the means by which [they] reserve [their] freedom *not* to speak" because it "may not yet be time." Mystics recognize "the necessity to guard the secret, to protect the revelation that is not ready to be made known."[82] Similar to the mystics, in silent waiting, women of color reserve the right to withhold the details of what they experience and what they feel until the right moment ripens. When attuned to contemplation, silence can motivate and support women of color's desire for freedom and connection and can work against the harmful silence that keeps them in suppression and complicity. While coercive silence prevents connection with others, the mystical freedom not to speak is practiced in the loving presence of the divine and trustful others. While complicit silence manufactures a misconceived autonomy and perpetuates veiled repression, contemplative silence creates space to patiently encourage one's desire to be themselves and to accept others as they are.

Just as mystics' silence enabled union with the divine mystery, so silence leads women of color to see and hear each other and form trusting relationships with each other. In mystical and contemplative waiting, the relationship grows resilient enough to overcome anxiety and fear and mature enough to willingly accept the limitation and incompleteness of full understanding. In this waiting, our shared vulnerability turns into an occasion to build intimacy. The built-in expectation of effective and clear communication can be rejected in this waiting because the ardent desire to truly see and listen to each other is stronger than the desire to resort to hastily prescribed meanings and assumptions. Such a wait resists the hope fabricated by shallow rhetoric and false conviction. Perhaps it is a "wait without hope," as T. S. Eliot writes, yet it may hold them in "echoed ecstasy" and enfold them in the shared "agony of death and birth."[83]

The practice of listening in silent waiting, in this regard, is more than just listening to what the other needs to say; it becomes a shared dream in which the listener and the silent other each reject the impulse to seek power over the other. Silence embraces them outside and inside, creating an infinity of distance that does not lock them within intrasubjectivity but instead stretches them toward the divine unknown. The unassimilability between them does not send them into a sense of failure. Rather, it connects them with the divine incomprehensible that cannot be reduced into any one's end and never ceases to reinvigorate a new possibility. The desire for an ever-renewed relationship keeps the listener and the silent other prioritizing relationship over practicality, presence over outcome, silence over superfluous words.

In waiting, therefore, we witness mystical and contemplative silence stretching outward toward engagement with transformative social action and becoming a resource with which we can prepare our hearts to resist the forces that silence us and close our ears. We also behold that mystical and contemplative silence inspires women of color not to be limited to the much-demanded confrontation against the force of illusion and injustice. Rather, such silence offers a gateway for different groups of women of color to dream and love together beyond the pursuit of solution-oriented utility and productivity. It encourages women of color to see and generates open-ended questions that vitalize curiosity about each other and that allow us to envision a better world together. Thus, the silence of women of color connects to the silence of the divine who patiently waits, the God who listens to the silences of those who have lost their voices, those who cannot express themselves but by crying and screaming, and those who protect themselves by refusing to speak. In waiting we listen to God, who listens to the silenced core of ourselves and others.

NOTES

1. Minh-ha, *Woman, Native, Other*, 20.
2. Bovon, "The Empty Tomb," 349.
3. Fiorenza, *In Memory of Her*, 50; D'Angelo, "Women in Luke–Acts," 441–61.
4. Reid, "The Gospel of Luke," 5.
5. Karris, "Women and Discipleship in Luke," 16.
6. Perkins, *Roman Imperial Identities*, 19–21; and Choi, *Postcolonial Discipleship*, 56–57.

7. Quintilian, *Institutio Oratoria*, as quoted in Choi, *Postcolonial Discipleship*, 48–59.
8. Ilan, *Jewish Women in Greco-Roman Palestine*, 163–66.
9. Barry, *Beginning Theory*, 122, 125; Green and LeBihan, *Critical Theory and Practice*, 245–49, 266; Clair, *Organizing Silence*, 20, as quoted in Choi, *Postcolonial Discipleship*, 145.
10. Elkins, *Trauma and the Memory*, 8.
11. Spivak, "Can the Subaltern Speak?" 28–37.
12. The term "body language" refers to the nonverbal communication that takes place between people as a result of the movements of their bodies, such as nodding one's head, blinking one's eyes, waving one's hands, or shrugging one's shoulders. "Paralanguage" refers to a variety of vocal features that serve to express and reflect the speaker's mood, including voice, intonation, pitch, pause, volume, emphasis, and signs, all used to express enthusiasm, confidence, worry, and the speaker's mental state and disposition. Laughing, crying, yelling, moaning, whining, belching, and yawning are also examples of paralanguage. Spatial communication or proxemics refer to space or territory. A significant amount of communication takes place in a non-vocal manner as we use the space around us in certain ways, for example, creating intimate space, personal space, social space, or public space. For more information, see Dunning, "Research in Nonverbal Communication"; Hymes, "Models of the Interaction of Language," 35–71; and Kirch, "Non-Verbal Communication across Cultures," 416–23.
13. Reid, "The Gospel of Luke," 1.
14. For more information about the research on this subject, see Jin Young Choi, *Postcolonial Discipleship*; Tolbert, *Sowing the Gospel*; and Larry W. Hurtado, "The Women, the Tomb, and the Climax of Mark," in *A Wandering Galilean: Essays in Honour of Seán Freyne*, ed. Zuleika Rodgers, Margaret Daly-Denton, and Anne Fitzpatrick-McKinley (Leiden: Brill, 2009), quoted in Liew, *Politics of Parousia*, 142–43.
15. Hua and Junn, "Amidst Pandemic and Racial Upheaval," 16–32.
16. Gover, Harper, and Langton, "Anti-Asian Hate Crime," 647–67.
17. Sundstrom and Kim, "Xenophobia and Racism," 20–45.
18. Adrienne Rich quoted in Kramarae, *Women and Men Speaking*, 25.
19. Sundstrom and Kim, "Xenophobia and Racism," 39.
20. Fujiwara and Roshanravan, "Weaponizing Our (In)visibility," 263; Wu, *Color of Success*, 171.
21. Junn, "From Coolie to Model Minority," 355–73.
22. Kim, "Racial Triangulation," 105–38; Hua and Junn, "Amidst Pandemic and Racial Upheaval."
23. Fanon, *Black Skin*, 111, 112.
24. Hong, *The Rupture of American Capital*, xvii.
25. Woolley, "Silence Itself," 272–73.
26. Deirdre Lashgari, "Introduction," in Lashgari, *Violence, Silence, and Anger*, 8.
27. Keating, "Resistant Silence," 32–33.
28. De Waele, Claeys, and Cauberghe, "The Organizational Voice," 1026–49.
29. Montoya, "Silence and Silencing," 289.
30. For more information about select research on nonverbal communication, see Burgoon, Guerrero, and Floyd, *Nonverbal Communication*; Philippot, Feldman, and Coats, *Nonverbal Behavior in Clinical Settings*; Knapp and Hall, *Nonverbal Communication in Human Interaction*; Shea, *Psychiatric Interviewing*; and Ekman and Friesen, *Unmasking the Face*.
31. Holmes, *Joy Unspeakable*.
32. Holmes, 51.

33. For more testimonies of captured Africans who became enslaved by Whites, see Blassingame, *Slave Testimony*.
34. Hopkins, *Down, Up, and Over*, 141.
35. Holmes, *Joy Unspeakable*, 52.
36. Noel, "Call and Response," 73; Holmes, *Joy Unspeakable*, 50.
37. Holmes, *Joy Unspeakable*, 50.
38. Ruth. A. Sasaki, *The Loom and Other Stories* (Minneapolis: Graywolf, 1991), cited in Fredericksen, "Muted Colors," 301.
39. Fredericksen, 301.
40. Kadi, "Speaking (about) Silence," 539–45.
41. Fredericksen, "Muted Colors," 301.
42. Stoler, "Colonial Aphasia," 125.
43. Titchkosky, "Life with Dead Metaphors," 271.
44. Freud, "Mourning and Melancholy," 584–89.
45. Butler, *Gender Trouble*, 63.
46. Chow, *Not Like Native Speakers*, 47.
47. Chow, 72.
48. Gayatri Spivak's critically acclaimed article "Can the Subaltern Speak?" (24–28) raises the question to challenge the power of the intellectual and argues that the subaltern can only speak through such intellectual interlocutors, which is then used to reproduce and manipulate them. Chandra Mohanty ("Under Western Eyes," 61–88) further indicates that such a colonial gaze can be practiced even among feminist scholars and activists by challenging feminist international relations experts for objectifying non-Western women in their pursuit to stand up for those who they believe are being silenced. See also Beverley, "*Testimonio*, Subalternity, and Narrative Authority"; and Enloe, *Curious Feminist*, 21.
49. Chow, *Not Like Native Speakers*, 11, 59.
50. Observance of the National Day of Silence to support LGBTQIA+ individuals is one example of the resistant potential of silence, but this chapter focuses more broadly on the experiences of women of color.
51. Adrienne Rich, "Twenty-One Love Poems," in *Dream of a Common Language* (New York: W. W. Norton, 1978), 25, 29, as quoted in Brown, "In the 'Folds of Our Own Discourse,'" 193.
52. Jacobs, *Incidents in the Life of a Slave Girl*.
53. Dalton, "Devil and the Virgin," 38–40.
54. Cheung, *Articulate Silences*. Patti Duncan's book *Tell This Silence* also examines the resistant potential of silence in the context of Asian American women.
55. Cheung, *Articulate Silences*, 4–5.
56. Brown, "In the 'Folds of Our Own Discourse.'"
57. Holmes, *Joy Unspeakable*, 58.
58. Carrillo Rowe and Malhotra, "Still the Silence," 1–2.
59. Roberts, "Paradox of Silence," 343–44.
60. Merton, *Contemplative Prayer*, 68.
61. Clair, "Introduction," xv, xvi.
62. Buber, "Distance and Relation," 206–13.
63. Ballif, Davis, and Mountford, "Toward an Ethics of Listening," 937.
64. Irigaray and Marder, *Building a New World*, 260–61.
65. Ballif, Davis, and Mountford, "Toward an Ethics of Listening," 937.

66. Rich, "Turning," quoted in Kramarae, *Women and Men Speaking*, 25.
67. Rich, 25.
68. In her article "Phrónēsis," Jin Young Choi also explores the practice of listening in the context of Asian American women leadership.
69. Sontag, "The Aesthetics of Silence," 194, 195.
70. Kun Jong Lee quoted in Cha, *Dictee*, 175; Lee, "Rewriting Hesiod, Revisioning Korea," 77–99.
71. Theresa Hak Kyung Cha, undated statement (after 1976), Communicating the Intermedia Archive: the Theresa Hak Kyung Cha Collection, accessed December 1, 2022, http://dnaanthology.com/anvc/dna/cha-section-5.7.
72. Cha, "Artist's Statement/Summary of Work," 1978, Theresa Hak Kyung Cha Collection, Berkeley Art Museum and Pacific Film Archive, University of California, Berkeley, accessed July 10, 2018, https://oac.cdlib.org/ark:/13030/tf4j49n6h6/?brand=oac4; Kim and Alarcón, *Writing Self, Writing Nation*.
73. Bertrand August, interview by Constance M. Lewallen, November 1, 2000, cited by Lewallen, *Dream of the Audience*.
74. Lewallen, *Dream of the Audience*, 34.
75. Cha, *Audience Distant Relative*.
76. Hetherington, "Second-Handedness," 159; Hetherington, "The Unsightly," 187–205.
77. Freud, "The 'Uncanny,'" 241.
78. Wilson, "Reading Theresa Hak Kyung Cha's 'Dictee,'" 3.
79. Theresa Hak Kyung Cha, unpublished statement, 1975, Theresa Hak Kyung Cha Archive, Berkeley Art Museum, cited by Lewallen, *Dream of the Audience*, 3.
80. Robert Atkins, "Other Things Seen, Other Things Heard (Ailleurs)," from an unpublished review for the *San Francisco Bay Guardian*, 1978, Cha Archive, cited by Lewallen, *Dream of the Audience*, 3.
81. Cha, *Dictee*, 3, 32.
82. Evans, "Silence and the Mystical Encounter," 292.
83. T. S. Eliot, "East Coker," in Eliot, *Four Quartets*, 23–34.

5

THE SILENT JOY OF THE EMPTY TOMB

Attention to the Void

> Grace fills the empty spaces but it can only enter where there is a void to receive it, and it is grace itself which makes this void.
> —Simone Weil, *Gravity and Grace*

> How to tell a shattered story? By slowly becoming everybody. No. By slowly becoming everything.
> —Arundhati Roy, *The Ministry of Utmost Happiness*

Amid the ebb and flow of our daily lives, suffering and joy often stand at opposite ends of the spectrum, unable to reconcile. As we bear witness to the lives of trauma survivors in the aftermath of violence and women of color in the United States, silence seems far from joy, aligning itself with suffering. Alongside the silences stemming from human suffering, the silence of nature—eerie stillness, devoid of birdsong and the colorful melodies of flowers—speaks of pain and death too. It was an ominous silence of spring that first alerted Rachel Carson to the catastrophic effects of pesticides on the environment, a world out of balance due to human interference and the violent exploitation of other living beings. The prospect of seeking joy in the face of our own or others' pain can feel like a far-off horizon, a distant shore that remains out of reach. Joy in the experience of suffering seems inappropriate, if not impossible.

However, if we look and listen more closely, we may find that silence can also express ineffable joy in the midst of life's struggles. It is in the serene stillness of a newborn baby sleeping in our arms, in the hushed awe of sunrise or sunset, in the humble gratitude exchanged between the eyes of those who give and receive kindness, in the tender embrace of strangers with no need for words, and in the communication of two silent lovers where a shared glance or touch is the most sublime language. In the midst of life's chaos and noise, a profound and indescribable joy can abound, transcending language. And it is in these moments of silence that we are enlightened with the beauty and wonder of the world around us. The tranquility brought about by silence has the distinct ability to soothe the jagged edges of our words and thoughts and transform fear and anxiety into a gentle, flowing energy. Silence creates space with extraordinary fullness that enables us to feel the instantaneous and intimate presence of others without hurting them with our words, desires, needs, wants, beliefs, and expectations. The exterior space created by silence becomes an interior sanctuary where we commune and bond with others and, furthermore, with the divine.[1]

The mystics of Christian traditions, too, celebrated joyful silence and especially encouraged us to celebrate it amid our daily struggles. We saw in chapter 2 that, for mystics such as Evagrius and Hadewijch, joy is not a fleeting emotion that offers temporary respite from suffering, nor is it a mere source of happiness or pleasure that fades away with time. Rather, it is a steadfast state of the soul that arises from union with God and serves as a resilient and enduring foundation that keeps us in communion with the divine. Silence accompanied the mystics in times not only of despair and lamentation but also of enchantment and exuberance. A mystical and contemplative gaze enabled them to see a life to celebrate even in the ruins and brokenness. Among affliction and despair, they trusted in the consoling love of silent God and immersed themselves in joy. They burst out in tears of joy in their encounter with God at the loss of language. They sang, as the psalmist did, "God, praise silently awaits you" (Psalm 65:1a).

Hence, in this final chapter I ask: How can we, just as the mystics did, integrate ineffable joy into our lived reality filled with inexplicable suffering? If silence can serve as a medium to transform suffering into joy, can we discover ways to use it as a resource to sustain ourselves and others in a world rife with violence, hatred, bigotry, and killing? Additionally, how can we differentiate genuine joy from narcotic or escapist pleasures that seek to evade the reality of pain? How can we understand that joy, instead of isolating us in our well-being, opens us to being accountable to the reality of suffering that affect others and ourselves? I expand upon these questions by revisiting concerns I left behind in previous chapters: As we struggle with the silence of the world that stems from suffering, how can we engage with and attune our ears to the silent whispers of God? How can we attain the joyfulness of silence in God without succumbing to burnout, self-sabotage, and self-destruction in the midst of suffering?

This chapter engages with these questions by exploring the mystical concept of ecstasy, which is characterized by its ineffability: silence. I begin by revisiting the women disciples around Jesus's empty tomb and observing their experience, which overtook them not only with fear and grief but also with awe and amazement. Working through the lens of ecstasy, I describe the disciples' experience at the tomb as a state of *jouissance*—a state that transcends the symbolic order of language and brings individuals an awareness of the interconnectedness of all existences, fostering a profound form of relationality rooted in union with the divine. I reject the idea of ecstasy as an esoteric concept disconnected from the reality of suffering and instead seek to investigate its significance in the context of political powerlessness as a means of pursuing liberating joy in face of oppression.

Along with the women disciples at the tomb, I consider the work of Simone Weil (1909–1943) and Arundhati Roy (1961–), two women writers who have ardently engaged with and responded to the poignant and soulful struggle against adversity in different times and cultures, in my reflection on the wonders and joys of mystical and contemplative silence in the midst of suffering. Pairing Weil, a French philosopher, activist, and mystic from the early twentieth century, with Roy, a contemporary Indian writer and activist, may seem like an unlikely combination, particularly when it comes to the topic of silence. However, the two writers share a common focus: they pay utmost attention to the silenced who experience extreme suffering, with Weil referring to them as "the afflicted" and Roy as "the unconsoled." Indeed, silence, a significant theme in both their writings, takes on both oppressive and contemplative forms and reveals a mystical potential to connect people in a transcendental and subversive way, ultimately inviting them to embrace joy. I particularly focus on the places of silence in these authors' works: Weil's concept of void and Roy's depiction of the graveyard, in her novel *The Ministry of Utmost Happiness*, in parallel with the empty tomb.

I then explore the concept of silent attention as manifested in the void and the graveyard. Attention is a practice and exercise through which one can experience ecstasy in union with the silent God, attained by directing our focus toward the reality of the silenced. Silent attention takes the practice of listening discussed in the previous chapter into a more radical dimension. It enables us to embrace the void; release ourselves from self-projections, consumptive imagination, and attachment to privilege; and encounter the silent God, who amplifies the presences of the silenced. Weil's and Roy's writings suggest that the process of unlearning and letting go of one's ego through attention is ecstatic, leading to a deep sense of communion with God and others. By suspending our expectation that God will serve our personal needs and renouncing any temptation to wield power over others for our own needs, silent attention creates space for God to work through us. Silent attention, therefore, is an intrinsic component of mystical and contemplative silence as well as a venue for union with the silent God and for a communion with others silenced in a violent world. Through attention, we are united with both the silent God and the silenced, slowly yet unwaveringly transforming faint sighs into the language of love. Let us first turn our gaze back to Jesus's empty tomb.

TERROR AND AMAZEMENT IN JESUS'S EMPTY TOMB

The silence of the women disciples in Jesus's empty tomb upon witnessing the vanishment of Jesus's body in the place of death and the following announcement of Resurrection was not prompted only by ominous fear and confusion. The evangelists Mark, Matthew, and John offer their descriptions of the affective response of women disciples to the tomb, eliciting mixed emotions that seem opposite in valence. Mark states, "For terror and *amazement* had seized them" (16:8a, emphasis added); Matthew writes, "So they left the tomb quickly with fear and *great joy*" (28:8, emphasis added); and John adds a story of a dramatic encounter between Jesus and Mary Magdalene that is full of complex emotions. The three evangelists observe that the silence of the first witnesses was a response to terror as well as overwhelming joy. What is this mysterious emotion of joy that they felt in the tomb of Jesus, even though they were initially and remained overpowered by fear? We may look into Mark's and Matthew's portrayals.

The original Greek that Mark adopts to describe the disciples' emotions in the tomb scene is "terror and amazement" (τρόμος καὶ ἔκστασις).[2] While the disciples felt a "terror" (τρόμος) as they witnessed the mystery of the Resurrection, they were also in "amazement," or more precisely "ecstasy," which is translated from the Greek word ἔκστασις. The biblical usage of ἔκστασις refers to a peculiar state that involves the numinous, a spiritual dimension that transcends one's rational capacity. It is a state of bewilderment that keeps one from comprehending miracles done by Jesus or the disciples (Mark 5:42, 16:8; Luke 5:26; Acts 3:10), or an experience of trance in which one is transported out of oneself during prayer (Acts 10:10, 11:5, 22:17). In the place of Mark's ἔκστασις, Matthew uses χαρά. Associated with χάρις (grace, favor, or gift), χαρά appears in the New Testament more frequently than ἔκστασις, ranging from the nativity story (Matt. 2:10) to the stories of the apostles in Acts (13:52, 15:3, 20:24). In the biblical usage, χαρά refers to extreme joy, often directly and explicitly received from the Holy Spirit.[3] It is not a fleeting sensation of great pleasure but a profound affection originating from the divine that brings one to ravishment, entrancement, and rapture. For both Mark and Matthew, the disciples' strange and uplifted feeling in the tomb is connected with something godly. They were thrown off not only because of fear and terror but because of exhilarating joy, or the fear and terror that they felt already included overwhelming joy. It was an experience of ecstasy, something like *mysterium tremendum et fascinans*, using Rudolf Otto's description for the nature of the Holy, a mystery before which human beings both tremble and are fascinated, are both repelled and irresistibly captivated.[4] The disciples lapsed into silence in a state of ecstatic bliss.

The meaning of "ecstasy" can differ depending on the context, but for the purposes of this chapter, I adopt the definition provided by Dorothee Sölle. Her definition takes into account not only religious experiences of ecstasy, but also encompasses a wide range of mystical experiences that occur in daily life. Sölle describes ecstasy as an experience of "the uttermost freedom from what determines our lives." According to Sölle, this experience of "stepping out from oneself" or "taking-leave of one's sense" is simultaneously an experience "to plunge down to the very ground or to submerge oneself."[5] In ecstasy an immanence opens itself to transcendence and participates in it, and the soul experiences itself as a unity in the wholeness and boundlessness. The disciples at Jesus's empty tomb, then, experienced a sense of utter freedom upon witnessing the disappearance of his body and being informed of the Resurrection. In the state of ecstasy, their sense of fear and seclusion was shattered, and they were instead exposed to the unknown that extends beyond the boundaries of the physical world—the Resurrection.

The limited capacity of language is a characteristic of mystical ecstasy. Since conventional language is in service of "purpose, calculation, and dominion," it is helpless to convey the experience of ecstasy that goes beyond all those imposed boundaries. Sölle cites Meister Eckhart's idea of *sunder warumbe*, meaning "without a why or a wherefore," as an indispensable expression of ecstasy. According to Eckhart, seeking God through a particular way may be fruitless, whereas living a mystical life entails simply losing oneself in God and embracing existence for what it is. "Life is lived for its own sake and emanates from its own sources; hence it is lived entirely without whys or wherefores, because it lives for itself," says Eckhart.[6] At the heart of every mystical love of God is *sunder warumbe*, and ecstasy involves breaking open one's self to attain this freedom. The joy the disciples experienced at the site of the empty tomb, not despite but because of the initial loss and sorrow, was of this nature. The sight of the empty tomb and the Resurrection unshackled the disciples from all constraints of measure and control, and brought them a sense of freedom. They fell silent because they found it impossible to express their experience of newfound freedom. However, this silence carries a deeper meaning beyond a mere pretentious or elitist display of passion. It radiates a sense of togetherness and unity that surpasses all the separations of the world, even transcending the divide between life and death. This silence reaches toward the ultimate silence of God, the perfect stillness that requires no language, discussed in chapter 2. I explore this relational nature of the silence in the empty tomb through the concept of *jouissance*, particularly its mystical and contemplative aspect that transforms pains and sorrows into a profound experience of freedom and unity.

In his essay "Haunting Silence: Trauma, Failed Orality, and Mark's Messianic Secret," biblical scholar Tat-siong Benny Liew discusses the inarticulability of the women disciples resulting from their encounter with the empty tomb and the Resurrection. Reading the tomb narrative as a testimony of trauma and engaging with the Freudian trauma theory, Liew argues that the women disciples' silence is "their failed orality" rather than failed discipleship. The silence of the tomb scene highlights not only the tragic and traumatic weight of the Jesus narrative but also the disciples' peculiar experience of being unable to comprehend "the level of that gravity or the lingering, open-ended effects and affects of their connection with that trauma." In other words, the miracle of Resurrection overwhelmed the disciples and struck them so hard that they failed to understand it rationally or speak about it legibly. They beheld an event that was both "excruciating and exhilarating" and left in silence; however, their traumatic remembrance became an intractable memory that would return to haunt them over and over.[7]

Whereas Liew's argument focuses on the reconstruction of the disciples' trauma as their repressed desire that perpetually implored them to find an expression, what draws my attention is his interpretation of their silence as an instance of *jouissance*. "Jouissance" is a psychoanalytic term developed by Freud and extended by Lacan that refers to a traumatic enjoyment involving both pleasure and pain, suffering and satisfaction, to be "presented as a single packet."[8] Jouissance is an experience so intense that it disrupts one's sense of coherence and causes language to break down. Nonetheless, it exposes forcefully what lies outside language and law: the underlying tensions, fragmentation, and incoherence that are often unnoticed but underpin the foundation of the subjectivities as well as the society that they belong to. In this respect, the silence of the women disciples in the empty tomb signifies jouissance, or the ineffable feeling of both pain and pleasure in the recognition that Jesus and his story will "continue to live on in *this* world" though his body is gone.[9]

Viewing the women disciples' silence as a form of jouissance reinforces the transformative aspect of mystical and contemplative silence, particularly in relation to the silence of God, that is, the joyful union with God in silence. Before delving into it, we need to glance at the connection between jouissance and mystical ecstasy. In his Seminar 20, *Encore*, Lacan distinguishes between "phallic" jouissance and "Other" jouissance, with the latter being associated with mysticism and femininity. According to Lacan, the phallic jouissance is marked by "the impossibility of establishing as such, anywhere in the enunciable, the sole One that interests us." Lacan's term "the One" refers to the presumed unity of the male subject who takes a sexual object as the cause of his desire and relies upon his phallic nature to attain it. Masculine jouissance, Lacan continues, remains inadequate, because it is inevitably subsumed by the phallic function and thus fails to merge with the Other's desire. On the feminine side, however, subjects have access both to sexual (phallic) jouissance and to a form of jouissance beyond phallus precisely because they are "not-all" (*pas-toute*) in the symbolic order and lack this "whole." By exemplifying Hadewijch of Antwerp, Saint John of the Cross, and Saint Teresa of Ávila, Lacan positions mystics, male or female, on the "feminine" side and establishes the connection between feminine jouissance and mysticism. The mystics reach *ek-stasis*, displacement, when they become one with the Other, merging their experience with the Other's desire but knowing nothing about what they experience.[10] In other words, through jouissance women and mystics are able to access the real, the unknown that exists outside the realm of symbolic representation. Feminine or mystical jouissance is thus not governed by the symbolic order or masculine "laws," especially in the realms of speech, language, and discourse.

Lacan's elaboration of feminine or mystical jouissance has been criticized by many, including the French feminist philosopher Luce Irigaray, who vehemently rejected his idea, arguing that it was simply another example of the unyielding reduction of women to passive objects of the male gaze and ignoring many works written by women mystics. Though Irigaray follows Lacan in viewing mysticism as the site of a jouissance that transcends the phallus, she repudiates his description of the "feminine" subject to be lacking or "not-all." She argues that in Lacan's description of the jouissance of the Other, the feminine imaginary still relies on the God-Man, and thus eventually is brought back into the symbolic order governed by the phallus.[11] Irigaray demands that women need their own divine instead of the God-Man in order to achieve subjectivity and thus presents alternative metaphors in the place of phallus, such as feminine lips.

Irigaray's discussion of women has been criticized even among feminist scholars, as it can be read as an essentialist attempt to homogenize all women's experiences. With some reservation, however, I agree with theologian Amy Hollywood's critique against the claims that Irigaray is essentialist, which are based on empirical observations of women. As Hollywood says, Irigaray makes it clear that "women" in her discussion are "a philosophical construct both absent from and in excess of male discourse" and this "must be understood within the framework of her historicizing presumptions."[12] In the context of my discussion on silence as the manifestation of union with God outside the symbolic order of heteropatriarchy, I find Irigaray's reinterpretation of feminine jouissance to be beneficial, as it offers an alternative way to envision the concept of union with God beyond the limitations of phallic unity. However, Irigaray's female subjectivity still needs to be challenged since it ignores the experiences of transgender and gender-nonconforming people, focusing only on the lives and experiences of cisgender women. Her description of women also does not account for the diverse experiences of women across the intersections of race and class. My discussion considers Irigaray's concept of the feminine and aims to expand upon it, despite its limitations. By using her approach to deconstruct phallic unity, I emphasize the apophatic dimension of her description of the feminine, allowing it to be used as a critique of the heteropatriarchal language that underpins the understanding of the divine union as a totalizing oneness.

In *Speculum of the Other Woman*, Irigaray argues for the existence of women-as-other, the repressed underside of masculine subjectivity and rationality, demonstrating how the feminine imaginary can radically decenter masculine subjectivity.[13] Irigaray's discussion on the mystics' body in *Speculum* continues the idea of Lacanian feminine jouissance as the mystics embrace the unconscious, which lies beyond language and represents the repressed aspect of consciousness, reason, and masculine dominance. Nonetheless, while Lacan maintains that mystics rely on the symbolic, specifically the God-Man, to access reality, Irigaray challenges this notion by asserting that the feminine imaginary constitutes the real, which highlights a fundamental difference in their views on the relationships between subjectivity, gender, and the ways in which the real is experienced and constructed.[14] For Irigaray, the jouissance experienced in mysticism involves encountering an unfathomable and incomprehensible other that she refers to as the feminine, which challenges male fantasies of achieving totality and mastery.[15] Instead of returning the mystics into the phallocentric symbolic order, mystical ecstasy provides access to a whole that transcends the symbolic order but manifests itself as unfathomable abyss.[16]

Irigaray's reassessment of the Lacanian jouissance to illuminate the incomprehensible "feminine" other sheds light on my discussion of the women disciples' silence as a response to the absence of Jesus's body. Irigaray presents the divine as a "feminine" other, experienced through feminine ecstasy or mystical inwardness—termed "enstasy." She posits this as the negativity of masculine subjectivity, challenging its presumed universality and dominance.[17] Woman or the mystic are united with no-thing, the "expansion that she neither is nor will be at any moment as definable universe."[18] Yet, for Irigaray, this "feminine" other is not a simple lack or replacement of the masculine. Rather, it is constructed as "man's negative mirror," which re-presents and repeats men's speaking subjectivity by reflecting men's words and images back with a difference.[19] The supposed singularity and homogeneity of the symbolic are shattered by its negative image, which is characterized by multiplicity, fluidity, and relationality. To enter ecstasy with the "feminine" other is to surpass the boundaries and limitations of the current social constructs that shape one's understanding of the world around them. The mystical soul speaks thus: "A living mirror, this am I to your resemblance as you are mine. We are both singular and plural."[20] When united with this divine no-thingness, the soul undergoes *sunder warumbe*, an experience that cannot be found in a phallocentric world. Ecstasy, in this regard, brings about an increased awareness of the interconnectedness of all existences, which nurtures a profound form of relationality rooted in the silence of being united with the divine nothingness.

The image of a mirror or perfectly still water is a metaphor familiar to the Christian mystical tradition. As we saw in chapter 2, Evagrius adopts the still water metaphor to describe the perfect prayer—silence. The soul becomes still water when it is united with God after negating all its perceptions and imaginations. Similarly, Amy Hollywood connects Irigaray's imagery to the mirror image in the mystical theology of Marguerite Porete, a fourteenth-century Beguine and the author of *The Mirror of Simple Souls*. Just as Evagrius highlights still water as the state of a soul in union with God, Porete describes a mirror becoming a reflection of the divine by emptying all its createdness. Porete holds an understanding that God is "the all," and Evagrius believes that the soul in perfect prayer restores the sense of wholeness,[21] both of which seem to suggest that union with God is still inscribed within the One that reduces alterity to sameness. Amy Hollywood's Irigarayan reading of mysticism, however, interprets it otherwise: the soul must become nothing in order to reflect the divine because "God is also nothing."[22] In other words, the God who is nothing is free of the masculine order that values autonomy, self-identity, omnipotence, and omniscience.[23] This God is the God of apophatic mysticism, who is undefinable except negatively, whose wholeness is not a universal structure encompassing the entire field of human action and existence but transcends the field. By negating the masculine symbolic, the soul becomes nothing and unites with God, who is also nothing.

The women disciples' silence at the tomb scene where the Logos, the Word Incarnate, is gone indicates their union with this divine nothingness, which goes beyond the constraints of language because language is rooted in the masculine symbolic. The silence left in the tomb without the corpus of the Word is the manifestation of the divine as nothing, allowing the women disciples to form a new relationship with Jesus, who is resurrected as an ineffable other that cannot be represented by the language and image of the existing order. The empty tomb signifies the Resurrection of God in God's radical relationality, beyond the God who is domesticated in the patriarchal symbolic. Resurrection is not a continuation of life passing through death, nor is the belief in it limited to the possibility of resuscitation of a dead body. Rather, it is an awakening of a sense of otherness inside oneself, breaking away from the self that has been tamed by societal norms and conventions.[24] Precisely at this juncture, the women disciples experienced jouissance. Their silence is a response to the God who is resurrected as the other, who "causes a crisis in language, an overthrow of logic, and rapturous release of *jouissance*."[25] The silence of God in this respect is a speculum or boundless space that recasts old beliefs so that new meanings and new possibilities can arise. By breaking down the old language for the divine, the silent God manifested in the empty tomb bears the ineffable relationship with the resurrected divine. The silence of the tomb, the divine nothingness, presents a "speculative opportunity that is beyond discourses of domesticated and revised hope."[26]

An Irigarayan understanding of jouissance, then, offers a source of alterity that enables the transformation of the oppressive features of the masculine order into a profound sense of relationality and joy, which suggests an alternative understanding of the emptiness of the tomb. By surpassing the boundaries imposed by the existing order, the empty tomb presents a more expansive sense of wholeness that reorients us toward union with God, just as it did for the women disciples. This wholeness is not a separate reality detached from the world but rather an intrinsic quality of our relationship with others we live with and the world we inhabit. It is the ground of all relationships facilitated by each of our relationships with others that allows for exploration of a broader, interconnected reality that goes beyond our individual experiences. Mystical and contemplative silence originates from and returns to this fathomless divine nothingness by transforming our mode of thinking, speaking, and writing about God and engaging with others.

The Johannine version of the empty tomb narrative, which focuses the experience of Mary Magdalene, highlights the significance of the silence in the tomb as a site of jouissance and further extends it by adding the Eucharistic dimension. Mary in John's Gospel continues searching the corpse of Jesus, the dead God, the evidence of terror as well as the remainder of her love, hoping that it might help her make a sense. Then, Jesus reveals himself to Mary:

> Jesus said to her, "Woman, why are you weeping? Whom are you looking for?" Supposing him to be the gardener, she said to him, "Sir, if you have carried him away, tell me where you have laid him, and I will take him away." Jesus said to her, "Mary!" She turned and said to him in Hebrew, "Rabbouni!" (which means "Teacher"). Jesus said to her, "Do not hold on to me, because I have not yet ascended to the Father. But go to my brothers and say to them, 'I am ascending to my Father and your Father, to my God and your God'" (John 20:15–17, emphasis added).

In this scene filled with strong emotions and betrayed expectations, Jesus calls Mary's name but does not allow her to grasp his body. By calling her name, Jesus reminds her of the intimate relationship he shared with her, yet his refusal to be held elucidates that a return to the past is no longer possible and that the complete graspability of truth has come to an end. Instead, truth is directed toward the community of people who follow Jesus in the manner of the Eucharist through which the body of God is broken into pieces and united with multifarious bodies. In other words, the ungraspability of God's body allows for God's Resurrection to occur through the multifarious bodies of God's people. The relational wholeness is dispersed into the multifarious relationships among people.

Jesus shifts Mary's desire to hold his physical body, directing her focus instead toward the community of his followers, who will continue his work and carry his message to the world. Despite his physical absence, or precisely because of the absence, he will remain in unbreakable relationship with her—"I am ascending to my Father and your Father, to my God and your God." The jouissance of the traumatized, perplexed, and bewildered Mary pushes her to transcend herself in her insight into "what God is/not."[27]

Her ineffableness merges into the ineffability of the mystery around the tomb and is united with the abysmal depth of the silence of God—a fluid, unfixed, placeless, and porous abyss. As such, the silence of the tomb creates an opportunity for the Resurrection to come into the lives of the multitude. In a way similar to the distribution of Jesus's body in the Eucharist, it allows for the emergence of new words that resist being confined to a single, definitive meaning. This new beginning cannot be initiated without the silence of the empty tomb, a pause in the manner of letting go of what was and making space for the arrival of something new.

In a similar train, de Certeau saw the epitome of Christian belief in Mary's experience of the empty tomb. He argues that "Christianity was founded upon the loss of a body—the loss of the body of Jesus Christ."[28] For de Certeau, Mary is the "eponymous figure of the modern mystic" who internalize this experience of seeking and not holding, who "cannot stop walking, and with the certainty of what is lacking, knows every place and object that it is not that." The graspability of the Word is replaced with what is unknown, unspeakable, unpossessable, which incessantly drives Mary's desire and those of the mystics who followed in her footsteps. De Certeau says the mystics are "'drunk with what they have not drunk': inebriation without drinking, inspiration from one knows not where, illumination without knowledge. They are drunk with what they do not possess. Drunk with desire. Therefore, they may all bear the name given to the work of Angelus Silesius: *Wandersmann*, the 'wanderer.'"[29]

And it is this desire that lays Mary and the mystics open and vulnerable to the advent of joy in freedom. By effacing the place of the Word of God, the silence of the tomb becomes space for her longing. Affirmed by Jesus's command not to hold onto him, the tomb's silence reoriented Mary's desire from obsession with definable and apprehensible truth to insatiable longing that cannot be resolved but is constantly renewed toward the divine nothingness who is intimate and irreducible.[30] The silence of God in the tomb embraces mystics, those who follow Mary, while permanently distancing them from both tame and hasty promises of words and at once putting them in a mode of searching.[31] No one can grasp, possess, fill, or claim this silence, yet it enraptures and allows the mystic to reflect the divine, like a mirror or perfectly still water. The dislocation of the Word of God then entices us to *ek-statis*, the silence of God where one is enthralled in joy. Such was a "perfect place of prayer" for Evagrius and "the abyss of Love" for Hadewijch.[32]

I seek to apply the jouissance of silence in the tomb to our experience of silence in daily struggles by contextualizing it within the reality of suffering. The silence of the tomb is a prime example that embraces both sorrow and joy rooted in the divine love. Just as the silence of the tomb transformed the fear and agony of the women disciples into resilient strength and enabled them to forge a new way of finding joy in their relationship with God and others, I believe that silence in our daily struggle can also muster in us the courage necessary to withstand fear and uncertainty and to rebuild trust in those who come to stay with others, forming community. Silence can help us resist the rhetoric of both triumphalism and indifference built upon our tendency to create divisions and maintain control over others by keeping us in relation with the silent God and the silenced.

Simone Weil and Arundhati Roy use the potency of silence to create transformative and joyful space in the midst of various painful contexts, from social and political activism to personal struggle with despondency and despair. By paying silent attention to the smallest beings in the throes of loss and death, Weil and Roy show how we can cultivate a sense of prayerful connection with others amid suffering and envision a new hope that transcends the dominant structures of power.

SILENCE, VOID, AND ATTENTION

Throughout her brief life, which coincided with the turbulent periods of the Great Depression and World War II, Simone Weil was consistently marked by social and political activism, throwing herself into the very margins of society, where suffering pervaded. In her philosophical and spiritual pursuit, Weil placed a strong emphasis on the role of suffering, or, in her terms, "affliction (*malheur*)"—the extreme condition of human misery that entails physical suffering as well as social and psychological degradation beyond one's control and comprehension.[33] I first discuss Weil's understanding of silence, and then explore her concept of void and attention in parallel with the notion of ecstasy, bringing together the idea of the silent God with the silenced suffering of humanity.

Silence as God's Language and the Expression of Affliction

The importance of silence in Weil's writing can be discerned in both the style and content of her works. Her aphoristic style is characterized by the use of ellipses, pauses, and incomplete sentences, which creates space for readers to connect with both the ineffable nature of mystery and the inexpressible nature of suffering. Nonetheless, her writing takes up the impossible task of portraying the nature of divine love, inviting us to a theological inquiry into its relation to silence. Similar to Evagrius and Hadewijch, Weil sees the nature of God in the act of self-emptying and maintains that silence is God's language of love.

Weil's concept of silence is intertwined with the notion of divine power, or more precisely divine powerlessness, in her theological thought. Her political involvement and insights on social mechanisms, especially the way they affected the lives of members of the working class, led her to conclude that wielding human power for emancipation is inevitably destructive and that divine power was needed to purify oppressive human existence. Weil contends that divine power is not about domination and conquest; instead, it is the power of self-emptying, of *kenosis*, that lets others live and thrive by relinquishing itself. Divine power manifests primarily through the act of Creation. In Creation, according to Weil, God did not use force, power, or imposition. Creation is "not an act of self-expansion but of restraint and renunciation."[34] God surrenders the divine privilege of being everything in order to allow something else to exist. Creation is "an act of love, and it is something which is going on perpetually."[35]

Weil believed that because the God of self-emptying is present with the soul through absence, the language that can capture the essence of God is only found in silence. God communicates with the soul through silence. Weil says: "The speech of created beings is with sounds. The word of God is silence. God's secret word of love can be nothing but silence. Christ is the silence of God. Just as there is no tree like the cross, so there is no harmony like the silence of God. . . . In this world, necessity is the vibration of God's silence."[36]

Weil's analogy of necessity as the vibration or sound of Creation, and silence as the language of God, is noteworthy. Just as the absence of God is a fundamental and implicit aspect of the universe and the basis for everything that exists, the silence of God constitutes the tacit ground of the observable world of human experience filled with the sound of necessity. In this sense, Weil says, silence is not a mere lack of sound but "the object of a positive sensation, more positive than that of sound." Noises can reach us only after "crossing this silence."[37] The ground of sound is silence, and there would be no sound to hear without silence; likewise, the necessity of Creation cannot be heard without the silent God. True joy arises when we consent to the silent God and the silence of our soul converges with God's silence. For sound is not in God's nature, but silence is. Perfect and infinite joy exists only within God. Only when we subdue the sound of our soul can we become united with the divine silence and discover joy. "If we find fullness of joy in the thought that God is, we must find the same fullness in the knowledge that we ourselves are not, for it is the same thought." We cannot experience joy even as a distinct emotion since there is no room for the self to attain it.[38] In this regard, silence for Weil is the means and end for finding joy in God. The mystical aspect of silence in which one listens to God within and beyond our horizon merges into contemplative silence in which one listens in God. This union is joy.

However, Weil thought that the sound of necessity has its role to play in union with God. God created the universe out of love by becoming everything, and similarly, God renders the divine self a necessity to facilitate human beings' encounter with God.[39] The necessity's mediation is unavoidable because it is a sign of God's love pinning itself down to the world.[40] Weil says that necessity is the "screen [*l'écran*] set between God and us so that we can be. Necessity is, however, to pierce through the screen so that we cease to be."[41] In other words, to listen to the silent God, we must first contact the sound of necessity as a medium to penetrate. Nonetheless, necessity holds no value in itself; it is only to break through so that we unite with God.

What grabs my focus is the way Weil links affliction with silence as it offers insight into the relationship between the silent God and the silenced. Weil thought affliction was a manifestation of necessity in the most brutal form, which means it can also mediate us to encounter God. Weil never romanticizes or spiritualizes affliction. As Maria Clara Bingemer describes in her book, she yearned to deeply understand the struggles of society's least fortunate, seeking to immerse herself in their reality and feel their hardships firsthand, as tangibly and authentically as possible. She was steadfast in her belief that to fight injustice, one must get close to it and live it from within. She perceived her factory work project as one that came to "shape her life in increasingly concrete ways."[42] While living as a factory worker, she had an astute sense of observing the destructive force of affliction that diminishes one's capacity for love and hope, reducing them to the states of being akin to "half-crushed worms" or "pinned-alive butterflies."[43] Despite this destructive nature, Weil is convinced that affliction presents an opportunity for us to contact God, and that it even brings us joy. This paradoxical potential of affliction lies in its character of silence. For Weil, the extremity of affliction is defined by its ability to forcefully strip away from individuals all they possess, including their dignity and language, eroding their sense of self-worth both in their own perception and in others'. The inability to communicate with others is a fundamental aspect of affliction because its impact defies both description and understanding.[44] Affliction perpetuates silence by creating a sense of isolation in the afflicted. Both the afflicted and others may struggle to empathize with each other, as the afflicted are consumed by their own suffering, while others may feel repelled by their reminder of human frailty. The afflicted end up harming themselves and others by disseminating a feeling of brokenness and wishing to see others suffering exactly as they suffer.[45] The essential trait of affliction is silence. The afflicted are the silenced, those who have no foundation to claim their agency or voice.

Weil sees the essential trait of joy as silence as well. For Weil, silence is an indispensable feature and quality of both joy and affliction, existing in the height of divine love and the depths of human suffering. In Weil's view, the contradictory condition of silence can be attributed to the state of the soul in both joy and affliction where the sense of self is suspended. Just as affliction arises when the sense of self is stripped away, joy emerges when one relinquishes the sense of self. The state of perfect joy, like that of affliction, allows no language to capture it or room for the self because it is beyond the realm of one's comprehension and control. As such, affliction and joy share common expression in the form of silence that arises from removing the self. The difference between the two silences, however, is as immeasurable as that between coercive silence and mystical and contemplative silence. While affliction is ineffable in a manner that leads to the erasure of one's value and to a sense of worthlessness, joy is ineffable because it represents an experience of ultimate freedom that allows one to unite with the divine nothingness, transcending the false sense of self and world that requires no language to explain.

The challenge that remains is how to differentiate and shift the silence of affliction toward the silence of joy. What sets apart Weil's perspective on silence in the conventional practice of spirituality is her recognition of the mystical and contemplative potential inherent in affliction, rather than seeking to avoid or overcome it. To grasp Weil's perspective on the interplay between the two silences, we must delve deeper into two of her key concepts: void, which serves as a locus for uniting the ineffable divinity and inexplicable suffering, and attention, which enables one to hear the silence of God through the silence of affliction.

Void and Attention

The void (*le vide*), for Weil, is the emptiness created by the condition of affliction, such as loss, suffering, or death. The void bears a resemblance to the emptiness of Jesus's tomb. Just like the tomb, the void in Weil's thought is a state of soul devoid of the influence of the projection of self, such as attachments to personal and collective privilege, idols, or even superficial consolations that rather numb the mind. Just like the tomb, the void is a state robbed of the power of language and filled with dejected silence. Efforts to deny the utter emptiness of the void prove futile. The experience of the void evokes a deep sense of vulnerability and fragility, exposing the transient nature of our existence and the limits of our control. Yet, just as the emptiness of the tomb becomes a locus of the joy of Resurrection, the void, too, contains the potential for a radical shift. Weil observed her coworkers in a factory resorting to cruelty toward others and themselves or to simply daydreaming in order to avoid the fearful and precarious feeling of the void. She thought that if they learned to accept the void, their work could become a means to connect with the divine.[46] Therefore, for Weil, the void represents a crucial space for transforming the silence of affliction into the silence of joy and uniting the silenced with the silent God, just as the empty tomb becomes a place for resurrection.

To accept or endure the void, Weil says one is "not to exercise all the power at one's disposal."[47] This does not mean that one tolerates or complies with the dehumanizing conditions of labor and society. In a world warped and broken by violence, the most vulnerable bear the brunt of all the violence of classism, racism, heteropatriarchy, and environmental destruction. To accept the void does not mean staying put in the status quo or remaining silent by retreating into narcotic spiritual therapy and by forgetting everything in momentary anesthetic, as if salvation is given from above. Instead, Weil urges us to prevent ourselves from being consumed by the very conditions that debase and destroy the world and to resist the impulse to confront them with hatred and violence toward others. Such actions only perpetuate the very evil we aim to overcome. Our natural inclination is to become entangled in the mechanisms of the world, which Weil refers to as the order of "gravity" (*la pesanteur*). Gravity is the force that pulls us away from our connection with God. It drives us to strive for anything that can maintain or expand our well-being at the expense of others and to exercise our power to achieve these goals. Gravity leads us either to surrender ourselves to the forces of suppression or turn them into a weapon to harm others. To accept the void means breaking free from the order of gravity that makes us rely on the privileged and powerful, who are responsible for breaking a world beyond repair. It means rejecting the system and mechanisms that make us numb to the sight of others dying and falling apart, ensuring our survival to their detriment. It means acknowledging that we cannot find hope in the order of gravity because it will eventually leave us all in brokenness and void. Only by accepting and acknowledging the void, and by setting ourselves apart from the order that supports power, can we make any difference.

Acceptance of the void, therefore, is to shift the mode of our existence and the way of our thinking and acting away from the mechanism of the world. Once embraced, the void can serve as a necessary condition for us to actually see the futility of the order of gravity and enter a new order that is divine in nature. Weil believed that accepting the void requires some kind of energy that is not derived from our own will or the means of the world. The energy must come from a different order, the action of the supernatural called "grace" (*la grâce*). When we are attached to something else, we cannot receive grace. The void thus enables us to open toward grace because it separates us from gravity. What is required of us is to quiet the distractions caused by our will, so that we can become truly receptive to grace.[48] We can observe Weil's mysticism here:

> Grace is something that we receive without doing anything positive; except that we have to keep ourselves exposed towards [it]; that is to say, to keep our attention oriented with love towards the good. The rest, whether painful or sweet, takes place in us without our cooperation. It is the fact of this second element which proves that it is truly a mysticism.[49]

Weil's concept of grace surpasses the traditional language of Christian doctrine such as divine providence, divine retribution, or heavenly rewards. In Weil's view, those concepts are rooted in the order of gravity and hinder us from receiving grace. Relying on God for comfort and reward can create a barrier between the soul and genuine connection with God. Adhering to these concepts may prevent us from truly loving God, just as Hadewijch chose unfaith over faith in God to intensify her love for God (chapter 2). On the contrary, the order of grace calls for a profound transformation in our way of living and being. This metamorphosis can only occur if we silence our will and surrender to the God of nothingness, who has emptied the divine self in order to have others exist. Hence, the void, the experience of total emptiness and silence in the midst of affliction, gives us an opportunity for a supernatural transformation, which involves converting ourselves from belonging to the order of gravity to the order of grace. Silence is at work in the void, opening us to grace and leading us to contemplative silence in union with God.

Weil inarguably subscribes to the belief that one must remain passive, which seems to conflict with my attempt to facilitate silence as a source of both spiritual nourishment and political catalysis in our struggle against the forces of suppression, especially against women and those made vulnerable.

Furthermore, her strong emphasis on passivity in the face of affliction appears to result in a devaluation of the agency necessary for transformation.[50] Weil's employment of the term "decreation" underscores this aspect. She defines "decreation" as the act of self-renunciation during moments of attention. This process involves the created self undergoing decreation to respond to God, who renounced the divine self out of love. Weil's kenotic self, in particular, seems to contrast sharply with Irigaray's understanding of feminine jouissance. Irigaray seems to oppose a sacrificial narrative often imposed on women, emphasizing instead the affirmation of women's identity, subjectivity, and bodily pleasure. Weil, conversely, appears to prioritize concepts such as self-emptying and the loss of self, especially in service to others. This apparent divergence raises questions about the appropriateness of applying Irigaray's concept of feminine jouissance in interpreting Weil's perspective on attention. However, I argue that their perspectives, while seemingly distinct, might offer potentially complementary insights into the nature of women's experience and mysticism.

I see the similarity between the two philosophers in their understanding of the relationship between the divine and the self. For Irigaray, the self, imitating the negativity attributed to women, becomes an empty vessel, an abyss where all identities and attributes are swallowed by the divine's radiant touch. This process transforms the feminine body into a "living mirror" of the divine, becoming fluid and permeable to the divine presence.[51] Similarly, Weil's approach showcases a radical self-annihilation in which the "I" must be negated in the process of decreation. For both, the mystical self forges a distinct relationship with the divine, one that deviates from traditional systems, enabling women to express insights independently of institutional and social constraints. In other words, in the philosophies of both Weil and Irigaray, there is a departure from the autonomy typically sought by heteropatriarchal men. They challenge the heteropatriarchal framework of abstract selfhood and envision a new form of self that transcends the prevailing system of dominance.

While both scholars see mystical pursuits as pathways to a new relationship between the self and the divine, and the self and the other, there are notable differences in their approaches. Irigaray's perspective leans toward kataphasis, highlighting the redemption of the body and its connection to divine transcendence. Conversely, Weil adopts an apophatic approach, exploring the paradoxical idea of self-annihilation in relation to God and others. Irigaray sees mysticism as a tool for overcoming women's oppression, emphasizing the body's constructive role, whereas Weil's mysticism involves becoming "no-thing" to unite with God, who is nonanthropomorphic and noncorporeal. Weil would not agree with Irigaray's linking of mysticism with sexual differences. Nonetheless, Weil and Irigaray align with each other in rejecting a masculine deity and oppose a hierarchical interpretation of divine power. For both, God is love, moving toward others rather than exerting dominance. This view of the divine leads to a self that is destabilized and made permeable, reflecting a shift away from traditional power structures.[52]

In addressing critiques of perceived passivity in Weil's work, which some believe might reinforce women's subordination, Sarah K. Pinnock's nuanced analysis of Weil's understanding of power and its potential harms may support my argument. Pinnock clarifies that, for Weil, power in everyday life often serves purposes of domination, conquest, subordination, exploitation, and control. This concept of force, frequently attributed to God, mirrors the absolute authority and control characteristic of divine omnipotence in classical Western theism, thereby elevating collective force to unprecedented heights. Weil, however, challenges this depiction of divinity and its associated dehumanizing societal force.[53] Her perspective, while aligning firmly with the traditions of Christian women mystics such as Marguerite Porete and Teresa of Ávila, who perceive passivity not merely as a diminishment but as a wellspring of transformation, also resonates with the insights of contemporary feminist theologians like Catherine Keller and Sarah A. Coakley. These thinkers, drawing inspiration from apophatic traditions, critically examine the perpetuation of prevailing power structures and their intrinsic characteristics.[54] These theologians, resonating with Weil's stance, oppose the bolstering and justification of hierarchical power exerted by any gender. Moreover, there is a pressing need to confront the oversight of women's potential as oppressors, as well as the neglect of social class and global inequality. Such issues are becoming increasingly central to feminists, particularly those focusing on the oppression of minority groups and those in the Global South.

I also argue that the traits of passivity in Weil's works must be understood in the context of her active proclivity to stand in solidarity with those in affliction. Weil's concept of accepting the void should not be interpreted solely in terms of "thought time" but also in terms of "lived time," referring to her life, in which she personally encountered and freely immersed herself in solidarity with the afflicted and avidly fought against the violence of the world. She denies the idea that justice is an unattainable utopian dream. Instead, she contends that justice is something that can be experienced and understood in a participatory, experimental manner.[55] For Weil, the concept of justice is with a form of love that has the ability to empathize with others who are different, without resorting to objectification or appropriation often seen in such empathetic connections. To grasp this counterintuitive nature of Weil's philosophy and life, it is crucial to consider her concept of attention, which indicates a lucid distinction between compliance with the order of gravity and freedom to be embraced by the order of grace.

Silent attention, according to Weil, is the only legitimate act of agency available in the void. Unlike passive endurance of time, attention requires reorienting one's focus from self to the object of attention by "suspending [one's] thought, leaving it detached, empty, and ready to be penetrated by the object."[56] The act of paying attention does not involve any exertion or mobilization of one's action or knowledge toward achieving a certain goal, apart from quietly looking. By focusing our gaze on an object, we are ready to receive it as it is, in all its reality. According to Weil, the creative potential of attention arises paradoxically from the act of self-renunciation, which is the acceptance of void. Attention embarks on mystical silence as it allows us to perceive what is invisible and hear what is unheard due to the order of gravity; then it turns itself into a creative energy that enables us to respond to the reality of suffering by embracing the order of grace, which reaches to contemplative silence. Weil's portrayal of the Good Samaritan parable exemplifies how attention can foster creativity:

> One of the two is only a little piece of flesh, naked, inert, and bleeding beside a ditch; he is nameless; no one knows anything about him. Those who pass by this thing scarcely notice it, and a few minutes afterward do not even know that they saw it. Only one stops and turns his attention toward it. The actions that follow are just the automatic effect of this moment of attention. The attention is creative. But at the moment when it is engaged it is renunciation.[57]

Through his attention, the Good Samaritan breathed life into the abandoned person who had been robbed of his existence. The act of Creation began with his attention that let him be penetrated by the other. In this way, the Good Samaritan mirrors the divine Creation, in which the self is emptied in order to give life to another. However, this act is not achieved through his own willpower but rather by surrendering to the work of love, the domain of God.

Weil's notion of attention emphasizes the importance of renouncing oneself to assume responsibility for the afflicted, as personal agendas are likely to interfere when actions are driven solely by one's will. By placing the object of attention at the center, Weil suggests we can free ourselves from the impulse to prioritize our own needs or the conviction that our own way is the only right way, and instead align ourselves with the divine act of renunciation that underlies all true acts of Creation. In this respect, the act of paying attention sets both mystical silence and contemplative silence in motion by taking us beyond our confinement and connecting us with others and the divine. The ethical responsibility that arises from this mysticism of silent attention, therefore, not only confronts the injustices resulting from self-expansion projects that pervade society, but also combats our own temptation to use force to dismantle them. At the heart of this temptation lies an admiration for power that contradicts the divine nature.

To fully see and listen to others and recognize our responsibility to them, we must ground that responsibility solely in their humanity without additional conditions or prerequisites. In other words, ethical responsibility must involve relinquishing the sovereign notion of one's agency in response to claims "made by those one does not fully know and did not fully choose."[58] If our responsibility is based on our own will, we may lose sight of our shared humanity because we tend to find a proximity between ourselves and others, which manifests itself as a totalizing force. According to Weil, the act of willing, even if the intention is good, uses such a totalizing force and eventually magnifies one's ego. In this respect, silent attention to the reality of suffering radicalizes the notion of human rights. Typically, the notion of rights is based on a legal framework that emphasizes agency and property ownership. However, as Weil notes, this approach to rights is marked by a "commercial flavor" that relies on force in the background.[59] By contrast, silent attention grounds our motivation in alignment with God's self-emptying nature—the divine nothingness that allows everything to exist as it is and connects everything as it is, without totalizing them.

The transformative effect of silent attention is mystical in this sense because it is only possible when we become fully receptive to the divine, who works through us. It is contemplative because it attunes us to others by negating distractions centered on ourselves. Our responsibility is to attend fully to the afflicted, allowing them to penetrate us deeply while resisting our innate tendency to shape them to fit our expectations or to turn away from them when they do not meet our needs. Silent attention is simply to let God's love flow through us to the afflicted as we remove ourselves from the equation: "the sufferer and the other love each other, starting from God, through God, but not for the love of God; they love each other for the love of the one for the other. This is an impossibility. That is why it comes about only through the agency of God." Attention facilitates an encounter and loving connection between God—the God present within ourselves and the God within the afflicted. Thus, for Weil, attention is inherently ecstatic in nature. When we love others, we do not love them personally, but "it is God in us who loves them."[60] Attention removes the veil that is the falsified sense of ourselves, so that God can love God. Our true agency lies in being willing to let go of the shackles of self and letting God love God through us. "May God grant me to become nothing. In so far as I become nothing, God loves himself through me," says Weil.[61] The ecstatic nature of silent attention establishes a crucial connection between two seemingly conflicting concepts: self-renunciation and ethical responsibility toward the reality of suffering, unleashing its creative potential. By embracing this connection, we can avoid the pitfall of mere compliance and instead foster a generative response to the world around us that affects both ourselves and others.[62]

The ecstatic character of Weil's perspective on attention inevitably requires radical transformations of one's perspective and way of living. However, it does not demand a perfect disposition in order to attend to others. Rather, the act of paying attention shapes one into a relational self that cherishes authentic connections and avoids treating others as mere instruments for their own purposes. Meanwhile, taking care of others does not necessarily mean neglecting one's own need for self-care. While Weil "prioritizes the self-direction of the other, even at the cost of the self," this other-oriented attention involves a conversion of self that finds joy in loving.[63] By loving others we enable God to come into contact with God in us. God does not harm nor use force to destroy anything, including self. Thus, Weil's understanding of self-renunciation is not an act of self-harm or self-sabotage but rather a means of bringing God to life within both oneself and others. The necessary pain of losing one's consumptive and ego-driven habit brings joy to seeing oneself in relation to others and finding joy in loving them. Therefore, even in the midst of affliction, joy is attainable. Or, more precisely, "the transforming power of suffering and joy are equally indispensable."[64] The result is jouissance—the painful joy of encountering and letting the unfathomable divine lead oneself. One is cast toward *sunder warumbe*.

At this juncture, Weil's perspective on void and attention carries significant implications that resonate with the empty tomb. Just as the empty tomb was a place of jouissance for the disciples, so the void is for Weil. The women disciples were exuberated by the painful joy of accepting the silent void of God in the tomb and simultaneously being directed toward a new relationship with God and others in joy; likewise, Weil describes that when the void is accepted and redirected toward God through attention, it becomes a place of transformation. Indeed, Weil believed that this paradox of joy and pain was precedented in the Crucifixion event where Christ stripped away of his sense of self on the cross and let divine love overflow. Weil's depiction of

Crucifixion exemplifies jouissance and at the same time shows how silence is the only language that can bear jouissance. The silence of Christ on the cross is the manifestation of his silent attention to God as an act of consenting to God, and the silence of God at the moment of Christ's death is God's attention to Jesus as an act of listening to his silent cries and transforming them into joy. It is a profound dialogue between the silent God and the silenced. Those who also consent to God through silence hear how "the dialogue of Christ's cry and the Father's silence echoes perpetual in a perfect harmony."[65]

The silent empty tomb stands as a enduring reminder of the dialogue between the silent God and the silenced by presenting the paradox of suffering and joy and by connecting to the places of void in our world. And it entices and redirects our attention toward the glimpse of joy in affliction, as it did to the women disciples, Weil, and all the mystics who stayed and had their gaze fixed in the void. Thus, we may be encouraged to say that the utter void made by the violence of our time can always signify a place of new departure as long as we pay attention to the afflicted in that midst. We may even dare to say, like Weil, "the one who has known pure joy is the only one for whom affliction is something devastating." They will uncover deep beneath "the sound of their own lamentation . . . the pearl of the silence of God." The more fully we can conceive of the nature of true joy, the more acute and intense our experience of suffering and our compassion for others will be. Silent attention in the void can open a fissure for us to witness the silent God being united with us in silence. In this regard, we can understand Weil's statement that "silence is the answer." In silent attention, we can consent, surrender, and move toward grace and let God love God.[66] With the glimmer of this new hope in mind, we may listen to another story of people who stayed with a void filled with both agony and ecstasy—the stories brought by the graveyard portrayed in Arundhati Roy's novel *The Ministry of Utmost Happiness*.

ATTENTION TO THE SMALL THINGS IN GRAVEYARDS

Before delving into the significance of the graveyard in Arundhati Roy's novel, it is necessary to acknowledge the relevance of her writing to my discussion of silence. Given her political activism and writings Arundhati Roy may seem far from silence. She has been unapologetically vocal in criticizing government and corporate attempts to homogenize complex realities and exploit minorities. She is an avid seeker of language as well. Both her fictional and nonfictional writings feature an abundant use of multiple languages. She says in an interview, "I'll have to find a language to tell the story I want to tell. By language I don't mean English, Hindi, Urdu, Malayalam, of course. I mean something else. A way of binding together worlds that have been ripped apart."[67] However, I believe that her unyielding devotion to language and passionate engagement with the people who were silenced keep her in a perpetual mode of searching for a new word, and this very pursuit paradoxically allows her to understand the significance of silence and its mystical and contemplative dimension.

Silence plays a role as pertinent as language in Roy's novels. She often contests language by choosing not to describe, rationalize, or validate. Silence takes the lead in her novels when language is not appropriate. Many of her chapters end with foreboding rhetorical ellipses. Some of the most important moments and relationships in her novels are contained in silence. While the spectacle of tragic massacres, protests, and environmental degradation make her readers feel as if they are witnessing a series of devastating historical events in India, the novel's focus on the spaces of marginalized people encourages readers to hush their own voices and listen to the silenced existences—of both human and nonhuman communities—in their attempts to establish a foothold in life.[68] She reveals how coercive silence can be weaponized, leaving individuals vulnerable to death, while also showcasing the life-giving potential of alternative forms of silence, such as loud, melancholic, and defiant silences, as embodied by her characters. And, through her description of the silenced, she shows how attentive engagement among the vulnerable in the broken world can envision a mode of living and being together, witnessing "the God of small things" who renounced privilege to become one of the silenced.[69]

Dedicated to the "unconsoled," Roy's novel *The Ministry of Utmost Happiness* achieves such a delicate balance and dynamic interplay between the use of language and the potency of silence in her illustration of the atrocities taking place across the Indian subcontinent, spanning from Old Delhi to the rural areas of Kashmir and beyond. The novel brings attention to the affliction of the minority communities, including Muslims and *hijras* (South Asian third-gender individuals), the subjugation of women, the worsening ecological imbalance, and the extremism that has become increasingly entangled with religious and political conflicts in present-day India.[70] The novel interweaves two main narratives and various subplots, all of which explore the challenges of identity, belonging, and justice in rapidly changing

India. The first centers around Anjum and her struggles as a *hijra* and Muslim in Indian society. Assigned male when she was born to a Muslim family in Delhi, she chooses to live as a woman and becomes a member of Khwabgah, a community of hijras. Eventually, she finds her home in a dilapidated Muslim cemetery in Delhi meant for departed souls. The second narrative follows Tilo, an architect and journalist who is the child of unmarried parents, a Dalit father and a Christian mother of Syrian origin. Tilo's story unfolds with her travel to Kashmir to see Musa, her lover and a freedom fighter who is involved in the Muslim separatist movement. They grapple with the complex politics of Kashmir and the deteriorating state of nature in the region. The third part of the novel brings these two narratives together at Anjum's new home in the graveyard, where the characters' lives intersect and their stories converge. Anjum builds a small guesthouse in the graveyard and names it Jannat, meaning "paradise" in Hindi. She rents space there to a group of diverse outcasts, including Tilo, and welcomes those in need without judgment.

The graveyard plays a significant role in *The Ministry of Utmost Happiness*, serving as both a symbolic and narrative anchor. It marks the beginning and end of the novel. It embodies the life conditions of those on the margins of Indian society. Yet it eventually becomes a place of rejuvenation and remembrance for those who have been silenced, whether they are among the living or the dead. Life and death, joy and sorrow, smiling and weeping—all these captivating dualities that the characters bear merge into the graveyard and burst into jouissance. Roy describes these moments using both poignantly beautiful language and profound mystical and contemplative silence. In the following section, I examine the purport of the graveyard, connect it to the silence amid the violence of the contemporary world, and draw parallels with the notions of the void and the empty tomb.

Roy remarked in a lecture that *The Ministry of Utmost Happiness* is a dialogue between two graveyards—one in Delhi, where Anjum creates a home and builds Jannat Guest House, and the other in war-torn Kashmir, which is covered in graveyards after thirty years of conflict.[71] Negative forms of silence pervade both: the dejected silence of the graveyard in Delhi, where the fragile presences of people at the margin of society are hidden, and the coercive and complicit silence of Kashmir, where the majority tries to cover up the political crimes damaging the life conditions of human and nonhuman communities. As places for the "others" of society, the graveyards in *The Ministry of Utmost Happiness* are a haunting reminder of Weil's concept of the void and Jesus's empty tomb. Deprived of life and of all the privileges attached to power, the graveyards are desolate and barren landscapes that evoke a sense of loss and emptiness. Yet, when Anjum embraces the void, the graveyards are transformed into a place where bereft individuals congregate and find a glimpse of new life and joy in loving each other.

The Ministry of Utmost Happiness is a story of the silenced. Anjum was a child born outside of language. When her mother discovered that her newborn baby had intersex characteristics, everything she had been sure of until then ceased to make sense to her. She asked herself whether it was "possible to live outside of language." All the identities and languages constructed by society escaped the baby. Anjum was destined to the life of a "soundless, embryonic howl."[72] Growing up, Anjum faced persistent social exclusion, ridicule, lack of recognition, and physical and sexual abuse. The silencing imposed upon Anjum's life is shared by most of the characters in the novel, including Tilo and Musa, and Saddam, a Dalit whose family was victim to fanatic religious beliefs. Through genocides, ecocides, wars, and impoverishment, these characters are pushed into affliction and thrown into a void that does not allow them to have an identity secured by society or a language to express themselves.

Anjum's acceptance of the void, represented by her move into the graveyard in Delhi, marks a pivotal moment in her life. This turning point follows a harrowing experience during her pilgrimage to Gujarat, where she became embroiled in a violent riot instigated by Hindu nationalists, resulting in the massacre of thousands.[73] Being a *hijra*, Anjum's life was spared, for killing her would bring bad luck. Yet the trauma of the event remained etched in her memory as "thirty thousand voices chimed together" in a cacophony of terror, panic, weeping, quivering, and the humiliation of being unkilled. Anjum retreated into silence like a "fugitive absconding from herself."[74] She could not communicate with anyone because there was no language to describe her experience. Anjum eventually leaves her *hijra* finery in Khwabgah and moves into a nearby graveyard, where her family is buried. Affliction creates an enormous pause in her life, leading her to a graveyard, the place of void. The silenced Anjum merges into the silence of the forgotten dead and yet eventually builds a "paradise" among the dead and living-dead.

The creation of the Jannat Guest House was, however, a collaborative effort by a group of individuals who found strength in each other's vulnerability. Initially, Anjum existed like a ghost in a tin hut near her family's burial site. However, her fellow outcasts, also robbed of their identity and language by society, gradually enticed her out of isolation by exposing their own wounds to her. With the establishment of the guesthouse, the void of the graveyard becomes a reservoir for new possibilities, precisely because it remains empty and free from attachment to prestige and manufactured hope.

Each new guest brings a unique set of differences that become a "necessity," in Weil's terminology, to be heard and penetrated by the attention of others. Each guest's acceptance of the void enables them to see the unseen and hear the unheard. The void disrupts the fixation on the labels marked by society. In this setting, neither the absence of the identities needed to fit in the dominant society nor the lack of language to describe oneself in dominant language is seen as a deficiency but as an opportunity to be embraced and explored together.

The community of the silenced in the graveyards extends beyond the realm of the living, as the silences of the residents are intrinsically linked to the silenced memories in history.[75] The story of Jannat's "presiding deity," Hazrat Sarmad Shaheed, prefigures the kind of community of the silenced, both living and dead, that Roy envisions. Sarmad, a Jewish Armenian merchant who traveled from Persia to Delhi in the seventeenth century, renounced Judaism for Islam. Then, after falling in love with a Hindu boy, he renounced orthodox Islam for love. He lived on the streets as a naked fakir reciting love poems, mocked and humiliated, until he was publicly executed. The memory of Sarmad is diluted and mostly forgotten, remembered only selectively by people in dominant society. However, to Anjum and her fellows, "Hazrat Sarmad's blood has not been washed away." He is "the Saint of the Unconsoled, Solace of the Indeterminate, Blasphemer among Believers, Believer among Blasphemers."[76] The residents of Jannat live on the saint's legacy by embracing his narrative as a whole and emulating his example, hosting a series of burials for the abandoned and anonymous dead. The Jannat Guest House, once abandoned, evolves into a vast space that facilitates the remembrance of those who have been silenced, whether living or dead.[77] Bearing the void and not eliminating it, each room of Jannat encloses a grave. Precisely because of its capacity to hold the void, Jannat is able to accommodate multifarious memories, giving them significance for the living.

The heart of transformation for the characters of *The Ministry of Utmost Happiness* lies in their attention to each other, which undertakes mystical and contemplative silence. In the novel, attention is portrayed as a life-giving energy that unites the shattered pieces of the residents' lives. Attention blossoms from the tiniest of beings—the delicate newborns, the curious kittens Khanum and Agha, the rooster Sultan, the smelly old dog Biroo, and the humble dung beetle Guih Kyom. They hold within them a captivating energy that draws in the characters in the novel and opens their eyes to the wonder and beauty of the world. By quieting themselves, the characters check on those little beings day and night, making sure they have survived the day.

They are amazed by these small creatures' ability to persevere through hardship. These creatures are an integral part of the circle of life in Jannat, and the characters know that they must place their trust in fragility. Attending to these minuscule beings is an act of trust strong enough to sustain the graveyard residents through the day and to find joy in it, even as they continue to exist within perilous societal structures. For they know, they will "save the world in case the heavens fall."[78]

The Ministry of Utmost Happiness illustrates how the habit of silent attention can guide one toward joy even amid affliction, echoing Weil's idea that attention is a creative energy that breathes life into those who are bereft. Silent attention brings the characters to moments of ecstatic jouissance as they willingly or forcefully dispossess themselves from the order of gravity ingrained in society in order to be fully present with others. It allows them to let go of self-centered interests and open themselves to tiny and fragile life forms around them. It involves quieting their own presence to listen to others, being "ready to receive in its naked truth the object that is to penetrate it," as Weil describes.[79] Attention in Jannat is not just a passive observation but a radical act of communion in the midst of affliction, a mystical force that allows the residents to transcend their individual selves and merge into a shared existence. Through this act of silent attention, they become vessels of creativity, open to the infinitely small yet explosive moments of ecstasy that would otherwise be ignored. Silent attention reveals the interconnectedness of all beings and offers a space for the silenced to flourish and thrive. As Weil wrote, "The share of the supernatural here on earth is that of secrecy, silence, the infinitely small. But the operation of that something infinitely small is decisive," and in Jannat, this is where the mysticism of attention operates.[80]

The fragile and marginalized beings in Roy's novel find joy through attention itself. Roy's characters understand, as Weil did, that without love and attention, life withers away, leaving them disengaged and stagnant. Attention may not have a tangible force to wield, but its revolutionary potential lies in its ability to inspire us to resist the destructive forces that threaten vulnerable lives. By instilling trust in the smallest of beings, attention redirects our focus toward life rather than death and reminds us that the joy of life is found in the very act of loving others. Joy is a state reserved for the fragile, filled with the wonders of life at the margins. It is a state where we can embrace both laughter and tears, rejoicing with each other in loving attention and protesting against the forces that destroy it simultaneously. The more we experience joy, the more alive we become, and the more open we are to the sorrows of others. This is the dialectic of an affirmed and loved life, and it is the life that Weil lived, and that Anjum and others in the graveyard live. Perhaps it is a life that we too can embrace, finding joy in silently attending to the smallest of moments and offers resistance to the forces that intimidate us all. There, amid the ruins, lies a hope—the kind of hope that the writer and activist Rebecca Solnit finds in her attention to the ruins of the world: "To awaken from sleep, to rest from awakening, to tame the animal, to let the soul go wild, to shelter in darkness and blaze with light, to cease to speak and be perfectly understood."[81]

Jannat Guest House is not a utopian abode in which the residents can live without threat from outside and conflicts from inside. In no way is a romantic happy ending secured for the residents. What Roy envisions is not a grand agenda to satisfy all or an organized solidarity summoned together with a single narrative. Such a thing is neither possible nor desirable, not only in the novel, but also in the reality we live in. Roy makes it clear: "Never again will a single story be told as though it's the only one."[82] What we can witness here is more likely a concentric circle like Theresa Hak Kyung Cha dreamed of. As we gather together in concentric circles to pay attention to each other and listen to each other, the unattainability of a utopia and of neatly organized solidarity becomes a potential to enlarge our circle bit by bit and nurture our capacity to embrace a multitude of dreams, enabling us to appreciate the creativity stemming from differences, clashes, and conflicts. Such a moment of attentively gathering in concentric circles will always remind us that the choices we make and the meaning we derive from our experiences are determined by what we attend to and how we pay attention, not by an effective agenda to find a solution. Then, it will constantly return us to mystical and contemplative silence, where we are slowly but deeply challenged to be aware of our tendency to categorize and label things within the restricted system of permissions, exclusions, and concealment that governs our lives. Our journey may remain always precarious but will not end in despair because the silent God, who sees, listens to, and is present with the silenced, will sustain us with an inexhaustible source of joy. The fragility of our existences in the void paradoxically makes us strong because we know, just like Roy's characters, that we cannot live without relying on each other and that we cannot continue living without loving each other. Rather than erasing the void from our sight—because there will always be fragile beings left in the void waiting for our attention—we can learn to cultivate our silent attention, rejoicing in each moment of growing together, as Roy writes: "How to tell a shattered story? By slowly becoming everybody. No. By slowly becoming everything."[83]

JOY FOR THE SILENT GOD AND THE SILENCED

As we bring this final chapter to a close, we are left with a departure point that will never lead us to the grand triumphalist finale. Instead, we can depart anew at each moment when we encounter the void in our lives, fixing our gaze on the voids of the world and emulating the gaze of the silent God. Through silent attention and immersion in the void, we attain the possibility of seeing and hearing what has been hidden by society's labels and homogenization. We recognize the sorrows and pains of each other and listen to the ever-present silence of God. Even amid the wreckage, joy can arise, revealing its mystical and contemplative nature. Through the empty tomb narrative and its connection to the stories of people in unique suffering, we learn that silence can sustain us resiliently, when no hasty promises can be made. In attention, we are both consoled and awakened by the silent God, who embraces the silence of fragile beings.

Thus, the silent God and the silenced unite in the empty tomb and the voids of the world, which become our place to come and stay, with all our brokenness and ineffable wounds. We widen the concentric circle of fragile beings, where we become able to see and hear anew, write anew, resist anew, and rest anew, opening ourselves to the never-ending unheard and untold stories of each other and the silent God. In this place of jouissance, numerous faint voices arise and sing together, disrupting the loud unison voice that tries to intimidate and assimilate our shattered voices. The song of shattered voices may sound chaotic, but we can find beauty in it if we patiently listen to each other by quieting our own voices, humbly recognizing our limits, and placing our trust in the most vulnerable part of ourselves, where our wounds lie. As we learn to attune ourselves to the humble awe and wonder of mystery in silence, this awe and wonder turn into silence again—the ineffable mystery of God, "as all music does."[84]

NOTES

1. Sardello, *Silence*, 54.
2. "Seized with trembling and bewilderment" (NAB) or "terror and amazement had seized them" (NRSV).
3. For example, "And the disciples were filled with *joy* and with the Holy Spirit" (Acts 13:52; emphasis added); "For the kingdom of God is not a matter of eating and drinking, but of righteousness, peace and *joy* in the Holy Spirit: (Rom. 14:17, emphasis added); "You became imitators of us and of the Lord, for you welcomed the message in the midst of severe suffering with the *joy* given by the Holy Spirit" (1 Thess. 1:6, emphasis added).

4. Ott, *The Idea of Holy*, 19–37.
5. Sölle, *Silent Cry*, 27, 29–33.
6. Sölle, 59–60; Eckhart quote from Quint, *Meister Eckhart*, 227.
7. Liew, "Haunting Silence," 99–123, 113, 112.
8. Lacan, *Ethics of Psychoanalysis*, 189.
9. Liew, "Haunting Silence," 114, 116.
10. Lacan, *Encore*, 7, 73–77.
11. Irigaray, *This Sex*, 60–67, 98.
12. Hollywood, *Sensible Ecstasy*, 189. See also Irigaray, *Marine Lover of Friedrich Nietzsche*, 86.
13. Irigaray, *Speculum*.
14. Hollywood, *Sensible Ecstasy*, 201.
15. Priest, "Woman as God," 4.
16. Irigaray, *Speculum*, 191–92.
17. According to Irigaray (*I Love to You*, 105), while "ecstasy" means standing outside the self, "enstasy" moves between and among subjects.
18. Irigaray, *Speculum*, 299.
19. Irigaray, 54; Hollywood, *Sensible Ecstasy*, 195.
20. Irigaray, *Speculum*, 195.
21. Porete, *The Mirror of Simple Souls*, 63–223; Evagrius, *Philokalia*, VI.33, quoted in Laird, *Sunlit Absence*, 43.
22. Hollywood, *Sensible Ecstasy*, 195.
23. Deutscher, "'The Only Diabolical Thing,'" 94.
24. French philosopher Jean-Luc Nancy (*Noli Me Tangere*, 26) says in his reading of the empty tomb narrative: "The resurrection is not an apotheosis; to the contrary, it is the kenosis continued. It is the emptiness or in the emptying out of presence that the light shines. And this light does not fill in that emptiness but hollows it out even more."
25. Priest, "Woman as God," 23.
26. Thate, *Godman and the Sea*, 10.
27. Jantzen, *Power, Gender, and Christian Mysticism*, 283.
28. de Certeau, *Mystic Fable*, 81–82.
29. de Certeau, 81–82, 299.
30. Jean-Luc Nancy (*Noli Me Tangere*, 52) also describes this paradox of Jesus's command at the tomb as he explores the characteristic of Christian love.
31. Inspired by Jean-Luc Nancy's (*Noli Me Tangere*, 16) description of Jesus's appearance before Mary.
32. See chapter 2.
33. Simone Weil, "The Love of God and Affliction," in Weil, *Waiting for God*, 118–19.
34. Weil, *Gravity and Grace*, 32.
35. Weil, *First and Last Notebook*, 81.
36. Weil, *Simone Weil Reader*, 467.
37. Simone Weil, "Spiritual Autobiography," in Weil, *Waiting for God*, 72.
38. Weil, *Gravity and Grace*, 37, 31.
39. Weil, 38.
40. A. Rebecca Rozelle-Stone and Benjamin P. Davis, "Simone Weil," *Stanford Encyclopedia of Philosophy*, accessed March 2023, https://plato.stanford.edu/entries/simone-weil/.
41. Weil, *Gravity and Grace*, 33.

42. Bingemer, "Simone Weil and Liberation Theology," 215. For additional insights into Weil's integration of her life with the plight of the impoverished, refer to Bingemer, *Simone Weil*.
43. Weil, *Love in the Void*, 92.
44. Weil, 120.
45. Weil, *Gravity and Grace*, 27; Weil, *Love in the Void*, 69–70.
46. Weil, *Gravity and Grace*, 9–11.
47. Weil, 10.
48. Rozelle-Stone and Stone, *Simone Weil and Theology*, 24.
49. Weil, *On Science*, 127.
50. Elshtain, "Vexation of Weil," 22–23.
51. Pinnock, "Simone Weil and French Feminist Philosophy," 210.
52. Pinnock, 209–10.
53. Pinnock, "Simone Weil and French Feminist Philosophy," 215.
54. Keller, *Cloud of the Impossible* and *On the Mystery*; and Coakley, *Powers and Submissions* and *New Asceticism*.
55. De Chavez, "'It Is Only Watching,'" 103; Duttenhaver, "Love's Labor," abstract.
56. Weil, *Gravity and Grace*, 33; Weil, *Waiting for God*, 111–12.
57. Weil, *Waiting for God*, 146–47.
58. Cha, *Decreation and the Ethical Bind*, 9.
59. Simone Weil, "Human Personality," in Weil, *Selected Essays*, 18, 28, 30.
60. Simone Weil, "Love of Our Neighbor," in Weil, *Waiting for God*, 151; Weil, *Waiting for God*, 93–94.
61. Weil, "Decreation," in *Gravity and Grace*, 32–34.
62. Veto, *Religious Metaphysics of Simone Weil*, 42.
63. Veto, 47–48.
64. Simone Weil, "Last Thought," in Weil, *Waiting for God*, 89.
65. Weil, *First and Last Notebook*, 94.
66. Weil, *The Simone Weil Reader*, 466–68.
67. Parul Sehgal, "Arundhati Roy's Fascinating Mass," *The Atlantic*, July/August 2017, https://www.theatlantic.com/magazine/archive/2017/07/arundhati-roys-fascinating-mess/528684/.
68. Baishya, "Review of 'The Ministry of Utmost Happiness,'" 71–72.
69. *The God of Small Things* is the title of Roy's first novel, which also narrates the stories of the silenced.
70. Roy, *Ministry of Utmost Happiness*, vii; Nanda, "Hijras of India," 35–54.
71. Roy, "Graveyard Talks Back."
72. Roy, *Ministry of Utmost Happiness*, 8.
73. The novel refers to the 2002 Gujarat riots instigated by Hindu nationalists allegedly instigated by the state's chief minister, Narendra Modi, who had fueled anti-Muslim sentiment. The violence lasted for three days and resulted in the deaths of as many as two thousand individuals.
74. Roy, *Ministry of Utmost Happiness*, 57, 56.
75. My interpretation of the graveyards in Roy's novel was inspired by Leila Essa's essay, "Of Other Spaces," 744–49. In this essay, Essa presents the Jannat Guest House as an example of Foucauldian "heteropias."
76. Roy, "Graveyard Talks Back"; Roy, *Ministry of Utmost Happiness*, 8, 382.

77. Essa, "Of Other Spaces," 771.
78. Roy, *Ministry of Utmost Happiness*, 405.
79. Weil, *Waiting for God*, 73.
80. Weil, *Oppression and Liberty*, 166.
81. Solnit, *Storming the Gates of Paradise*, 167.
82. In the words of John Berger, noted in the epigraph of Roy's first novel, *The God of Small Things*.
83. Roy, *Ministry of Utmost Happiness*, 402–3.
84. Mary Oliver, "When Death Comes," in *Devotions*, 285.

EPILOGUE

The Concentric Circle of Listening and Paying Attention to Silence

Silence.

I pause and take a still moment to savor what my journey of writing this book has instilled in me. Yet even in this brief moment of silence, the din of the world outside intrudes into my mind, already filled with many noises. A cacophony of war drums from numerous locations around the globe. Mass shootings near and far that have become a daily routine. Divisive politics that blatantly attack others in self-promotion. Constant buzzes from social media that pour out a barrage of self-expansion. And fear and anxiety rattling in my mind as a response to all those noises. Amid this tumultuous uproar are delicate voices quivering and struggling to be heard, overshadowed by the constant din of conflict and dissonance. I yearn for silence, to listen to the silenced core of these vulnerable existences and to my own. To attend to them. To look more closely. Otherwise, they will be drowned out by all the noise.

The inspiration that propelled me to write this book originated from my yearning to connect with those faint and trembling voices and to discover the transformative potential of silence in their midst—not merely as a fleeting escape from the commotion but as a way to tune in to the depth of others' struggles that are too intricate and painful to be expressed. I sought to understand how the profound sense of connection that silence offers could shield me from being consumed by the clamor that surrounds me. I hoped to immerse myself in the silent God who listens to the grief, sorrow, and anger of the silenced, whose resilient presence becomes a source of joy for us, even when we cannot find a word. I aspired for my silence to merge with that of the silent God and the silenced, to become a conduit for them to be heard.

Yet, delving into the presence of both the silent God and the silenced, I realized that I did not have ears trained to hear nor eyes trained to see what silence was revealing. The first two chapters of the book were, therefore, my effort to prepare myself to listen and engage with silence in the midst of suffering, drawing inspiration from the wisdom and expertise of the mystics in the Christian spiritual traditions, in particular Evagrius Ponticus and Hadewijch of Antwerp. There, I have named the mystical and contemplative dimensions of silence: the former as a fount of epiphany that leads us to encounter the transcendent through the silences in the life contexts of suffering people, the latter as the fundamental ground where divine silence resides, shaping and disposing us to remain attuned to God and others in silence. Both mystical and contemplative silences require that we quiet the noises within and around us, and let go of our habitual attachment to blaring, powerful, and efficient voices, opening ourselves up to the discovery of the unknown.

The remaining three chapters of the book represent my effort to facilitate the use of mystical and contemplative silence as both a source of inspiration and a spiritual practice in our struggle to listen to each other, build community together, and dream together, while recognizing the silent space within each of us. The mysterious silence of Jesus's empty tomb served as my point of departure for each chapter, compelling me to reconsider and reshape my perspectives on how I think, speak, and write about God and the struggles of humanity. From there, I explored the silence of people in the aftermath of South Korea's ferry disaster, learning the role of mystical and contemplative silence as a space to foster the practice of unsaying for the subjugated, openness for the transcendent, and capacity to build communion with others and the divine. Second, I explored the silence experienced by marginalized communities, with a special emphasis on the experiences of women of color in the United States, a topic that resonated with me due to its intersection with my own experiences. I suggested that in our endeavor to form a community, we must learn how to listen to each other's silence, not only to each other's speech. I highlighted "loud" silence, melancholic silence, and defiant silence as forms of silence that contain complicated layers in the silence of women of color yet reveal mystical and contemplative dimensions that can be a source of resistance. Finally, I searched for ways to discover joy through mystical and contemplative silence amid suffering, as it was crucial for me not to turn to escapism, avoidance, self-sabotage, or self-isolation. By pairing the women disciples' experience at Jesus's empty tomb with the writings of Simone Weil and Arundhati Roy, I discussed the significance of ecstatic jouissance, which can be found in the place of suffering and loss and opens us to love freely. They taught me that by attending to the smallest of existences around us, we learn to discover joy in the act of loving.

As I close the pages of this book, an image forms in my mind. It is a series of concentric circles of people connected by strands of thread made from the pain we experience in our daily lives.[1] Each of us inhabits a unique intersection of struggles, a place where our life contexts converge. While our paths and experiences may differ, we are not solitary entities within this circle. Rather, we behold one another in a spiral. There is no linear or hierarchical arrangement of seating in the circle. The beauty of the open spiral of a concentric circle lies in its ability to surpass the enclosure of individual bubbles, forging a threshold that connects us with others through our shared struggles and aspirations. What holds the circle together is a respectful, communal silence that contains mystical and contemplative opportunities. As we sit in the concentric circle, we hush our own voices in order to listen and see together. Then we finally begin to perceive the soft sighs, mournful murmurs, and poignant cries of each other—minuscule sounds that only silence can give voice to.

In the circle, mystical and contemplative silence are "the beginning of devotion," as the poet Mary Oliver says.[2] It is a devotion to remaining open to the unknown and uncertain nature of others and the divine beyond our immediate grasp. It is an act of refusing to place ourselves at the center and instead finding ourselves in the shattered and scattered sighs, murmurs, and cries of others. It is an act of confiding our trust in the most vulnerable and intimate aspects of ourselves and others while questioning the power of the strong and well-developed. This also requires trust in the powerlessness—rather than the power—of God, the God who renounced the divine self for the sake of Creation, the God who was stripped of divinity on the cross, and the God who remains present within our vulnerability through silence. Ultimately, we remain in union with God through our silence, because only in silence we can recognize that it is our vulnerability that carries the silent God within us.

Even as a communal devotion of people who join the concentric circles, the transformative potential of silence first germinates within oneself, rather than in others or the world. For mystical and contemplative silence is rooted in divine love, and it is the nature of love that transforms the self before it transforms others. Like all love, however, we never achieve perfection or become fully formed individuals in our pursuit of transformation through silence. Instead, we allow ourselves to be transformed by silence. The effect of silence is not deferred until some later point but begins immediately upon practice, first by serving as a break from the ordinary way of seeing, acting, and being. And it eventually leads to change within ourselves and in our relations with others, ultimately having an impact on the world.

Perhaps the transformation brought about by silence in the concentric circle always remains unsatisfied and unfulfilled because its goal is not to find a solution. The truth can never be fully articulated; it exists as an ever-present possibility within the unique and dynamic contexts of each individual. Mystical and contemplative silence neither provides a binary opposite to counteract a perceived threat nor does it necessarily offer an immediate alternative. However, it reveals previously unseen and unheard areas, exposes unrecognized limitations, and inspires us to explore what lies beyond our current understanding. Even in the most obscure moments, when all other solutions have failed, it provides us with a space to come together and hold on patiently. Taking apparent failure into silence may enable us to distance ourselves from destructive feelings and instead endure together while waiting for new possibilities to take shape from the void. This can be achieved through mutual agreement within the concentric circle to move away from the notion that our personal agenda is exceptional, to avoid comparing the weight of each other's pain, and to release ourselves from the obligation to lead. Rather, we can relax and breathe in silence, staying curious toward each other, and allowing ourselves to be vulnerable together by listening to others.

From there, we have an opportunity to rekindle our theological language as a poetic fervor that recognizes the value of both speaking and unspeaking. This language knows that silence cracks open the rusty architecture of our perceptions, freeing us to God. This language is born out of a prayerful attention to God's silence that reveals the subtlest nuances of fragile existence. This language knows when, where, and how to unspeak, which requires just as much courage as it takes to speak. The task of theologians is not only to highlight what humans are capable of but also to acknowledge our limitations. It is not to exalt our achievements or strive for victory but rather to draw our attention to the scenes behind the facade of success. In this way, theology must find a way to discipline members of the community to listen to the voices that have been erased from the grandiose narratives of the human ego. For it is these voices that bear and emulate the silent God.

At last, silence returns to the silence of God—the ineffable love. It is in this inexhaustible love that mystical and contemplative silence enable us to continue loving. And it is through this unwavering pursuit of love that we find the deepest joy—the joy that remains ineffable, just like God.

So, where shall I go from here? I sit here first. I quiet my words. I get myself ready to listen.

NOTES

1. "Concentric circle" is a concept formed by Theresa Hak Kyung Cha, which I describe in chapter 4.
2. Oliver, *Upstream*, 8.

BIBLIOGRAPHY

Achino-Loeb, Maria-Luisa, ed. *Silence: The Currency of Power*. Oxford: Berghahn, 2005.
Aguilar, Paloma. "Agents of Memory: Spanish Civil War Veterans and Disabled Soldiers." In *War and Remembrance in the Twentieth Century*, edited by Jay Winter and Emmanuel Sivan, 84–103. Cambridge, UK: Cambridge University Press, 1999.
Arico, Carol J. *A Taste of Silence: Centering Prayer and the Contemplative Journey*. New York: Lantern, 2015.
Baishya, Amit R. "Review of 'The Ministry of Utmost Happiness.'" *World Literature Today* 91, no. 6 (November/December 2017): 71–72.
Ballif, Michelle, D. Diane Davis, and Roxanne Mountford. "Toward an Ethics of Listening." *JAC* 20, no. 4 (Fall 2000).
Balthasar, Hans Urs von. *Man in History: Theological Study*. London: Sheed and Ward, 1982.
Balthasar, Hans Urs von. *Mysterium Paschale: The Mystery of Easter*. Translated by Aidan Nicholas. San Francisco: Ignatius Press, 2000.
Barnard, Leslie W. "Did Athanasius Know Antony?" *Ancient Society* 24 (1993): 139–49.
Barry, Peter. *Beginning Theory: An Introduction to Literary and Cultural Theory*. Manchester, UK: Manchester University Press, 2009.
Barth, Karl. *Church Dogmatics*. Vol. 5. London: Bloomsbury, 2004.
Basso, Keith H. "'To Give Up on Words': Silence in Western Apache Culture." *Southwestern Journal of Anthropology* 26, no. 3 (Autumn 1970): 213–30.
Beverley, John. "*Testimonio*, Subalternity, and Narrative Authority." In *Handbook of Qualitative Research*, edited by Norman K. Denzin and Yvonna S. Lincoln, 547–58. Thousand Oaks, CA: Sage, 2000.
Bhabha, Homi K. *The Location of Culture*. London: Routledge, 2012.
Bianco, Frank. *Voices of Silence: Lives of The Trappists Today*. Norwell, MA: Anchor, 1992.
Bingemer, Maria Clara. "Simone Weil and Liberation Theology." In *Relevance of the Radical: Simone Weil*, edited by A. Rebecca Rozelle-Stone and Lucian Stone. New York: Continuum, 2010.

Bingemer, Maria Clara. *Simone Weil: Mystic of Passion and Compassion*. Eugene, OR: Cascade, 2015.

Blassingame, John, ed. *Slave Testimony: Two Centuries of Letters, Speeches, Interviews, and Autobiographies*. Baton Rouge: Louisiana State University Press, 1977.

Bocken, Inigo. "Nomad and Layman." In *Spiritual Spaces: History and Mysticism in Michel de Certeau*, edited by Inigo Bocken, 111–24. Leuven-Paris-Walpole, MA: Peeters, 2013.

Boesel, Chris, and Catherine Keller, eds. *Apophatic Bodies: Negative Theology, Incarnation, and Relationality*. New York: Fordham University Press, 2010.

Bonhoeffer, Dietrich. *Berlin: 1932–1933*. Translated by Isabel Best, David Higgins, and Douglas W. Stott. Edited by Larry L. Rasmussen. Dietrich Bonhoeffer Works 12. Minneapolis: Fortress, 2009.

Boseker, Barbara J., and Sandra L. Gordon. "What Native Americans Have Taught Us as Teacher Educators." *Journal of American Indian Education* 22, no. 3 (May 1983): 20–24.

Bovon, François. "The Empty Tomb and the Fullness of the Message (23:56b–24:12)." In *Luke 3: Commentary on 19:28–53*, edited by Helmut Koester, translated by James E. Crouch. Minneapolis: Fortress, 2012.

Brink, Andre, "Stories of History: Reimagining the Past in Post-Apartheid Narrative." In *Negotiating the Past: The Making of Memory in South Africa*, edited by Sarah Nuttall and Carli Coetzee. Cape Town: Oxford University Press, 2000.

Bronx, Jane. *Silence: A Social History of One of the Least Understood Elements of Our Lives*. Boston: Marine, 2019.

Brown, Wendy. "In the 'Folds of Our Own Discourse': The Pleasures and Freedom of Silence." *University of Chicago Law School Roundtable* 3, no. 1 (1996): 185–97.

Buber, Martin. "Distance and Relation." In *The Martin Buber Reader*, edited by Ashe D. Biemann, 206–13. New York: Palgrave Macmillan, 2002.

Burgoon, Judee K., Laura K. Guerrero, and Kory Floyd. *Nonverbal Communication*. Boston: Allyn and Bacon, 2009.

Burney, C. F. *Notes on the Hebrew Text of the Book of Kings*. Oxford: Oxford University Press, 1903.

Burrows, Mark S. "Words That Reach into the Silence: Mystical Languages of Unsaying." In *Minding the Spirit: The Study of Christian Spirituality*, edited by Elizabeth A. Dreyer and Mark S. Burrows. Baltimore, MD: Johns Hopkins University Press, 2005.

Burrus, Virginia. "Praying Is Joying: Musings on Love in Evagrius Ponticus." In *Toward a Theology of Eros: Transfiguring Passion at the Limits of Discipleship*, edited by Virginia Burrus and Catherine Keller. New York: Fordham University Press, 2006.

Butler, Judith. "Afterword: After Loss, What Then?" In *Loss: The Politics of Mourning*, edited by David L. Eng and David Kazanjian. Berkeley: University of California Press, 2003.

Butler, Judith. *Gender Trouble: Feminism and the Subversion of Identity*. New York: Routledge, 2006.
Butler, Judith. *Precarious Life: The Powers of Mourning and Violence*. Brooklyn: Verso, 2006.
Bynum, Caroline Walker. *Holy Feast and Holy Fast: The Religious Significance of Food to Medieval Women*. Berkeley: University of California Press, 1988.
Byron, John. "Abel's Blood and the Ongoing Cry for Vengeance." *Catholic Biblical Quarterly* 73, no. 4 (October 2011): 743–56.
Byung-Mu, Ahn. "The Story of Cain and Abel." *Salim* 52 (1993).
Cage, John. *Silence*. Middletown, CT: Wesleyan University Press, 2011.
Caputo, John D. *Specters of God: An Anatomy of the Apophatic Imagination*. Bloomington: Indiana University Press, 2022.
Carlson, Eric S. *I Remember Julia: Voices of the Disappeared*. Philadelphia: Temple University Press, 1996.
Carrillo Rowe, Aimee. "Be Longing: Toward a Feminist Politics of Relation." *NWSA Journal* 17, no. 2 (Summer 2005): 15–46.
Carrillo Rowe, Aimee, and Sheena Malhotra. "Still the Silence: Feminist Reflections at the Edges of Sound." In *Silence, Feminism, Power: Reflections at the Edges of Sound*, edited by Sheena Malhotra and Aimee Carrillo Rowe. New York: Palgrave Macmillan, 2013.
Casiday, Augustine M. *Evagrius Ponticus*. London: Routledge, 2006.
Catechism of the Catholic Church. 2nd ed. Washington, DC: United States Conference of Catholic Bishops, 2011. Accessed April 17, 2023. https://www.usccb.org/sites/default/files/flipbooks/catechism/654/.
Cavanaugh, William. *Theopolitical Imagination*. London: T&T Clark, 2002.
Cavanaugh, William. *Torture and the Eucharist: Theology, Politics, and the Body of Christ*. New York: Wiley-Blackwell, 1998.
Celan, Paul. "The Meridian." In *Paul Celan: Collected Prose*, translated by Rosemary Waldrop. New York: Routledge, 2003.
Cha, Theresa Hak Kyung. *Dictee*. Berkeley: University of California Press, 1999.
Cha, Yoonsook. *Decreation and the Ethical Bind: Simone Weil and the Claim of the Other*. New York: Fordham University Press, 2017.
Chariton, Igumen. *The Art of Prayer: An Orthodox Anthology*. New York: Farrar, Straus and Giroux, 1997.
Cheung, King-Kok. *Articulate Silences: Hisaye Yamamoto, Maxine Hong Kingston, and Joy Kogewa*. Ithaca, NY: Cornell University Press, 1993.
Chireau, Yvonne. *Black Magic: Religion and the African American Conjuring Tradition*. Berkeley: University of California Press, 2003.
Choi, Chungmoo. "The Politics of War Memories toward Healing." In *Perilous Memories: The Asia-Pacific War(s)*, edited by T. Fujitani, Geoffrey M. White, and Lisa Yoneyama, 395–409. Durham, NC: Duke University Press, 2001.
Choi, Jin Young. *Postcolonial Discipleship of Embodiment: An Asian and Asian American Feminist Reading of the Gospel of Mark*. London: Palgrave Macmillan, 2015.

Choi, Jin Young. "Phrónēsis, the Other Wisdom Sister." In *Leading Wisdom: Asian and Asian North American Women Leaders*, edited by Su Yon Pak and Jung Ha Kim, 105–14. Louisville, KY: Westminster John Knox Press, 2017.

Chow, Rey. *Not Like Native Speakers: On Language as a Postcolonial Experience*. New York: Columbia University Press, 2014.

Chrétien, Jean-Louis. "The Hospitality of Silence." In *The Ark of Speech*, translated by Andrew Brown. London: Routledge, 2003.

Christie, Douglas E. *The Blue Sapphire of the Mind: Notes for a Contemplative Ecology*. New York: Oxford University Press, 2012.

Cixous, Hélène. "The Laugh of the Medusa." In *New French Feminisms*, edited by Elaine Marks and Isabelle de Courtivron. New York: Schocken, 1981.

Clair, Robin Patric. *Organizing Silence: A World of Possibilities*. Albany: State University of New York Press, 1998.

Coakley, Sarah A. *New Asceticism: Sexuality, Gender and the Quest for God*. London: Bloomsbury, 2015.

Coakley, Sarah A. *Powers and Submissions: Spirituality, Philosophy and Gender*. Oxford: Wiley-Blackwell, 2002.

Cooke, Thomas N., and Sophia Dingli. *Political Silence: Meanings, Functions, and Ambiguity*. New York: Routledge, 2018.

Copeland, M. Shawn. "Theology at the Crossroads: A Meditation on the Blues." In *Uncommon Faithfulness: The Black Catholic Experience*, edited by M. Shawn Copeland. Ossining, NY: Orbis, 2009.

Corrigan, Kevin, and Gregory Yuri Glazov. "Compunction and Compassion: Two Overlooked Virtues in Evagrius of Potus." *Journal of Early Christian Studies* 22, no. 1 (Spring 2014).

Crosby, Wendy Theresa. "The Spirit of a Weak God: Reimagining Divine Providence after the Critique of Ontotheology." PhD diss., Loyola University, 2017. https://ecommons.luc.edu/cgi/viewcontent.cgi?article=3790&context=luc_diss.

Dalton, Anne B. "The Devil and the Virgin: Writing Sexual Abuse in 'Incidents in the Life of a Slave Girl.'" In *Violence, Silence, and Anger: Women's Writing as Transgression*, edited by Deirdre Lashgari. Charlottesville: University Press of Virginia, 1995.

D'Angelo, Mary Rose. "Women in Luke–Acts: A Redactional View." *Journal of Biblical Literature* 109, no. 3 (1990): 441–61.

Dauenhauer, Bernard P. "On Silence." *Research in Phenomenology* 3, no. 1 (1973): 9–27.

Dauenhauer, Bernard P. *Silence: The Phenomenon and Its Ontological Significance*. Bloomington: Indiana University Press, 1980.

Dauenhauer, Bernard P. "Silence: The Phenomenon and Its Ontological Significance." *International Journal for Philosophy of Religion* 13, no. 4 (1982): 229–30.

Davis, Bruce. *Monastery without Walls: Daily Life in the Silence*. Bloomington, IN: iUniverse, 2001.

Davis, Stephen T. *Logic and the Nature of God*. Grand Rapids, MI: Eerdmans, 1983.
de Certeau, Michel. *The Mystic Fable*. Translated by Michael B. Smith. Chicago: University of Chicago Press, 1992.
de Certeau, Michel. *The Practice of Everyday Life*. Berkeley: University of California Press, 1988.
De Chavez, Jeremy. "'It Is Only Watching, Waiting, Attention': Rethinking Love with Alain Badiou and Simone Weil." *KEMANUSIAAN: The Asian Journal of Humanities* 22, no. 2 (2015): 93–116.
de la Barre, Jorge, and Blagovesta Momchedjikova. "Introduction: Sounds and Silence in the Pandemic City." *Streetnotes* 28 (2022): 1–8. Accessed August 26, 2023. https://escholarship.org/content/qt3p86145k/qt3p86145k_noSplash_d8b1c409879a1ae061dea5bf376c2c3c.pdf?t=r8y0z7.
Derrida, Jacques. *Dissemination*. Translated by Barbara Johnson. Chicago: University of Chicago Press, 1981.
Derrida, Jacques. *Margins of Philosophy*. Translated by Alan Bass. Chicago: University of Chicago Press, 1982.
Derrida, Jacques. *Of Grammatology*. Translated by Gayatri Spivak. Baltimore: Johns Hopkins University Press, 1988.
Derrida, Jacques. *Speech and Phenomena*. Translated by D. B. Allison and N. Garner. Evanston, IL: Northwestern University Press, 1973.
Derrida, Jacques. *Writing and Difference*. Translated by Alan Bass. Chicago: University of Chicago Press, 1978.
De Waele, Aurélie, An-Sofie Claeys, and Verolien Cauberghe. "The Organizational Voice: The Importance of Voice Pitch and Speech Rate in Organizational Crisis Communication." *Communication Research* 46, no. 7 (October 2019): 1026–49.
Deutscher, Penelope. "'The Only Diabolical Thing about Women . . .': Luce Irigaray on Divinity." *Hypatia* 9, no. 4 (Autumn 1994): 88–111.
Dønen, Tomas Sundnes. "Christian Migrant Communities." *Method & Theory in the Study of Religion* 30, no. 3 (2018).
Dreyer, Elizabeth A., and Mark S. Burrows, eds. *Minding the Spirit: The Study of Christian Spirituality*. Baltimore, MD: Johns Hopkins University Press, 2005.
Dreyer, Elizabeth A., and Mark S. Burrows. "Preface." In *Minding the Spirit: The Study of Christian Spirituality*, edited by Elizabeth A. Dreyer and Mark S. Burrows, xi–xviii. Baltimore, MD: Johns Hopkins University Press, 2005.
Duncan, Patti. *Tell This Silence*. Iowa City: University of Iowa Press, 2004.
Dunning, G. B. "Research in Nonverbal Communication." *Theory into Practice* 10, no. 4 (October 1971): 250–58.
Duttenhaver, Krista E. "Love's Labor: The Relational Self in Simone Weil's Mystical-Political." PhD diss., University of Notre Dame, April 2010.
Edgar, A. "Music and Silence." In *Silence: Interdisciplinary Perspectives*, edited by Adam Jaworski, 311–28. Berlin: Mouton de Gruyter, 1997.

Ekman, Paul, and Wallace V. Friesen. *Unmasking the Face*. Englewood Cliffs, NJ: Prentice-Hall, 1975.
Eliot, T. S. *Four Quartets*. New York: HarperCollins, 2014.
Elkins, Janet. *Trauma and the Memory of Politics*. Cambridge, UK: Cambridge University Press, 2003.
Elshtain, Jean Bethke. "The Vexation of Weil." In *Power Trips and Other Journeys: Essays in Feminism as Civic Discourse*, edited by Jean Bethke Elshtain, 13–23. Madison: University of Wisconsin Press, 1990.
Enloe, Cynthia. *The Curious Feminist: Searching for Women in a New Age of Empire*. Berkeley: University of California Press, 2004.
Epiphanius. "An Ancient Homily for Holy Saturday: Christ's Descent into Hell." In *Best Sermons Ever*, compiled by Christopher Howse. New York: Bloomsbury Academic, 2004.
Esaki, Brett J. *Enfolding Silence: The Transformation of Japanese American Religion and Art under Oppression*. New York: Oxford University Press, 2016.
Esparza, Marcia, Henry R. Huttenbach, and Daniel Feierstein, eds. *State Violence and Genocide in Latin America: The Cold War Years*. New York: Routledge, 2011.
Essa, Leila. "Of Other Spaces and Others' Memories: Reading Graveyards in Arundhati Roy's 'The Ministry of Utmost Happiness' and Reina Scheer's 'Machandel.'" *Comparative Literature Studies* 58, no. 4 (2021): 744–49.
Evagrius Ponticus. *The Praktikos and Chapters on Prayer*. Translated by John Eudes Bamberger. Kalamazoo, MI: Cistercian, 1981.
Evans, Jean N. "Silence and the Mystical Encounter: A Consideration." *Spiritus: A Journal of Christian Spirituality* 22, no. 2 (Fall 2022): 291–95.
Fanon, Frantz. *Black Skin, White Masks*. New York: Grove, 1967.
Farley, Wendy. *Beguiled by Beauty: Cultivating a Life of Contemplation and Compassion*. Louisville, KY: Westminster John Knox Press, 2022.
Farmer, Frank. *Saying and Silence*. Logan: Utah State University Press, 2001.
Ferrari, Martina. "Questions of Silence: On the Emancipatory Voice and the Coloniality of Silence." *Hypatia* 35 (2020): 123–42.
Fiorenza, Elisabeth Schüssler. *In Memory of Her: A Feminist Theological Reconstruction of Christian Origins*. New York: Crossroad, 1983.
Flanagan, Kieran. "Liturgy, Ambiguity, and Silence: The Ritual Management of Real Absence." *British Journal of Sociology* 36, no. 2 (June 1985): 193–223.
Ford, David F. "Apophasis and the Shoah: Where was Jesus Christ at Auschwitz?" In *Silence and the Word: Negative Theology and Incarnation*, edited by Oliver Davies and Denys Turner, 185–200. Cambridge, UK: Cambridge University Press, 2008.
Foss, Karen, and Sonja Foss. *Women Speak: The Eloquence of Women's Lives*. Long Grave, IL: Waveland Press, 1991.
Foucault, Michel. *The Archaeology of Knowledge and the Discourse on Language*. New York: Pantheon, 1972.

Foucault, Michel. *Discipline and Punish*. New York: Pantheon, 1977.
Foucault, Michel. *The History of Sexuality*. Vol. 1, *An Introduction*. London: Penguin, 1978.
Foucault, Michel. *The History of Sexuality*. Vol. 1, *The Will to Knowledge*. London: Penguin, 1988.
Fredericksen, Elaine. "Muted Colors: Gender and Classroom Silence." *Language Arts* 77, no. 4 (March 2000): 301–8.
Freud, Sigmund. *Modern Classics on Murder, Mourning, and Melancholia*. Edited by Shaun Whiteside. London: Penguin Classics, 2005.
Freud, Sigmund. "Mourning and Melancholy." In *The Freud Reader*, edited by Peter Gay, 584–89. New York: W. W. Norton, 1989.
Freud, Sigmund. "The 'Uncanny.'" In *The Complete Psychological Works*, vol. 17. London: Hogarth, 1955.
Frohlich, Mary. "Contemplation." In *Prayer in the Catholic Tradition: A Handbook of Practical Approaches*, edited by Robert J. Wicks, 65–76. Cincinnati: Franciscan Media, 2016.
Fujiwara, Lynn, and Shireen Roshanravan. "Weaponizing Our (In)visibility: Asian American Feminist Ruptures of the Model-Minority Optic." In *Asian American and Women of Color Politics*, edited by Lynn Fujiwara and Shireen Roshanravan, 261–82. Seattle: University of Washington Press, 2018.
Gandsman, Ari. "The Limits of Kingship Mobilizations and the (A)politics of Human Rights in Argentina." *Journal of Latin American and Caribbean Anthropology* 17, no. 2 (2012): 193–214.
Gates-Madsen, Nancy J. *Trauma, Taboo, and Truth-Telling: Listening to Silence in Postdictatorship Argentina*. Madison: University of Wisconsin Press, 2016.
General Instruction of the Roman Missal. Vatican City: The Holy See, 2003. Last modified March 17, 2003. https://www.vatican.va/roman_curia/congregations/ccdds/documents/rc_con_ccdds_doc_20030317_ordinamento-messale_en.html.
Glenn, Cheryl. *Rhetoric Retold: Regendering the Tradition from Antiquity through the Renaissance*. Carbondale: Southern Illinois University Press, 1997.
Glenn, Cheryl. *Unspoken: A Rhetoric of Silence*. Carbondale: Southern Illinois University Press, 2004.
Gooch, Paul W. *Reflections on Jesus and Socrates: Word and Silence*. New Haven, CT: Yale University Press, 1996.
Gorman, George H. *The Amazing Fact of Quaker Worship*. London: Quaker Home Service, 1973.
Gover, Angela R., Shannon B. Harper, and Lynn Langton. "Anti-Asian Hate Crime during the COVID-19 Pandemic: Exploring the Reproduction of Inequality." *American Journal of Criminal Justice* 45 (2020): 647–67.
Green, Keith, and Jill LeBihan. *Critical Theory and Practice: A Coursebook*. New York: Routledge, 1996.

Greene, Alice B. *The Philosophy of Silence*. New York: Richard R. Smith, 1940.
Guest, Tanis M. *Some Aspects of Hadewijch's Poetic Form in the Strofische Gedichten*. The Hague, Netherlands: Matinus Nijhoff, 1975.
Guillaume, Xavier. "How to Do Things with Silence: Rethinking the Centrality of Speech to the Securitization Framework." *Security Dialogue* 49, no. 6 (2018).
Guroian, Vigen. "Seeing Worship as Ethics: An Orthodox Perspective." *Journal of Religious Ethics* 13, no. 2 (Fall 1985): 332–59.
Hadewijch. *Hadewijch: The Complete Works*. Translated by Columba Hart. Mahwah, NJ: Paulist Press, 1980.
Haraway, Donna. "Situated Knowledge: The Science Question in Feminism and the Privilege of Partial Perspective." *Feminist Studies* 14, no. 3 (Autumn 1988): 575–99.
Hart, Kevin. *The Trespass of the Sign: Deconstruction, Theology, and Philosophy*. 2nd ed. New York: Fordham University Press, 2000.
Hart, Matthew J. "Calvinism and the Problem of Hell." In *Calvinism and the Problem of Evil* edited by David E. Alexander and Daniel M. Johnson, 248–72. Eugene, OR: Pickwick, 2016.
Hatzisavvidou, Sophia. "Disturbing Binaries in Political Thought: Silence as Political Activism." *Social Movement Studies* 14, no. 5 (2015): 509–22.
Heidegger, Martin. *On the Way to Language*. San Francisco: HarperOne, 1982.
Heber-Percy, Colin. "Exploring the Spiritualty of School Chapel: Space, Silence and the Self." *Spiritus: A Journal of Christian Spirituality* 16, no. 2 (Fall 2016): 215–34.
Hetherington, Kevin. "Second-Handedness: Consumption, Disposal, and Absent Presence." *Environment and Planning D: Society and Space* 22, no. 1 (2004): 157–73.
Hetherington, Kevin. "The Unsightly: Visual Impairment, Touch and the Parthenon Frieze." *Theory, Culture, and Society* 19, no. 5–6 (2002): 187–205.
Hillgardner, Holly. *Longing and Letting Go: Christian and Hindu Practices of Passionate Non-attachment*. Oxford: Oxford University Press, 2016.
Hollywood, Amy. "Love Speaks Here: Michel de Certeau's 'Mystic Fable.'" *Spiritus: A Journal of Christian Spirituality* 12, no. 2 (Fall 2012): 198–206.
Hollywood, Amy. Review of *Mystical Languages of Unsaying* by Michael A. Sells. *Journal of Religion* 75, no. 4 (October 1995): 564–65.
Hollywood, Amy. *Sensible Ecstasy*. Chicago: University of Chicago Press, 2001.
Holmes, Barbara A. *Joy Unspeakable: Contemplative Practices of the Black Church*. Minneapolis: Augsburg Fortress, 2004.
Hong, Grace Kyungwon. *The Rupture of American Capital: Women of Color Feminism and the Culture of Immigrant Labor*. Minneapolis: University of Minnesota Press, 2006.
Hopkins, Dwight. *Down, Up, and Over: Slave Religion and Black Theology*. Minneapolis: Fortress, 1999.
Heuertz, Phileena. *Mindful Silence: The Heart of Christian Contemplation*. Downers Grove, IL: IVP, 2018.

Hua, Whitney, and Jane Junn. "Amidst Pandemic and Racial Upheaval: Where Asian Americans Fit." *Journal of Race, Ethnicity, and Politics* 6, no. 1 (2021): 16–32.
Hymes, Dell. "Models of the Interaction of Language and Social Life." In *Directions in Sociolinguistics: The Ethnography of Communication*, edited by John J. Gumperz, 35–71. New York: Hold, Rinderhart and Winston, 1972.
Ilan, Tal. *Jewish Women in Greco-Roman Palestine: An Inquiry into Image and Status*. Peabody, MA: Hendrickson, 1996.
Irigaray, Luce. *I Love to You: Sketch of a Possible Felicity in History*. Translated by Alison Martin. New York: Routledge, 1996.
Irigaray, Luce. *Marine Lover of Friedrich Nietzsche*. Translated by Gillian C. Gill. New York: Columbia University Press, 1991.
Irigaray, Luce. *Speculum of the Other Woman*. Ithaca, NY: Cornell University Press, 1985.
Irigaray, Luce. *This Sex Which Is Not One*. Translated by Catherine Porter and Carolyn Burke. Ithaca, NY: Cornell University Press, 1985.
Irigaray, Luce. *To Be Two*. New York: Routledge, 2001.
Irigaray, Luce, and Michael Marder. *Building a New World: Luce Irigaray, Teaching II*. London: Palgrave Macmillan, 2015.
Jacobs, Harriet A. *Incidents in the Life of a Slave Girl*. Edited by Lydia Maria Francis Child. Boston: self-published, 1861. Accessed via Documenting the American South. https://docsouth.unc.edu/fpn/jacobs/jacobs.html.
Jantzen, Grace. *Power, Gender, and Christian Mysticism*. Cambridge, UK: Cambridge University Press, 1996.
Jaworski, Adam. *The Power of Silence: Social and Pragmatic Perspectives*. Newbury Park, CA: SAGE, 1993.
John of the Cross. "Maxims on Love, 21." In *the Collected Works of St. John of the Cross*. Translated by K. Kavannaugh and O. Rodriguez. Washington, DC: Institute of Carmelite Studies, 1979.
Johnson, Daniel M. "Calvinism and the Problem of Evil: A Map of the Territory." In *Calvinism and the Problem of Evil*, edited by David E. Alexander and Daniel M. Johnson, 19–55. Eugene, OR: Pickwick, 2016.
Johnson, Elizabeth. *Friends of God and Prophets: A Feminist Theological Reading of "The Communion of Saints."* New York: Continuum, 1999.
Jones, Rufus M. "Rethinking Quaker Principles." In *The Pendle Hill Reader*, edited by Herrymon Mauer, 65–88. New York: Harper and Brothers, 1950.
Junn, Jane. "From Coolie to Model Minority: US Immigration Policy and the Construction of Racial Identity." *Du Bois Review: Social Science Research on Race* 4, no. 2 (2007): 355–73.
Kadi, Joanna. "Speaking (about) Silence." In *Sing, Whisper, Shout, Pray! Feminist Visions for a Just World*, edited by M. Jacqui Alexander, Lisa Albrecht, Sharon Day, and Mab Segrest, 539–45. Fort Bragg, GA: Edgework, 2002.
Karlsson, Jenni. "Doing Visual Research with School Learners in South Africa." *Visual Sociology* 16, no. 2 (2003): 23–37.

Karris, Robert J. "Women and Discipleship in Luke." *Catholic Biblical Quarterly* 56, no. 1 (January 1994): 1–20.

Kasper, Walter. *Jesus the Christ*. Mahwah, NJ: Paulist Press, 1976.

Keating, Christine. "Resistant Silence." In *Silence, Feminism, Power: Reflections at the Edges of Sound*, edited by Aimee Carrillo Rowe and Sheena Malhotra, 25–33. New York: Palgrave Macmillan, 2013.

Keller, Catherine. *Cloud of the Impossible: Negative Theology and Planetary Entanglement*. New York: Columbia University Press, 2014.

Keller, Catherine. *On the Mystery: Discerning Divinity in Process*. Minneapolis: Fortress, 2008.

Kerr, Fergus. "The 'Essence' of Christianity: Notes after de Certeau." *New Blackfriars* 54, no. 643 (1973): 545–56.

Kim, Claire Jean. "The Racial Triangulation of Asian Americans." *Politics & Society* 27, no. 1 (1999): 105–38.

Kim, Elaine H., and Norma Alarcón, eds. *Writing Self, Writing Nation: A Collection of Essays on "Dictée" by Theresa Hak Kyung Cha*. Berkeley: Third Woman Press, 1994.

Kim, Heejung S. "We Talk, Therefore We Think? A Cultural Analysis of the Effect of Talking on Thinking." *Journal of Personality and Social Psychology* 83, no. 4 (2000): 828–42.

Kirch, Max S. "Non-verbal Communication across Cultures." *Modern Language Journal* 63, no. 8 (1979): 416–23.

Knapp, Karlfried, Werner Enninger, and Annelie Knapp-Potthoff, eds. *Analyzing Intercultural Communication*. Berlin: Mouton de Gruyter, 1987.

Knapp, Mark L., and Judith A. Hall. *Nonverbal Communication in Human Interaction*. 7th ed. Wadsworth, Canada: Cengage Learning, 2010.

Knepper, Timothy D. *Negating Negation: Against the Apophatic Abandonment of the Dionysian Corpus*. Eugene, OR: Wipf & Stock, 2013.

Kramarae, Cheris. *Women and Men Speaking*. Rowley, MA: Newbury House, 1981.

Kristeva, Julia. *Revolution in Poetic Language*. Ithaca, NY: Columbia University Press, 1984.

Kurzon, Dennis. *Discourse of Silence*. Amsterdam: John Benjamins, 1998.

Lacan, Jacques. *Encore: The Limits of Love and Knowledge*. Vol. 20 of *The Seminar of Jacques Lacan*, translated by Bruce Fink. New York: W. W. Norton, 1999.

Lacan, Jacques. *The Ethics of Psychoanalysis, 1956–1960*. Vol. 7 of *The Seminar of Jacques Lacan*, edited by Jacques-Alain Miller and translated by Dennis Porter. New York: W. W. Norton, 1992.

Laird, Martin. *Into the Silent Land: A Guide to the Christian Practice of Contemplation*. Oxford: Oxford University Press, 2006.

Laird, Martin. *A Sunlit Absence: Silence, Awareness, and Contemplation*. New York: Oxford University Press, 2011.

Lashgari, Deirdre, ed. *Violence, Silence, and Anger: Women's Writing as Transgression*. Charlottesville: University of Virginia Press, 1995.

Lee, Hyeon Jung. "The Struggle Surrounding the 4.16 Classrooms and the Construction of a New Placeness: Beyond the Memory of Victimhood." *Journal of Memory & Vision* 41 (2019): 145–88.

Lee, Kun Jong. "Rewriting Hesiod, Revisioning Korea: Theresa Hak Kyung Cha's 'Dictee' as a Subversive Hesiodic 'Catalogue of Women.'" *College Literature* 33, no. 3 (Summer 2006): 77–99.

Lee, So Hee, Jin-Won Noh, Kyoung-Beom Kim, Eun Ji Kim, Jihoon Oh, and Jeong-Ho Chae. "Factors Associated with Post-traumatic Stress Disorder among Bereaved Family Members and Surviving Students Two and Half Years after the Sewol Ferry Accident in South Korea." *Psychiatry Research* 296 (February 2021). https://doi.org/10.1016/j.psychres.2020.113666.

Lefebvre, Henri. *The Production of Space*. Hoboken, NJ: Willey-Blackwell, 1992.

Leloup, Jean-Yves. *Being Still: Reflections on an Ancient Mystical Tradition*. Translated by M. S. Laird. Mahwah, NJ: Paulist Press, 2003.

Lewallen, Constance M. *The Dream of the Audience: Theresa Hak Kyung Cha (1951–1982)*. Berkeley: University of California Berkeley Art Museum, 2001.

Lewis, Alan E. *Between Cross and Resurrection: A Theology of Holy Saturday*. Grand Rapids, MI: William B. Eerdmans, 2003.

Lewis, Jeff. *Cultural Studies—The Basics*. London: Sage, 2008.

Liew, Tat-siong Benny. "Haunting Silence: Trauma, Failed Orality, and Mark's Messianic Secret." In *Psychoanalytic Meditations between Marxist and Postcolonial Readings of the Bible*, edited by Tat-Siong Benny Liew and Erin Runions, 99–123. Semeia Studies 84. Atlanta: Society of Biblical Literature, 2016.

Liew, Tat-Siong Benny. *Politics of Parousia: Reading Mark Inter(con)textually*. Leiden: Brill, 1999.

Lloyd, Vincent. "Liturgy in the Broadest Sense." *New Blackfriars* 92, no. 1037 (January 2011): 71–89.

Lorde, Audre. *Your Silence Will Not Protect You*. San Jose: Silver, 2017.

MacCulloch, Diarmaid. *Silence: A Christian History*. New York: Penguin, 2013.

Maclear, Kyo. "Not in So Many Words: Translating Silence across 'Difference.'" *Fireweed*, no. 44–45 (Summer 1994): 6–11.

Malhotra, Sheena, and Aimee Carrillo Rowe, eds. *Silence, Feminism, Power: Reflections at the Edges of Sound*. New York: Palgrave Macmillan, 2013.

Malinger, Laurence P. "Hearing the Silent, Seeing the Invisible: Varyeira, Genesis 18:1–22:24." Union for Reform Judaism. Modified November 2006. https://reformjudaism.org/learning/torah-study/torah-commentary/hearing-silent-seeing-invisible.

McColman, Carl. *Befriending Silence: Discovering the Gifts of Cistercian Spirituality*. Notre Dame, IN: Ave Maria, 2015.

McGinn, Bernard. *The Flowering of Mysticism: Men and Women in the New Mysticism, 1200–1350*. New York: Crossroad, 1998.

McGinn, Bernard. *Foundations of Mysticism: Origins to the Fifth Century*. New York: Crossroad, 2004.

McGinn, Bernard. "The Letter and the Spirit: Spirituality as an Academic Discipline." In *Minding the Spirit: The Study of Christian Spirituality*, edited by Elizabeth A. Dreyer and Mark S. Burrows, 24–41. Baltimore: Johns Hopkins University Press, 2005.

McGinn, Bernard. "Unio Mystica/Mystical Union." In *The Cambridge Companion to Christian Mysticism*, edited by Amy Hollywood and Patricia Z. Beckman. New York: Cambridge University Press, 2012.

McGrath, Alister E. *Christian Spirituality*. Hoboken, NJ: Wiley-Blackwell, 2013.

McGrath, Alister E. *Christian Theology: An Introduction*. London: Blackwell, 2007.

McIntosh, Mark A. *Mystical Theology*. Oxford: Blackwell, 1998.

McIvor, David W. "Bringing Ourselves to Grief: Judith Butler and the Politics of Mourning." *Political Theory* 40, no. 4 (August 2012): 409–36.

McLauchlan, Richard. *Saturday's Silence: R. S. Thomas and Paschal Reading*. Cardiff, UK: University of Wales Press, 2016.

Merton, Thomas. *Conjectures of a Guilty Bystander*. New York: Doubleday, 1966.

Merton, Thomas. *Contemplative Prayer*. New York: Crown, 2009.

Merton, Thomas. *Echoing Silence: Thomas Merton on Vocation and Writing*. Boulder, CO: Shambala, 2007.

Merton, Thomas. *New Seeds of Contemplation*. Boulder, CO: Shambhala, 2003.

Merton, Thomas. *The Waters of Silence*. London: Hollis and Carter, 1950.

Meyer, Morgan. "A Space for Silence: Exhibiting and Materializing Silence through Technology." *Cultural Geographies* 23, no. 2 (Spring 2016).

Michaels, Anne. *Fugitive Pieces*. London: Bloomsbury, 1998.

Michelson, David A. "Philoxenos of Mabbug and the Simplicity of Evagrian Gnosis Competing Uses of Evagrius in the Early Sixth Century." In *Evagrius and His Legacy*, edited by Joel Kalvesmaki and Robin Darling, 175–205. Notre Dame, IN: University of Notre Dame Press, 2016.

Minh-ha, Trinh T. *When the Moon Waxes Red: Representation, Gender, and Cultural Politics*. London: Routledge, 1992.

Minh-ha, Trinh T. *Woman, Native, Other: Writing Postcoloniality and Feminism*. Bloomington: Indiana University Press, 2009.

Mohanty, Chandra Talpade. "Under Western Eyes: Feminist Scholarship and Colonial Discourses." *Feminist Review* 30, no. 1 (1988): 61–88.

Mommaers, Paul. *Hadewijch: Writer—Beguine—Love Mystic*. Louvain, Belgium: Peeters, 2004.

Mommaers, Paul. *Riddles of Christian Mystical Experience: The Role of the Humanity of Jesus*. Louvain, Belgium: Peeters, 2003.

Montoya, Margaret E. "Silence and Silencing: Their Centripetal and Centrifugal Forces in Legal Communication, Pedagogy and Discourse." *University of Michigan Journal of Law Reform* 263, no. 33 (2000).

Morris, Thomas V. *Our Idea of God: An Introduction to Philosophical Theology*. Downers Grove, IL: InterVarsity, 1991.

Nance, Kimberly A. *Can Literature Promote Justice? Trauma Narrative and Social Action in Latin American Testimonio.* Nashville: Vanderbilt University Press, 2006.
Nancy, Jean-Luc. *The Inoperative Community.* Edited by Peter Connor. Minneapolis: University of Minnesota Press, 1991.
Nancy, Jean-Luc. *Noli Me Tangere: On the Raising of the Body.* Translated by Sarah Clift. New York: Fordham University Press, 2008.
Nanda, Serena. "The Hijras of India: Cultural and Individual Dimensions of an Institutionalized Third Gender Role." *Journal of Homosexuality* 11, no. 3–4 (1985): 35–54.
Newman, Barbara. *God and the Goddesses: Vision, Poetry, and Belief in the Middle Ages.* Philadelphia: University of Pennsylvania Press, 2005.
Nhat Hanh, Thich. *The Power of Silence in a World Full of Noise.* New York: HarperCollins, 2015.
Nietzsche, Friedrich. *"The Anti-Christ," "Ecce Homo," "Twilight of the Idols," and Other Writings.* Edited by Aaron Ridley and Judith Norman. Translated by Judith Norman. Cambridge: Cambridge University Press, 2005.
Nietzsche, Friedrich. *The Birth of Tragedy and Other Writings.* Edited by Raymond Geuss and Ronald Speirs. Translated by Ronald Speirs. Cambridge: Cambridge University Press, 1999.
Nietzsche, Friedrich. *Human, All Too Human: A Book for Free Spirits.* Translated by R. J. Hollingdale. Cambridge: Cambridge University Press, 1996.
Noel, James A. "Call and Response: The Meaning of the Moan and Significance of the Shout in Black Worship." *Reformed Liturgy and Music* 28, no. 2 (Spring 1994): 72–76.
Oliver, Mary. *Devotions.* New York: Penguin, 2017.
Oliver, Mary. *Upstream: Selected Essays.* New York: Penguin, 2019.
Olsen, Tillie. *Silences.* 25th ed. New York: Feminist Press, 2003.
Oppenheimer, Joshua. "Director's Notes." *The Look of Silence.* Modified 2015. Accessed June 6, 2021. http://thelookofsilence.com/.
Oppenheimer, Joshua, dir. *The Look of Silence.* Drafthouse Films, 2014.
Orsi, Robert. "Everyday Miracles: The Study of Lived Religions." In *Lived Religions in America: Toward a History of Practices,* edited by David Hall. Princeton, NJ: Princeton University Press, 1997.
Ott, Rudolf. *The Idea of Holy: An Inquiry Into the Non-rational Factor in the Idea of the Divine and Its Relation to the Rational.* Translated by John W. Harvey. Pantianos Classics, 2017.
Pak, Su Yon, and Jung Ha Kim, eds. *Leading Wisdom: Asian and Asian North American Women Leaders.* Louisville, KY: Westminster John Knox Press, 2017.
Palmer, Parker. *The Courage to Teach: Exploring the Inner Landscape of a Teacher's Life.* Ann Arbor: University of Michigan Press, 1998.
Paris, Peter. *The Spirituality of African Peoples.* Minneapolis: Fortress, 1995.

Paul VI. *Sacrosanctum Concilium (Constitution on the Sacred Liturgy)*. Vatican City: The Holy See, 1963. www.vatican.va/archive/hist_councils/ii_vatican_council/documents/vat-ii_const_19631204_sacrosanctum-concilium_en.html.

Perkins, Judith. *Roman Imperial Identities in the Early Christian Era*. New York: Routledge, 2009.

Petroff, Elizabeth A. *Body and Soul: Essays on Medieval Women and Mysticism*. London: Oxford University Press, 1986.

Phan, Peter. "Liturgy of Life as the 'Summit and Source' of the Eucharistic Liturgy: Church Worship as Symbolization of the Liturgy of Life?" In *Incongruities: Who We Are and How We Pray*, edited by Timothy Fitzgerald and David A. Lysik, 257–78. Chicago: Liturgy Training, 2000.

Philippot, Pierre, Robert S. Feldman, and Erik J. Coats, eds. *Nonverbal Behavior in Clinical Settings*. New York: Oxford University Press, 2003.

Picard, Max. *The World of Silence*. Chicago: Henry Regnery, 1964.

Pinn, Anthony B. *Varieties of African American Religious Life*. Minneapolis: Augsburg Fortress, 1998.

Pinnock, Sarah K. "Simone Weil and French Feminist Philosophy." In *Relevance of the Radical: Simone Weil*, edited by A. Rebecca Rozelle-Stone and Lucian Stone, 205–20. New York: Continuum, 2010.

Porete, Marguerite. *The Mirror of Simple Souls*. Translated by Ellen Babinsky. Mahwah, NJ: Paulist Press, 1993.

Pranger, Burcht. "*Dimida Hora*: Liminal Silence in Bernard Clairvaux, Anselm of Canterbury, and Barack Obama." In *Images, Improvisations, Sound, and Silence from 1000 to 1800: Degree Zero*, edited by Babette Hellemans and Alissa Jones Nelson, 229–45. Amsterdam: Amsterdam University Press, 2018.

Prevot, Andrew. "Divine Opacity: Mystical Theology, Black Theology, and the Problem of Light-Dark Aesthetics." *Spiritus: A Journal of Christian Spirituality* 16, no. 2 (Fall 2016): 166–88.

Prevot, Andrew. *The Mysticism of Ordinary Life: Theology, Philosophy, and Feminism*. Oxford: Oxford University Press, 2023.

Priest, Ann-Marie. "Woman as God, God as Woman: Mysticism, Negative Theology, and Luce Irigaray." *Journal of Religion* 83, no. 1 (January 2003): 1–23.

Prochnik, George. *In Pursuit of Silence: Listening for Meaning in a World of Noise*. New York: Anchor, 2011.

Pseudo-Dionysius. *The Complete Works*. Translated by Colm Luibheid. Mahwah, NJ: Paulist Press, 1987.

Quashie, Kevin E. *The Sovereignty of Quiet: Beyond Resistance in Black Culture*. New Brunswick, NY: Rutgers University Press, 2012.

Quashie, Kevin E. "The Trouble with Publicness: Toward a Theory of Black Quiet." *African American Review* 43, no. 2–3 (Summer/Fall 2009): 329–43.

Quint, Josef, ed. *Meister Eckhart: Deutsche Predigten und Traktate*. Munich: C. Hanser, 1969.

Rahner, Karl. *The Mystical Way in Everyday Life: Sermons, Prayers and Essays*. Translated and edited by Annemarie S. Kidder. Maryknoll, NY: Orbis, 2010.
Rambo, Shelly. *Spirit and Trauma: A Theology of Remaining*. Louisville, KY: Westminster John Knox Press, 2010.
Ratcliffe, Krista. *Rhetorical Listening: Identification, Gender, Whiteness*. Carbondale: Southern Illinois University, 2006.
Ratzinger, Joseph Cardinal. *The Spirit of the Liturgy*. San Francisco: Ignatius, 2000.
Reid, Barbara E. "The Gospel of Luke: Friend or Foe of Women Proclaimers of the Word?" *Catholic Biblical Quarterly* 78, no. 1 (January 2016): 1–23.
Rich, Adrienne. *The Dream of a Common Language: Poems, 1974–1977*. New York: W. W. Norton, 1978.
Rich, Adrienne. *On Lies, Secrets and Silence*. New York: W. W. Norton, 1979.
Roberts, Dorothy. "The Paradox of Silence: Some Questions about Silence as Resistance." *University of Michigan Journal of Law Reform* 33, no. 3 (2002): 343–57.
Rodriguez, Dalia. "Un/Masking Identity: Healing Our Wounded Souls." *Qualitative Inquiry* 12, no. 6 (2003): 1067–90.
Rogers, Katherin A. *Christianity and Western Theism: Classical Approaches to the Hard Questions*. London: Routledge, 2023.
Rolheiser, Ronald. *The Holy Longing: The Search for a Christian Spirituality*. New York: Image, 2009.
Roy, Arundhati. *The God of Small Things*. New York: Random House, 1997.
Roy, Arundhati. "The Graveyard Talks Back: Arundhati Roy on Fiction in the Time of Fake News—What Is the Role of the Writer in a Time of Rising Nationalism?" Clark Lecture in English Literature, Trinity College, Cambridge, UK, February 12, 2020. Literary Hub. https://lithub.com/the-graveyard-talks-back-arundhati-roy-on-fiction-in-the-time-of-fake-news/.
Roy, Arundhati. *The Ministry of Utmost Happiness*. New York: Alfred Knopf, 2017.
Rozelle-Stone, A. Rebecca, and Lucian Stone. *Simone Weil and Theology*. New York: Bloomsbury T&T Clark, 2013.
Rubenstein, Mary-Jane. "Dionysius, Derrida, and the Critique of 'Ontotheology.'" *Modern Theology* 24, no. 4 (October 2008): 725–41.
Sanders, Theresa. *Tenebrae: Holy Week after the Holocaust*. Maryknoll, NY: Orbis, 2006.
Sardello, Robert. *Silence: The Mystery of Wholeness*. Berkeley: North Atlantic, 2008.
Schmemann, Alexander. *Liturgy and Tradition*. Crestwood, NY: St. Vladimir's Seminary Press, 1990.
Schneiders, Sandra M. "Approaches to the Study of Christian Spirituality." In *The Blackwell Companion to Christian Spirituality*, edited by Arthur Holder, 15–34. Hoboken, NJ: Wiley-Blackwell, 2011.
Schneiders, Sandra M. "A Hermeneutical Approach to the Study of Christian Spirituality." In *Minding the Spirit: The Study of Christian Spirituality*, edited by

Elizabeth Dreyer and Mark S. Burrows. Baltimore, MD: Johns Hopkins University Press, 2005.
Schneiders, Sandra M. "Religion and Spirituality: Strangers, Rivals, or Partners?" *Santa Clara Lectures* 6, no. 2 (February 6, 2000).
Schudson, Michael. "Dynamic of Distortion in Collective Memory." In *Memory Distortion: How Minds, Brains, and Societies Reconstruct the Past*, edited by Daniel L. Schacter, 346–64. Cambridge, MA: Harvard University Press, 1997.
Sells, Michael A. *Mystical Languages of Unsaying*. Chicago: University of Chicago Press, 1994.
Shea, Shawn Christopher. *Psychiatric Interviewing: The Art of Understanding*. 2nd ed. Philadelphia: Sanders, 1998.
Sheldrake, Philip. *The Exploration in Christian Spirituality: History, Theology, and Social Practice*. New York: Paulist Press, 2010.
Sheldrake, Philip, ed. *The New Westminster Dictionary of Christian Spirituality*. Louisville, KY: Westminster John Knox Press, 2013.
Sheldrake, Philip. *Spirituality and History: Questions of Interpretation and Method*. Ossining, NY: Orbis, 1991.
Sheldrake, Philip. *Spirituality and Theology: Christian Living and the Doctrine of God*. London: Darton, Longman and Todd, 1998.
Sim, Stuart. *Manifesto for Silence: Confronting the Politics and Culture of Noise*. Edinburgh: Edinburgh University Press, 2007.
Sölle, Dorothee. *The Silent Cry: Mysticism and Resistance*. Minneapolis: Fortress Press, 2001.
Solnit, Rebecca. *Storming the Gates of Paradise: Landscapes for Politics*. Berkeley: University of California Press, 2008.
Sontag, Susan. "The Aesthetics of Silence." In *A Susan Sontag Reader*. New York: Farrar, Straus and Giroux, 1982.
Spivak, Gayatri C. "Can the Subaltern Speak?" In *The Post-colonial Studies Reader*, edited by Bill Ashcroft, Gareth Griffiths, and Helen Tiffin. New York: Routledge, 1995.
Spivak, Gayatri C. *The Spivak Reader*. Edited by Donna Landry. London: Routledge, 1996.
Stang, Charles M. *Apophasis and Pseudonymity in Dionysius the Areopagite: "No Longer I."* Oxford: Oxford University Press, 2012.
Steiner, George. *Language and Silence*. New Haven, CT: Yale University Press, 2013.
Stoler, Ann Laura. "Colonial Aphasia: Race and Disabled Histories in France." *Public Culture* 23, no. 1 (2011): 121–56.
Stora, Benjamine. "The Algerian War in French Memory: Vengeful Memory's Violence." In *Memory and Violence in the Middle East and North Africa*, edited by Ussama Makdisi and Paul A. Silverstein, 151–74. Bloomington: Indiana University Press, 2006.
St. Victor, Richard. *Collected Works of Richard of St. Victor*. Jasper, FL: Revelation Insights, 2016.

Sundstrom, Ronald R., and David Haekwon Kim. "Xenophobia and Racism." In "Xenophobia and Racism," special issue, *Critical Philosophy of Race* 2, no. 1 (2014): 20–45.
Synod of Bishops: Special Assembly for Asia. *Lineamenta*. Vatican City: The Holy See, 1998. https://www.vatican.va/roman_curia/synod/documents/rc_synod_doc_01081996_asia-lineam_en.html.
Tannen, Deborah, and Muriel Saville-Troike. *Perspectives on Silence*. Norwood, NJ: Ablex, 1985.
Tenoudji, P. "Les gestes du silence." *Social Anthropology* 6, no. 3 (2006): 343–64.
Thate, Michael. *The Godman and the Sea: The Empty Tomb, the Trauma of the Jews, and the Gospel of Mark*. Philadelphia: University of Pennsylvania Press, 2019.
Thomas, R. S. *Collected Poems, 1945–1990*. London: Phoenix, 1993.
Titchkosky, Tanya. "Life with Dead Metaphors: Impairment Rhetoric in Social Justice Praxis." In *The Disability Studies Reader*, edited by Lennard J. Davis, 269–81. New York: Routledge, 2016.
Tolbert, Mary Ann. *Sowing the Gospel: Mark's World in Literary Historical Perspective*. Minneapolis: Fortress, 1989.
Treadway, Linzie M. "Freedom in the Wilderness between Two Worlds: A Native American Approach to Genesis 21:1–21." In *Reading Bible Texts Together: Pursuing Minoritized Biblical Criticism*, edited by Tai-sing Benny Liew and Fernando F. Segovia, 119–34. Atlanta: Society of Biblical Literature, 2022.
Turner, Denys. *The Darkness of God: Negativity in Christian Mysticism*. Cambridge: Cambridge University Press, 1995.
Ugolnik, Zachary. "Internal Liturgy: The Transmission of the Jesus Prayer in the 'Philokalia' and 'The Way of a Pilgrim (Rasskaz Strannika).'" *Religion & Literature* 48, no. 1 (Spring 2016): 99–133.
van Mierlo, Jozef, ed. *Hadewijch: Brieven*. 2 vols. Antwerp: Standaard, 1947.
van Mierlo, Jozef, ed. *Hadewijch: Mengeldichten*. Antwerp: Standaard, 1952.
van Mierlo, Jozef, ed. *Hadewijch: Strophische Gedichten*. 2 vols. Antwerp: Standaard, 1942.
van Mierlo, Jozef, ed. *Hadewijch: Visionen*. 2 vols. Louvain, Belgium: Vlaamsch Boekenhalle, 1924, 1925.
Veto, Miklos. *The Religious Metaphysics of Simone Weil*. Translated by Joan Dargan. Albany: State University of New York Press, 1994.
Vinitzky-Seroussi, Vered, and Chana Teeger. "Silence and Collective Memory." In *The Oxford Handbook of Cognitive Sociology*, edited by Wayne H. Brekhuhs and Gabe Ignatow, 663–74. Oxford: Oxford University Press, 2019.
von Sass, Hartmut, and Eric E. Hall. *Groundless Gods: The Theological Prospects of Post-Metaphysical Thought*. Eugene, OR: Pickwick, 2014.
Wainwright, Geoffrey. *Doxology, the Praise of God in Worship, Doctrine and Life: A Systematic Theology*. New York: Oxford University Press, 1980.
Walshe, Maurice O'C., trans. and ed. *The Complete Mystical Works of Meister Eckhart*. New York: Crossroad, 2009.

Ward, Benedicta. *The Wisdom of the Desert Fathers: The Apophthegmata Patrum*. Oxford: SLG, 1975.
Weil, Simone. *First and Last Notebook: Supernatural Knowledge*. Translated by Richard Reese. Eugene, OR: Wipf & Stock, 2015.
Weil, Simone. *Gravity and Grace*. Translated by Emma Crawford and Mario von der Ruhr. London: Routledge, 2002.
Weil, Simone. *Love in the Void: Where God Finds Us*. Walden, NY: Plough, 2018.
Weil, Simone. *On Science, Necessity, and the Love of God*. Translated by Richard Rees. London: Oxford University Press, 1968.
Weil, Simone. *Oppression and Liberty*. Amherst: University of Massachusetts Press, 1978.
Weil, Simone. *Selected Essays, 1934–1943*. Translated and edited by Richard Rees. London: Oxford University Press, 1962.
Weil, Simone. *The Simone Weil Reader*. Ann Arbor: University of Michigan Press, 1977.
Weil, Simone. *Waiting for God*. New York: Harper & Row, 1951.
West, Traci C., ed. *Solidarity and Defiant Spirituality: African Lessons on Religion Racism, and Ending Gender Violence*. New York: New York University Press, 2019.
Williams, Delores S. *Sisters in the Wilderness: The Challenge of Womanist God-Talk*. Maryknoll, NY: Orbis, 2013.
Williams, J. P. *Seeking the God Beyond: A Beginner's Guide to Christian Apophatic Spirituality*. Eugene, OR: Cascade, 2019.
Williams, Rowan. *The Edge of Words: God and the Habits of Language*. London: Bloomsbury, 2014.
Williams, Rowan. *Silence and Honey Cakes: The Wisdom of the Desert*. Oxford: Lion, 2004.
Williams, Rowan. *Where God Happens: Discovering Christ in One Another*. Boston: New Seeds, 2007.
Wilson, Rob. "Reading Theresa Hak Kyung Cha's *Dictee* as Spiritual Dictation: Falling into the Korean Uncanny." *Revista de Estudos e Culturais* 3 (2016): 9–18.
Winchakul, Thongchai. *Moments of Silence: The Unforgetting of the October 6, 1976, Massacre in Bangkok*. Honolulu: University of Hawaii Press, 2020.
Winter, Jay. *Sites of Memory, Sites of Mourning: The Great War in European Cultural History*. Cambridge, UK: Cambridge University Press, 2014.
Wittgenstein, Ludwig. *Tractatus Logico Philosophicus*. London: Routledge, 2001.
Wittgenstein, Ludwig. *Philosophical Investigations*. Hoboken, NJ: Wiley-Blackwell, 2009.
Wolfteich, Claire E. "Practices of 'Unsaying': Michel de Certeau, Spirituality Studies, and Practical Theology." *Spiritus: A Journal of Christian Spirituality* 12, no. 2 (2012): 161–71.
Woolley, Susan. "The Silence Itself Is Enough of a Statement: The Day of Silence and LGBTQ Awareness Raising." *Anthropology & Education Quarterly* 43, no. 3 (September 2021).

Wu, Ellen. *Color of Success: Origins of the Model Minority Myth*. Durham, NC: Duke University Press, 2015.
Wyman, Jason. "Constructive Theology: History, Movement, Method." In *What Is Constructive Theology? History, Methodologies, and Perspectives*, edited by Marion Grau and Jason Wyman, 9–30. London: Bloomsbury, 2020.
Yore, Su. *The Mystic Way in Postmodernity: Transcending Theological Boundaries in the Writings of Iris Murdoch, Denise Levertov and Annie Dillard*. Religion and Discourse 43. Bern, Germany: Peter Lang, 2009.

INDEX

Pages in *italics* refer to figures.

"an idle tale," 101, 104–8
anti-Blackness, 110
anti-Black racism, 109, 110
apatheia, 51
Articulate Silence (Cheung), 119
Audience Distant Relative (Cha), 127, *128*
Augustine of Hippo, 46

Ballif, Michelle, 122
Barth, Karl, 73
Basil the Great, 50
Biblical stories, 38–43
Bingemer, Maria Clara, 151
Black Lives Matter, 10, 19, 109
Bocken, Inigo, 64
Bonhoeffer, Dietrich, 43, 65n17
Bronx, Jane, 66n21
Buber, Martin, 122
Buddhism, 9
Burney, C. F., 65n3
Burrows, Mark S., 32n58
Burrus, Virginia, 52
Butler, Judith, 60, 95
Byung-Mu, Ahn, 65n4

Cage, John, 15
Carson, Rachel, 137
Cavanaugh, William T., 47, 66n28
Celan, Paul, 6, 31n10, 31n11
Cha, Theresa Hak Kyung, 104, 125–30, *128*, 135nn71–72, 166, 175n1
Cheung, King-Kok, 119
Choi, Jin Young, 107
Chow, Rey, 116–17, 134nn46–47
Chrétien, Jean-Louis, 13, 32n30, 32n31, 63
Christian liturgy, 38–43
Christian mystical tradition, 36, 37, 64, 123, 145
Christian spiritual traditions, 10, 17–20; mystical and contemplative silence, 25–30; spirituality of silence, 20–25
Christie, Douglas, 51
Cixous, Hélène, 7
Clair, Robin P., 121
The Cloud of Unknowing, 27
Coakley, Sarah A., 156
Compunction, 51
Confucianism, 9
Connell, Martin F., 76

Constantinople, 50
constructive theology, 24
contemplative listening, 131–32
Cooke, Thomas N., 32n54
Copeland, M. Shawn, 24
COVID-19 restrictions, 19

Dalton, Anne B., 118
D'Angelo, Mary Rose, 105
Dauenhauer, Bernard P., 16, 30n8
Davis, Benjamin P., 168n40
Davis, D. Diane, 122
de Certeau, Michel, 17, 26, 27, 32n48, 92, 148
Derrida, Jacques, 7
Deus absconditus, 38
Dictee (Cha), 125, 126
Dingli, Sophia, 32n54
discourse-oriented mourning, 87
diseuse, 130
Don't Say Gay bill, 8
Dreyer, Elizabeth A., 32n58

Eckhart, Meister, 28, 141
The Edge of Words (Lecture), 93
Edkins, Jenny, 107
Eliot, T. S., 101, 132
Elkins, Janet, 133n10
Encore, 143
Enfolding Silence: The Transformation of Japanese American Religion and Art under Oppression (Esaki), 11
Esaki, Brett J., 11–14, 30n3
Evagrius Ponticus, 35, 37, 48, 58, 61, 62, 138, 148, 150; compunction, 51–53; The Fifth Ecumenical Council's identification, 55; journey of the soul, 54; mystical and contemplative silence, 48–56; passionate distraction, 51; "place of God," 54; reality of suffering, 63–64; self-contradictory statement, 55; silence in hesychasm, 49, 50; spatial metaphors, 53
Evans, Jean N., 131

Fanon, Frantz, 110, 111
Farley, Wendy, 28
Farmer, Frank, 30n8
Feldman, Allen, 81
Ferrari, Martina, 5, 30n6
Fifth Ecumenical Council, 55
The Fifth Ecumenical Council's identification of Evagrius, 55
Fiorenza, Elisabeth Schussler, 105, 132n3
Flanagan, Kieran, 66n23
Floyd, George, 19
Ford, David F., 82
Foucault, Michel, 23
4.16 Memory Classroom, 83–88, 90
Fredericksen, Elaine, 134n39
Freud, Sigmund, 116
Frohlich, Mary, 28
"fruition" *(ghebruken)*, 57
Fugitive Pieces (Michaels), 82
Fujiwara, Lynn, 133n20

Gassam, Janice, 31n18
Gates-Madsen, Nancy J., 30n7, 69, 80, 81, 83, 98nn38–41
General Instruction of the Roman Missal, 44
Geun-hye, Park, 84
Glenn, Cheryl, 30n8
Gooch, Paul W., 41
Gorman, George H., 32n52
graveyards, 161–166
Gregory of Nazianzus, 50
Gwan-hong, Kim, 84

Hadewijch of Antwerp, 35, 37, 48, 68n74, 68nn76–89, 138, 143, 148, 150, 154; Beguine's life context, 56; bridal mysticism, 56; Christological perspective, 57; contemplative silence, 63; "fruition" (*ghebruken*), 57; idea of unfaith, 60; journey for Love, 60; Land of Love, 58; mystical and contemplative silence, 56–63; "non-fruition" (*ghebreken*), 57; reality of suffering, 63–64; remarkable resemblance, 61; spatial and topographical metaphor, 57; vocations and engage, 62

Haidt, Jonathan, 6, 31n9

Hall, Eric E., 98n14

Haraway, Donna, 32n64

"Haunting Silence: Trauma, Failed Orality, and Mark's Messianic Secret" (Liew), 142

Heber-Percy, Colin, 15, 32n38

Hebrew Bible, 63

Heske, Marianne, 14

hesychasmos, 49

Hillgardner, Holly, 60, 67nn71–72

Hinduism, 9

Hollywood, Amy, 144, 145

Holmes, Barbara A., 9, 10, 114, 133nn31–32

Holy Spirit, 52

Hopkins, Dwight, 114

Incidents in the Life of a Slave Girl (Jacobs), 118

In Pursuit of Silence (Prochnik), 12

Irigaray, Luce, 7, 143–144, 155, 168nn16–20

Jacobs, Harriet, 118, 119

Jesus's empty tomb, silence of, 72–77; communion with others, 94–96; drawing an analogy, 71; 4.16 Memory Classroom, 83–88, *90*; mysticism of silence and political struggle, 88–91; New Testament, 70; numerous empty tombs, 77–78; openness to transcendent, 93–94; political struggle, 96–97; practice of unsaying, 91–93; silence and collective memory, 78–80; silence and testimony, 80–83; spiritual practice, 96–97; terror and amazement, 140–49

Joseph of Arimathea, 72

joy for the silent god, 167

joy of the empty tomb: expression of affliction, 149–52; Jesus's empty tomb, 140–49; language of God, 149–52; mystics of Christian traditions, 138; silent attention, 139; void and attention, 152–60; women disciples at tomb, 139

Joy Unspeakable (Holmes), 9, 114

Kadi, Joanna, 115

Karlsson, Jenni, 32n44

Karris, Robert J., 132n5

Kasper, Walter, 73

Keating, Thomas, 27

Keller, Catherine, 156

Kerr, Fergus, 27

Kim, Claire Jean, 110

Kim, David Haekwon, 133n17, 133n19

Kingston, Maxine Hong, 119

Kogawa, Joy, 119

Kristeva, Julia, 7

Kyom, Guih, 164

Lacan, Jacques, 142–44, 168n8, 168n10

Laird, Martin, 14

Language and Silence (Steiner), 5

Lashgari, Deidre, 82, 112, 133n26

Lecture, Gifford, 93
Lee, Hyeon Jung, 87
Lee, Kun Jong, 126
Lefebvre, Henri, 16
lex orandi est lex credendi, 46, 47
lex vivendi, 47
Liew, Tat-siong Benny, 142
listening to silence: contemplative listening, 131–32; dream of the listener, 125–30; "echoed ecstasy," 132; ever-renewed relationship, 132; for linguistic minorities, 120; process of repression, 129; sense of distance, 122–25; unrecognized memories, 121
liturgical silence, 43–48
Logismoi, 50
Longing and Letting Go (Hillgardner), 60
The Look of Silence (Oppenheimer), 69
"The Loom," (Sasaki), 115
Lorde, Audre, 11
Luang, Sanam, 79

MacCulloch, Diarmaid, 65n11
Magdalene, Mary, 72, 101, 105, 147
Malhotra, Sheena, 32n57
McGinn, Bernard, 20, 32n60
McGrath, Alister E., 25
McLauchlan, Richard, 76, 97n6
Meninger, William, 27
Merton, Thomas, 1, 18, 27, 32n51, 55, 121
#MeToo movement, 10
Meyer, Morgan, 14
Michaels, Anne, 82
Minh-ha, Trinh T., 7, 101, 132n1
The Ministry of Utmost Happiness (Roy), 139, 160–65
The Mirror of Simple Souls (Porete), 145
Mommaers, Paul, 57
Mountford, Roxanne, 122
Mysterium Paschale (Balthasar), 76

mystical and contemplative silence: Christian spiritual traditions, 25–30; concentric circles, 173; defiant silence, 118–20; Evagrius suggestions, 48–56; Hadewijch's Christological perspective, 56–63; hesychast tradition's, 50; "loud" silence, 113–15; melancholic silence, 115–17
Mystical Languages of Unsaying (Sells), 92

Nance, Kimberly, 81
Nancy, Jean-Luc, 52, 168nn30–31
New Testament, 63
Nicodemus, 72
Nietzsche, Friedrich, 31n12
"non-fruition" (*ghebreken*), 57
numerous empty tombs, 77–78

Oliver, Mary, 172
Olsen, Tillie, 7
Oppenheimer, Joshua, 69
Organizing Silence (Clair), 121
Orsi, Robert, 22
Otto, Rudolf, 141

pathologized defiant Blackness, 110
Paul, Apostle, 44
paying attention to silence, 171–75
Pennington, Basil, 27
perpetual foreigners, 109
Phan, Peter, 46
Picard, Max, 12, 13, 32n29
Pinnock, Sarah K., 156, 169nn51–53
Porete, Marguerite, 145, 156
posture of vulnerability, 63
Practices of Everyday Life (de Certeau), 17
Precarious Life: The Powers of Mourning and Violence (Butler), 95
Prevot, Andrew, 21, 32n62

probationary citizens, 109
Prochnik, George, 12, 13, 31n28
Prosper of Aquitaine, 46
Pseudo-Dionysius, 63

Quashie, Kevin E., 8
Quintilian, 133n7

Rahner, Karl, 26
Rambo, Shelly, 73
Ratzinger, Joseph Cardinal, 65n18
Resurrection of God, 146
Resurrection of Jesus, 44
Rich, Adrienne, 123, 124
Rolheiser, Ronald, 32n59
Roshanravan, Shireen, 133n20
Rowe, Carrillo, 32n35, 32n57
Roy, Arundhati, 137, 139, 149, 160, 161, 164, 166, 169nn70–72, 172
Rozelle-Stone, Rebecca, 168n40
Rukun, Adi, 69, 70

Sacrosanctum Concilium, 46
Saint John of the Cross, 143
Saint Paul, 7
Saint Teresa of Avila, 143
Sasaki, Ruth A., 115
Schmemann, Alexander, 46, 66n26
Schneiders, Sandra M., 20, 21, 32n61, 33n71
Shaheed, Hazrat Sarmad, 164
"Shattered Love" (Nancy), 52
Sheldrake, Philip, 20, 23
silence: ambiguity of, 102; in biblical stories, 38–43; classed, 8; contemplation, 28–30; depictions of, 63; dominant culture, 2; in everyday life, 4–7; experience of vulnerable population, 7–11; gendered, 7–8;
human communication, 2; liturgy and prayer, 43–48; musical sense of, 15; personal experiences and expectations, 2; prevailing culture, 102; racialized, 8; segregated, 8–9; space in spirituality, 11–17; spatial sense of, 16; speech and silence, 1, 2; spirituality of, 20–25; spiritual traditions, 3; teaching and practice, 64; undefinable nature, 1
Silences (Olsen), 7
silent god, 38–43
silent meditation, 35
Silent Protest Parade, 91
The Silent Room (Heske), 14
Silesius, Angelus, 148
Sölle, Dorothee, 26, 65n1, 141
Solnit, Rebecca, 166
Sontag, Susan, 1, 125
South African Police Service, 91
The Sovereignty of Quiet (Quashie), 8
space in spirituality, 11–17
Speculum of the Other Woman (Irigaray), 144
Spirit and Trauma (Rambo), 73
Spirituality and Theology (Sheldrake), 24
spirituality of silence: belief and tradition, 21; Christian spirituality, 25; to claim and reclaim, 23; in daily life, 21; dominant cultural condition, 22; historical-contextual approach, 21; linguistic minorities, 23; theological approaches, 24; transcultural approach, 22
Spivak, Gayatri, 7, 107, 134n48
Steiner, George, 5, 30n5
Stevens, Dana, 97nn4–5
Sumida, Stephen H., 30n1
Sundstrom, Ronald R., 133n17, 133n19

Tauler, Johannes, 13
Teeger, Chana, 79
Tenebrae liturgy, 44, 45
Teresa of Avila, 156
Thate, Michael, 168n26
Thomas, R. S., 75, 76, 98nn17–18
Thurman, Howard, 31n23
Trauma, Taboo, and Truth-Telling (Gates-Madsen), 80
Treadway, Linzie M., 40
Tudor, David, 15

Ugolnik, Zachary, 66n35

Vinitzky-Seroussi, Vered, 79
Visions, Poems in Stanzas, Poems in Couplets (Hadewijch), 56
von Balthasar, Hans Urs, 74, 76, 77, 98nn22–23
von Sass, Hartmut, 98n14

Weil, Simone, 137, 139, 149–53, 155–60, 164–66, 168n33, 169n47, 169nn59–61, 169nn64–66, 170nn79–80, 172
West, Traci C., 25, 33n78
"White Silence Is Violence," 10
Williams, Delores, 40
Williams, Rowan, 33n65, 49, 93
Winichakul, Thongchai, 79
Winter, Jay, 78
women of color, United States, 108–13; concentric circle, 130; precariousness of speech, 130
The World of Silence (Picard), 12

Yamamoto, Hisaye, 119

ABOUT THE AUTHOR

MIN-AH CHO is a scholar of constructive theology and Christian spirituality. Critically engaging feminist and decolonial and postcolonial theories, the Christian mystical tradition, and Asian and Asian American religion and spirituality, Cho's research focuses on the forms of conflict, negotiation, and reconciliation between the spirituality of Christian individuals—particularly those made vulnerable and excluded—and the public and institutional representation of religion and theology. She is passionate about exploring how new and innovative theological languages, spiritual expressions, metaphors, works of art, and actions emerge from the various life contexts of Christian individuals in their relationship with the public sphere and the institutional church. Her greatest desire as a scholar and teacher is to bridge gaps between different cultures and to promote communication among people with different points of view. As a native of South Korea who has been educated in American institutions and as a theologian who has received training in both Protestant and Roman Catholic traditions, her experience sharpens her sensitivity to the various forms of human diversity and shapes her teaching philosophy. Before joining the faculty at Georgetown University in 2019, Cho taught at St. Catherine University, Saint Paul (2011–2015), and at Manhattan College in the Bronx (2018–2019).

www.ingramcontent.com/pod-product-compliance
Lightning Source LLC
Chambersburg PA
CBHW032043300426
44117CB00009B/1171